INTERACTION RITUAL

ERVING GOFFMAN was born in Canada in 1922. He received his B.A. from the University of Toronto, his M.A. and Ph.D. from the University of Chicago. He is the author of, among other books, *The Presentation of Self in Everyday Life* (A147) and *Asylums* (A277) and is Professor of Sociology at the University of California at Berkeley.

INTERACTION RITUAL

ESSAYS
ON FACE-TO-FACE BEHAVIOR
BY ERVING GOFFMAN

ANCHOR BOOKS
DOUBLEDAY & COMPANY, INC.
GARDEN CITY, NEW YORK

"On Face-Work: An Analysis of Ritual Elements in Social Interaction" is reprinted with permission from *Psychiatry: Journal for the Study of Interpersonal Processes*, Volume 18, Number 3, August 1955, pp. 213–31. Copyright © 1955 by the William Alanson White Psychiatric Foundation, Inc.

"Embarrassment and Social Organization" is reprinted with permission from *The American Journal of Sociology*, Volume 62, Number 3, November 1956, pp. 264–74.

"The Nature of Deference and Demeanor" is reprinted with permission from *American Anthropologist*, Volume 58, June 1956, pp. 473–502. Copyright © 1956 by the American Anthropological Association. All rights reserved.

"Alienation from Interaction" is reprinted with permission from *Human Relations*, Volume 10, Number 1, 1957, pp. 47–59.

"Mental Symptoms and Public Order" is reprinted with permission of the Walter Reed Army Institute of Research.

"Where the Action Is" was prepared with the assistance of a grant from the Youth Development Program of the Ford Foundation and the Center for the Study of Law and Society, University of California, Berkeley, under a grant from the Office of Juvenile Delinquency and Youth Development, Welfare Administration, U. S. Department of Health, Education and Welfare in cooperation with the President's Committee on Juvenile Delinquency and Youth Crime. Support was also received from the Institute of Human Development, University of California, Berkeley, and from the Center For International Affairs, Harvard University. Edwin Lemert has provided detailed criticisms for which I am very grateful. Comments on Nevada casino gambling are based on a study in progress.

The first four papers were published while I was a member of the Laboratory of Socio-environmental Studies, National Institute of Mental Health, and I am grateful for the Laboratory's support. For support in bringing this collection of six papers together for publication, I am grateful to the Center For International Affairs, Harvard University.

The Anchor Books edition is the first
publication of *Interaction Ritual*

Anchor Books edition: 1967

CONTENTS

INTERACTION RITUAL

INTRODUCTION

The study of face-to-face interaction in natural settings doesn't yet have an adequate name. Moreover, the analytical boundaries of the field remain unclear. Somehow, but only somehow, a brief time span is involved, a limited extension in space, and a restriction to those events that must go on to completion once they have begun. There is a close meshing with the ritual properties of persons and with the egocentric forms of territoriality.

The subject matter, however, can be identified. It is that class of events which occurs during co-presence and by virtue of co-presence. The ultimate behavioral materials are the glances, gestures, positionings, and verbal statements that people continuously feed into the situation, whether intended or not. These are the external signs of orientation and involvement—states of mind and body not ordinarily examined with respect to their social organization.

The close, systematic examination of these "small behaviors" has begun to develop, stimulated by impressive current studies of animals and of language, and supported by the resources available for the study of interaction in "small groups" and the psychotherapies.

One objective in dealing with these data is to describe the natural units of interaction built up from them, beginning with the littlest—for example, the fleeting facial move an individual can make in the game of expressing his alignment to what is happening—and ending with affairs such as week-long conferences, these being the interactional mastodons that push to the limit what can be called a social occasion. A second objective is to uncover the norma-

1

tive order prevailing within and between these units, that is, the behavioral order found in all peopled places, whether public, semi-public, or private, and whether under the auspices of an organized social occasion or the flatter constraints of merely a routinized social setting.* Both of these objectives can be advanced through serious ethnography: we need to identify the countless patterns and natural sequences of behavior occurring whenever persons come into one another's immediate presence. And we need to see these events as a subject matter in their own right, analytically distinguished from neighboring areas, for example, social relationships, little social groups, communication systems, and strategic interaction.

A sociology of occasions is here advocated. Social organization is the central theme, but what is organized is the co-mingling of persons and the temporary interactional enterprises that can arise therefrom. A normatively stabilized structure is at issue, a "social gathering," but this is a shifting entity, necessarily evanescent, created by arrivals and killed by departures.

The first five papers in this book appear in the order of their original publication with only a few editorial changes; the sixth, comprising almost half of the volume, is published here for the first time. I'm afraid there is not much that is botanical about them. But they do focus on one general issue that remains of interest to the ethnographer and will always have to receive some consideration.

I assume that the proper study of interaction is not the individual and his psychology, but rather the syntactical relations among the acts of different persons mutually present to one another. None the less, since it is individual actors who contribute the ultimate materials, it will always be reasonable to ask what general properties they must have if this sort of contribution is to be expected of them.

* I have made an attempt along these lines in *Behavior in Public Places* (New York, The Free Press of Glencoe, 1966).

What minimal model of the actor is needed if we are to wind him up, stick him in amongst his fellows, and have an orderly traffic of behavior emerge? What minimal model is required if the student is to anticipate the lines along which an individual, *qua* interactant, can be effective or break down? That is what these papers are about. A psychology is necessarily involved, but one stripped and cramped to suit the sociological study of conversation, track meets, banquets, jury trials, and street loitering.

Not, then, men and their moments. Rather moments and their men.

ON FACE-WORK*

An Analysis of
Ritual Elements in Social Interaction

Every person lives in a world of social encounters, involving him either in face-to face or mediated contact with other participants. In each of these contacts, he tends to act out what is sometimes called a *line*—that is, a pattern of verbal and nonverbal acts by which he expresses his view of the situation and through this his evaluation of the participants, especially himself. Regardless of whether a person intends to take a line, he will find that he has done so in effect. The other participants will assume that he has more or less willfully taken a stand, so that if he is to deal with their response to him he must take into consideration the impression they have possibly formed of him.

The term *face* may be defined as the positive social value a person effectively claims for himself by the line others assume he has taken during a particular contact. Face is an image of self delineated in terms of approved social attributes—albeit an image that others may share, as when a person makes a good showing for his profession or religion by making a good showing for himself.[1]

* This paper was written at the University of Chicago; for financial support in writing it, I am indebted to a U. S. Public Health Grant (No. M702[6]MH[5]) for a study of the characteristics of social interaction of individuals, headed by Dr. William Soskin of the Department of Psychology, University of Chicago.

[1] For discussions of the Chinese Conception of face, see the

A person tends to experience an immediate emotional response to the face which a contact with others allows him; he cathects his face; his "feelings" become attached to it. If the encounter sustains an image of him that he has long taken for granted, he probably will have few feelings about the matter. If events establish a face for him that is better than he might have expected, he is likely to "feel good"; if his ordinary expectations are not fulfilled, one expects that he will "feel bad" or "feel hurt." In general, a person's attachment to a particular face, coupled with the ease with which disconfirming information can be conveyed by himself and others, provides one reason why he finds that participation in any contact with others is a commitment. A person will also have feelings about the face sustained for the other participants, and while these feelings may differ in quantity and direction from those he has for his own face, they constitute an involvement in the face of others that is as immediate and spontaneous as the involvement he has in his own face. One's own face and the face of others are constructs of the same order; it is the rules of the group and the definition of the situation which determine how much feeling one is to have for face and how this feeling is to be distributed among the faces involved.

A person may be said to *have*, or *be in*, or *maintain* face when the line he effectively takes presents an image of him that is internally consistent, that is supported by judgments and evidence conveyed by other participants, and that is confirmed by evidence conveyed through im-

following: Hsien Chin Hu, "The Chinese Concept of 'Face,'" *American Anthropologist*, 1944, n.s. 46:45–64. Martin C. Yang, *A Chinese Village* (New York, Columbia University Press, 1945), pp. 167–72. J. Macgowan, *Men and Manners of Modern China* (London, Unwin, 1912), pp. 301–12. Arthur H. Smith, *Chinese Characteristics* (New York, Felming H. Revell Co., 1894), pp. 16–18. For a comment on the American Indian conception of face, see Marcel Mauss, *The Gift*, tr. Ian Cunnison (London, Cohen & West, 1954), p. 38.

personal agencies in the situation. At such times the person's face clearly is something that is not lodged in or on his body, but rather something that is diffusely located in the flow of events in the encounter and becomes manifest only when these events are read and interpreted for the appraisals expressed in them.

The line maintained by and for a person during contact with others tends to be of a legitimate institutionalized kind. During a contact of a particular type, an interactant of known or visible attributes can expect to be sustained in a particular face and can feel that it is morally proper that this should be so. Given his attributes and the conventionalized nature of the encounter, he will find a small choice of lines will be open to him and a small choice of faces will be waiting for him. Further, on the basis of a few known attributes, he is given the responsibility of possessing a vast number of others. His coparticipants are not likely to be conscious of the character of many of these attributes until he acts perceptibly in such a way as to discredit his possession of them; then everyone becomes conscious of these attributes and assumes that he willfully gave a false impression of possessing them.

Thus while concern for face focuses the attention of the person on the current activity, he must, to maintain face in this activity, take into consideration his place in the social world beyond it. A person who can maintain face in the current situation is someone who abstained from certain actions in the past that would have been difficult to face up to later. In addition, he fears loss of face now partly because the others may take this as a sign that consideration for his feelings need not be shown in the future. There is nevertheless a limitation to this interdependence between the current situation and the wider social world: an encounter with people whom he will not have dealings with again leaves him free to take a high line that the future will discredit, or free to suffer humiliations that would make future dealings with them an embarrassing thing to have to face.

A person may be said to *be in wrong face* when information is brought forth in some way about his social worth which cannot be integrated, even with effort, into the line that is being sustained for him. A person may be said to *be out of face* when he participates in a contact with others without having ready a line of the kind participants in such situations are expected to take. The intent of many pranks is to lead a person into showing a wrong face or no face, but there will also be serious occasions, of course, when he will find himself expressively out of touch with the situation.

When a person senses that he is in face, he typically responds with feelings of confidence and assurance. Firm in the line he is taking, he feels that he can hold his head up and openly present himself to others. He feels some security and some relief—as he also can when the others feel he is in wrong face but successfully hide these feelings from him.

When a person is in wrong face or out of face, expressive events are being contributed to the encounter which cannot be readily woven into the expressive fabric of the occasion. Should he sense that he is in wrong face or out of face, he is likely to feel ashamed and inferior because of what has happened to the activity on his account and because of what may happen to his reputation as a participant. Further, he may feel bad because he had relied upon the encounter to support an image of self to which he has become emotionally attached and which he now finds threatened. Felt lack of judgmental support from the encounter may take him aback, confuse him, and momentarily incapacitate him as an interactant. His manner and bearing may falter, collapse, and crumble. He may become embarrassed and chagrined; he may become shamefaced. The feeling, whether warranted or not, that he is perceived in a flustered state by others, and that he

8

is presenting no usable line, may add further injuries to his feelings, just as his change from being in wrong face or out of face to being shamefaced can add further disorder to the expressive organization of the situation. Following common usage, I shall employ the term *poise* to refer to the capacity to suppress and conceal any tendency to become shamefaced during encounters with others.

In our Anglo-American society, as in some others, the phrase "to lose face" seems to mean to be in wrong face, to be out of face, or to be shamefaced. The phrase "to save one's face" appears to refer to the process by which the person sustains an impression for others that he has not lost face. Following Chinese usage, one can say that "to give face" is to arrange for another to take a better line than he might otherwise have been able to take,[2] the other thereby gets face given him, this being one way in which he can gain face.

As an aspect of the social code of any social circle, one may expect to find an understanding as to how far a person should go to save his face. Once he takes on a self-image expressed through face he will be expected to live up to it. In different ways in different societies he will be required to show self-respect, abjuring certain actions because they are above or beneath him, while forcing himself to perform others even though they cost him dearly. By entering a situation in which he is given a face to maintain, a person takes on the responsibility of standing guard over the flow of events as they pass before him. He must ensure that a particular *expressive order* is sustained —an order that regulates the flow of events, large or small, so that anything that appears to be expressed by them will be consistent with his face. When a person manifests these compunctions primarily from duty to himself, one speaks in our society of pride; when he does so because of duty to wider social units, and receives support

---

[2] See, for example, Smith, footnote 1; p. 17.

from these units in doing so, one speaks of honor. When these compunctions have to do with postural things, with expressive events derived from the way in which the person handles his body, his emotions, and the things with which he has physical contact, one speaks of dignity, this being an aspect of expressive control that is always praised and never studied. In any case, while his social face can be his most personal possession and the center of his security and pleasure, it is only on loan to him from society; it will be withdrawn unless he conducts himself in a way that is worthy of it. Approved attributes and their relation to face make of every man his own jailer; this is a fundamental social constraint even though each man may like his cell.

Just as the member of any group is expected to have self-respect, so also he is expected to sustain a standard of considerateness; he is expected to go to certain lengths to save the feelings and the face of others present, and he is expected to do this willingly and spontaneously because of emotional identification with the others and with their feelings.[3] In consequence, he is disinclined to witness the defacement of others.[4] The person who can wit-

[3] Of course, the more power and prestige the others have, the more a person is likely to show consideration for their feelings, as H. E. Dale suggests in *The Higher Civil Service of Great Britain* (Oxford, Oxford Univ. Press, 1941), p. 126n. "The doctrine of 'feelings' was expounded to me many years ago by a very eminent civil servant with a pretty taste in cynicism. He explained that the importance of feelings varies in close correspondence with the importance of the person who feels. If the public interest requires that a junior clerk should be removed from his post, no regard need be paid to his feelings; if it is a case of an Assistant Secretary, they must be carefully considered, within reason; if it is a Permanent Secretary, his feelings are a principal element in the situation, and only imperative public interest can override their requirements."

[4] Salesmen, especially street "stemmers," know that if they take a line that will be discredited unless the reluctant customer buys, the customer may be trapped by considerateness and buy in order to save the face of the salesman and prevent what would ordinarily result in a scene.

ness another's humiliation and unfeelingly retain a cool countenance himself is said in our society to be "heartless," just as he who can unfeelingly participate in his own defacement is thought to be "shameless."

The combined effect of the rule of self-respect and the rule of considerateness is that the person tends to conduct himself during an encounter so as to maintain both his own face and the face of the other participants. This means that the line taken by each participant is usually allowed to prevail, and each participant is allowed to carry off the role he appears to have chosen for himself. A state where everyone temporarily accepts everyone else's line is established.[5] This kind of mutual acceptance seems to be a basic structural feature of interaction, especially the interaction of face-to-face talk. It is typically a "working" acceptance, not a "real" one, since it tends to be based not on agreement of candidly expressed heart-felt evaluations, but upon a willingness to give temporary lip service to judgments with which the participants do not really agree.

The mutual acceptance of lines has an important conservative effect upon encounters. Once the person initially

---

[5] Surface agreement in the assessment of social worth does not, of course, imply equality; the evaluation consensually sustained of one participant may be quite different from the one consensually sustained of another. Such agreement is also compatible with expression of differences of opinion between two participants, provided each of the disputants shows "respect" for the other, guiding the expression of disagreement so that it will convey an evaluation of the other that the other will be willing to convey about himself. Extreme cases are provided by wars, duels, and barroom fights, when these are of a gentlemanly kind, for they can be conducted under consensual auspices, with each protagonist guiding his action according to the rules of the game, thereby making it possible for his action to be interpreted as an expression of a fair player openly in combat with a fair opponent. In fact, the rules and etiquette of any game can be analyzed as a means by which the image of a fair player can be expressed, just as the image of a fair player can be analyzed as a means by which the rules and etiquette of a game are sustained.

presents a line, he and the others tend to build their later responses upon it, and in a sense become stuck with it. Should the person radically alter his line, or should it become discredited, then confusion results, for the participants will have prepared and committed themselves for actions that are now unsuitable.

Ordinarily, maintenance of face is a condition of interaction, not its objective. Usual objectives, such as gaining face for oneself, giving free expression to one's true beliefs, introducing depreciating information about the others, or solving problems and performing tasks, are typically pursued in such a way as to be consistent with the maintenance of face. To study face-saving is to study the traffic rules of social interaction; one learns about the code the person adheres to in his movement across the paths and designs of others, but not where he is going, or why he wants to get there. One does not even learn why he is ready to follow the code, for a large number of different motives can equally lead him to do so. He may want to save his own face because of his emotional attachment to the image of self which it expresses, because of his pride or honor, because of the power his presumed status allows him to exert over the other participants, and so on. He may want to save the others' face because of his emotional attachment to an image of them, or because he feels that his coparticipants have a moral right to this protection, or because he wants to avoid the hostility that may be directed toward him if they lose their face. He may feel that an assumption has been made that he is the sort of person who shows compassion and sympathy toward others, so that to retain his own face, he may feel obliged to be considerate of the line taken by the other participants.

By *face-work* I mean to designate the actions taken by a person to make whatever he is doing consistent with face. Face-work serves to counteract "incidents"—that is, events whose effective symbolic implications threaten face. Thus poise is one important type of face-work, for through poise the person controls his embarrassment and hence the embarrassment that he and others might have over his embarrassment. Whether or not the full consequences of face-saving actions are known to the person who employs them, they often become habitual and standardized practices; they are like traditional plays in a game or traditional steps in a dance. Each person, subculture, and society seems to have its own characteristic repertoire of face-saving practices. It is to this repertoire that people partly refer when they ask what a person or culture is "really" like. And yet the particular set of practices stressed by particular persons or groups seems to be drawn from a single logically coherent framework of possible practices. It is as if face, by its very nature, can be saved only in a certain number of ways, and as if each social grouping must make its selections from this single matrix of possibilities.

The members of every social circle may be expected to have some knowledge of face-work and some experience in its use. In our society, this kind of capacity is sometimes called tact, *savoir-faire*, diplomacy, or social skill. Variation in social skill pertains more to the efficacy of face-work than to the frequency of its application, for almost all acts involving others are modified, prescriptively or proscriptively, by considerations of face.

If a person is to employ his repertoire of face-saving practices, obviously he must first become aware of the interpretations that others may have placed upon his acts and the interpretations that he ought perhaps to place upon theirs. In other words, he must exercise perceptiveness.[6] But even if he is properly alive to symbolically con-

[6] Presumably social skill and perceptiveness will be high in groups whose members frequently act as representatives of wider social units such as lineages or nations, for the player here is gambling with a face to which the feelings of many persons are attached. Similarly, one might expect social skill

13

veyed judgments and is socially skilled, he must yet be willing to exercise his perceptiveness and his skill; he must, in short, be prideful and considerate. Admittedly, of course, the possession of perceptiveness and social skill so often leads to their application that in our society terms such as politeness or tact fail to distinguish between the inclination to exercise such capacities and the capacities themselves.

I have already said that the person will have two points of view—a defensive orientation toward saving his own face and a protective orientation toward saving the others' face. Some practices will be primarily defensive and others primarily protective, although in general one may expect these two perspectives to be taken at the same time. In trying to save the face of others, the person must choose a tack that will not lead to loss of his own; in trying to save his own face, he must consider the loss of face that his action may entail for others.

In many societies there is a tendency to distinguish three levels of responsibility that a person may have for a threat to face that his actions have created. First, he may appear to have acted innocently; his offense seems to be unintended and unwitting, and those who perceive his act can feel that he would have attempted to avoid it had he foreseen its offensive consequences. In our society one calls such threats to face *faux pas, gaffes,* boners, or bricks. Secondly, the offending person may appear to have acted maliciously and spitefully, with the intention of causing open insult. Thirdly, there are incidental offenses; these arise as an unplanned but sometimes anticipated by-product of action—action the offender performs in spite of its offensive consequences, although not out of spite.

---

to be well developed among those of high station and those with whom they have dealings, for the more face an interactant has, the greater the number of events that may be inconsistent with it, and hence the greater the need for social skill to forestall or counteract these inconsistencies.

From the point of view of a particular participant, these three types of threat can be introduced by the participant himself against his own face, by himself against the face of the others, by the others against their own face, or by the others against himself. Thus the person may find himself in many different relations to a threat to face. If he is to handle himself and others well in all contingencies, he will have to have a repertoire of face-saving practices for each of these possible relations to threat.

THE BASIC KINDS OF FACE-WORK

The avoidance process.—The surest way for a person to prevent threats to his face is to avoid contacts in which these threats are likely to occur. In all societies one can observe this in the avoidance relationship[7] and in the tendency for certain delicate transactions to be conducted by go-betweens.[8] Similarly, in many societies, members know the value of voluntarily making a gracious withdrawal before an anticipated threat to face has had a chance to occur.[9]

[7] In our own society an illustration of avoidance is found in the middle- and upper-class Negro who avoids certain face-to-face contacts with whites in order to protect the self-evaluation projected by his clothes and manner. See, for example, Charles Johnson, *Patterns of Negro Segregation* (New York, Harper, 1943), ch. 13. The function of avoidance in maintaining the kinship system in small preliterate societies might be taken as a particular illustration of the same general theme.

[8] An illustration is given by K. S. Latourette, *The Chinese: Their History and Culture* (New York, Macmillan, 1942): "A neighbor or a group of neighbors may tender their good offices in adjusting a quarrel in which each antagonist would be sacrificing his face by taking the first step in approaching the other. The wise intermediary can effect the reconciliation while preserving the dignity of both" (vol. 2: p. 211).

[9] In an unpublished paper Harold Garfinkel has suggested that when the person finds that he has lost face in a conversational encounter, he may feel a desire to disappear or "drop

Once the person does chance an encounter, other kinds of avoidance practices come into play. As defensive measures, he keeps off topics and away from activities that would lead to the expression of information that is inconsistent with the line he is maintaining. At opportune moments he will change the topic of conversation or the direction of activity. He will often present initially a front of diffidence and composure, suppressing any show of feeling until he has found out what kind of line the others will be ready to support for him. Any claims regarding self may be made with belittling modesty, with strong qualifications, or with a note of unseriousness; by hedging in these ways he will have prepared a self for himself that will not be discredited by exposure, personal failure, or the unanticipated acts of others. And if he does not hedge his claims about self, he will at least attempt to be realistic about them, knowing that otherwise events may discredit him and make him lose face.

Certain protective maneuvers are as common as these defensive ones. The person shows respect and politeness, making sure to extend to others any ceremonial treatment that might be their due. He employs discretion; he leaves unstated facts that might implicitly or explicitly contradict and embarrass the positive claims made by others.[10] He

---

through the floor," and that this may involve a wish not only to conceal loss of face but also to return magically to a point in time when it would have been possible to save face by avoiding the encounter.

[10] When the person knows the others well, he will know what issues ought not to be raised and what situations the others ought not to be placed in, and he will be free to introduce matters at will in all other areas. When the others are strangers to him, he will often reverse the formula, restricting himself to specific areas he knows are safe. On these occasions, as Simmel suggests, ". . . discretion consists by no means only in the respect for the secret of the other, for his specific will to conceal this or that from us, but in staying away from the knowledge of all that the other does not expressly reveal to us." See *The Sociology of Georg Simmel* (Kurt H. Wolff, tr. and ed.) (Glencoe, Ill., Free Press, 1950), pp. 320–21.

employs circumlocutions and deceptions, phrasing his replies with careful ambiguity so that the others' face is preserved even if their welfare is not.[11] He employs courtesies, making slight modifications of his demands on or appraisals of the others so that they will be able to define the situation as one in which their self-respect is not threatened. In making a belittling demand upon the others, or in imputing uncomplimentary attributes to them, he may employ a joking manner, allowing them to take the line that they are good sports, able to relax from their ordinary standards of pride and honor. And before engaging in a potentially offensive act, he may provide explanations as to why the others ought not to be affronted by it. For example, if he knows that it will be necessary to withdraw from the encounter before it has terminated, he may tell the others in advance that it is necessary for him to leave, so that they will have faces that are prepared for it. But neutralizing the potentially offensive act need not be done verbally; he may wait for a propitious moment or natural break—for example, in conversation, a momentary lull when no one speaker can be affronted—and then leave, in this way using the context instead of his words as a guarantee of inoffensiveness.

When a person fails to prevent an incident, he can still attempt to maintain the fiction that no threat to face has occurred. The most blatant example of this is found where

[11] The Western traveler used to complain that the Chinese could never be trusted to say what they meant but always said what they felt their Western listener wanted to hear. The Chinese used to complain that the Westerner was brusque, boorish, and unmannered. In terms of Chinese standards, presumably, the conduct of a Westerner is so gauche that he creates an emergency, forcing the Asian to forgo any kind of direct reply in order to rush in with a remark that might rescue the Westerner from the compromising position in which he had placed himself. (See Smith, footnote 1; ch. 8, "The Talent for Indirection.") This is an instance of the important group of misunderstandings which arise during interaction between persons who come from groups with different ritual standards.

the person acts as if an event that contains a threatening expression has not occurred at all. He may apply this studied nonobservance to his own acts—as when he does not by any outward sign admit that his stomach is rumbling—or to the acts of others, as when he does not "see" that another has stumbled.[12] Social life in mental hospitals owes much to this process; patients employ it in regard to their own peculiarities, and visitors employ it, often with tenuous desperation, in regard to patients. In general, tactful blindness of this kind is applied only to events that, if perceived at all, could be perceived and interpreted only as threats to face.

A more important, less spectacular kind of tactful overlooking is practiced when a person openly acknowledges an incident as an event that has occurred, but not as an event that contains a threatening expression. If he is not the one who is responsible for the incident, then his blindness will have to be supported by his forbearance; if he is the doer of the threatening deed, then his blindness will have to be supported by his willingness to seek a way of dealing with the matter, which leaves him dangerously dependent upon the cooperative forbearance of the others.

Another kind of avoidance occurs when a person loses control of his expressions during an encounter. At such times he may try not so much to overlook the incident as to hide or conceal his activity in some way, thus making it possible for the others to avoid some of the difficulties created by a participant who has not maintained face. Correspondingly, when a person is caught out of face because he had not expected to be thrust into interaction, or because strong feelings have disrupted his expressive mask, the others may protectively turn away from him or his activity for a moment, to give him time to assemble himself.

[12] A pretty example of this is found in parade-ground etiquette which may oblige those in a parade to treat anyone who faints as if he were not present at all.

The corrective process.—When the participants in an undertaking or encounter fail to prevent the occurrence of an event that is expressively incompatible with the judgments of social worth that are being maintained, and when the event is of the kind that is difficult to overlook, then the participants are likely to give it accredited status as an incident—to ratify it as a threat that deserves direct official attention—and to proceed to try to correct for its effects. At this point one or more participants find themselves in an established state of ritual disequilibrium or disgrace, and an attempt must be made to re-establish a satisfactory ritual state for them. I use the term *ritual* because I am dealing with acts through whose symbolic component the actor shows how worthy he is of respect or how worthy he feels others are of it. The imagery of equilibrium is apt here because the length and intensity of the corrective effort is nicely adapted to the persistence and intensity of the threat.[13] One's face, then, is a sacred thing, and the expressive order required to sustain it is therefore a ritual one.

The sequence of acts set in motion by an acknowledged threat to face, and terminating in the re-establishment of ritual equilibrium, I shall call an *interchange*.[14] Defining

[13] This kind of imagery is one that social anthropologists seem to find naturally fitting. Note, for example, the implications of the following statement by Margaret Mead in her "Kinship in the Admiralty Islands," *Anthropological Papers of the American Museum of Natural History*, 34:183–358: "If a husband beats his wife, custom demands that she leave him and go to her brother, real or officiating, and remain a length of time commensurate with the degree of her offended dignity" (p. 274).

[14] The notion of interchange is drawn in part from Eliot D. Chapple, "Measuring Human Relations," *Genetic Psychol. Monographs* (1940) 22:3–147, especially pp. 26–30, and from A. B. Horsfall and C. A. Arensberg, "Teamwork and Productivity in a Shoe Factory," *Human Organization* (1949) 8:13–25, especially p. 19. For further material on the interchange as a unit see E. Goffman, "Communication Conduct in an

a message or move as everything conveyed by an actor during a turn at taking action, one can say that an interchange will involve two or more moves and two or more participants. Obvious examples in our society may be found in the sequence of "Excuse me" and "Certainly," and in the exchange of presents or visits. The interchange seems to be a basic concrete unit of social activity and provides one natural empirical way to study interaction of all kinds. Face-saving practices can be usefully classified according to their position in the natural sequence of moves that comprise this unit. Aside from the event which introduces the need for a corrective interchange, four classic moves seem to be involved.

There is, first, the challenge, by which participants take on the responsibility of calling attention to the misconduct; by implication they suggest that the threatened claims are to stand firm and that the threatening event itself will have to be brought back into line.

The second move consists of the offering, whereby a participant, typically the offender, is given a chance to correct for the offense and re-establish the expressive order. Some classic ways of making this move are available. On the one hand, an attempt can be made to show that what admittedly appeared to be a threatening expression is really a meaningless event, or an unintentional act, or a joke not meant to be taken seriously, or an unavoidable, "understandable" product of extenuating circumstances. On the other hand, the meaning of the event may be granted and effort concentrated on the creator of it. Information may be provided to show that the creator was under the influence of something and not himself, or that he was under the command of somebody else and not acting for himself. When a person claims that an act was meant in jest, he may go on and claim that the self

Island Community," unpublished Ph.D. dissertation, Department of Sociology, University of Chicago, 1953, especially chs. 12 and 13, pp. 165–95.

that seemed to lie behind the act was also projected as a joke. When a person suddenly finds that he has demonstrably failed in capacities that the others assumed him to have and to claim for himself—such as the capacity to spell, to perform minor tasks, to talk without malapropisms, and so on—he may quickly add, in a serious or unserious way, that he claims these incapacities as part of his self. The meaning of the threatening incident thus stands, but it can now be incorporated smoothly into the flow of expressive events.

As a supplement to or substitute for the strategy of redefining the offensive act or himself, the offender can follow two other procedures: he can provide compensations to the injured—when it is not his own face that he has threatened; or he can provide punishment, penance, and expiation for himself. These are important moves or phases in the ritual interchange. Even though the offender may fail to prove his innocence, he can suggest through these means that he is now a renewed person, a person who has paid for his sin against the expressive order and is once more to be trusted in the judgmental scene. Further, he can show that he does not treat the feelings of the others lightly, and that if their feelings have been injured by him, however innocently, he is prepared to pay a price for his action. Thus he assures the others that they can accept his explanations without this acceptance constituting a sign of weakness and a lack of pride on their part. Also, by his treatment of himself, by his self-castigation, he shows that he is clearly aware of the kind of crime he would have committed had the incident been what it first appeared to be, and that he knows the kind of punishment that ought to be accorded to one who would commit such a crime. The suspected person thus shows that he is thoroughly capable of taking the role of the others toward his own activity, that he can still be used as a responsible participant in the ritual process, and that the rules of conduct which he appears to have broken are still sacred, real, and unweakened. An offensive act may arouse anxiety about the ritual code; the offender allays this anxiety by showing that both the code and he as an upholder of it are still in working order.

After the challenge and the offering have been made, the third move can occur: the persons to whom the offering is made can accept it as a satisfactory means of reestablishing the expressive order and the faces supported by this order. Only then can the offender cease the major part of his ritual offering.

In the terminal move of the interchange, the forgiven person conveys a sign of gratitude to those who have given him the indulgence of forgiveness.

The phases of the corrective process—challenge, offering, acceptance, and thanks—provide a model for interpersonal ritual behavior, but a model that may be departed from in significant ways. For example, the offended parties may give the offender a chance to initiate the offering on his own before a challenge is made and before they ratify the offense as an incident. This is a common courtesy, extended on the assumption that the recipient will introduce a self-challenge. Further, when the offended persons accept the corrective offering, the offender may suspect that this has been grudgingly done from tact, and so he may volunteer additional corrective offerings, not allowing the matter to rest until he has received a second or third acceptance of his repeated apology. Or the offended persons may tactfully take over the role of the offender and volunteer excuses for him that will, perforce, be acceptable to the offended persons.

An important departure from the standard corrective cycle occurs when a challenged offender patently refuses to heed the warning and continues with his offending behavior, instead of setting the activity to rights. This move shifts the play back to the challengers. If they countenance the refusal to meet their demands, then it will be plain that their challenge was a bluff and that the bluff has been called. This is an untenable position; a face for themselves cannot be derived from it, and they are left to bluster. To avoid this fate, some classic moves are open to them. For instance, they can resort to tactless, violent retaliation, destroying either themselves or the person who had refused to heed their warning. Or they can withdraw from the undertaking in a visible huff—righteously indignant, outraged, but confident of ultimate vindication. Both tacks provide a way of denying the offender his status as an interactant, and hence denying the reality of the offensive judgment he has made. Both strategies are ways of salvaging face, but for all concerned the costs are usually high. It is partly to forestall such scenes that an offender is usually quick to offer apologies; he does not want the affronted persons to trap themselves into the obligation to resort to desperate measures.

It is plain that emotions play a part in these cycles of response, as when anguish is expressed because of what one has done to another's face, or anger because of what has been done to one's own. I want to stress that these emotions function as moves, and fit so precisely into the logic of the ritual game that it would seem difficult to understand them without it.[15] In fact, spontaneously expressed feelings are likely to fit into the formal pattern of the ritual interchange more elegantly than consciously designed ones.

[15] Even when a child demands something and is refused, he is likely to cry and sulk not as an irrational expression of frustration but as a ritual move, conveying that he already has a face to lose and that its loss is not to be permitted lightly. Sympathetic parents may even allow for such display, seeing in these crude strategies the beginnings of a social self.

MAKING POINTS—THE AGGRESSIVE USE OF
FACE-WORK

Every face-saving practice which is allowed to neutralize a particular threat opens up the possibility that the threat will be willfully introduced for what can be safely gained by it. If a person knows that his modesty will be answered by others' praise of him, he can fish for compliments. If his own appraisal of self will be checked against incidental events, then he can arrange for favorable incidental events to appear. If others are prepared to overlook an affront to them and act forbearantly, or to accept apologies, then he can rely on this as a basis for safely offending them. He can attempt by sudden withdrawal to force the others into a ritually unsatisfactory state, leaving them to flounder in an interchange that cannot readily be completed. Finally, at some expense to himself, he can arrange for the others to hurt his feelings, thus forcing them to feel guilt, remorse, and sustained ritual disequilibrium.[16]

When a person treats face-work not as something he need be prepared to perform, but rather as something that others can be counted on to perform or to accept, then an encounter or an undertaking becomes less a scene of mutual considerateness than an arena in which a contest or match is held. The purpose of the game is to preserve everyone's line from an inexcusable contradiction, while scoring as many points as possible against one's adversaries and making as many gains as possible for oneself. An audience to the struggle is almost a necessity. The

[16] The strategy of maneuvering another into a position where he cannot right the harm he has done is very commonly employed but nowhere with such devotion to the ritual model of conduct as in revengeful suicide. See, for example, M. D. W. Jeffreys, "Samsonic Suicide, or Suicide of Revenge Among Africans," *African Studies* (1952) 11:118–22.

general method is for the person to introduce favorable facts about himself and unfavorable facts about the others in such a way that the only reply the others will be able to think up will be one that terminates the interchange in a grumble, a meager excuse, a face-saving I-can-take-a-joke laugh, or an empty stereotyped comeback of the "Oh yeah?" or "That's what you think" variety. The losers in such cases will have to cut their losses, tacitly grant the loss of a point, and attempt to do better in the next interchange. Points made by allusion to social class status are sometimes called snubs; those made by allusions to moral respectability are sometimes called digs; in either case one deals with a capacity at what is sometimes called "bitchiness."

In aggressive interchanges the winner not only succeeds in introducing information favorable to himself and unfavorable to the others, but also demonstrates that as interactant he can handle himself better than his adversaries. Evidence of this capacity is often more important than all the other information the person conveys in the interchange, so that the introduction of a "crack" in verbal interaction tends to imply that the initiator is better at footwork than those who must suffer his remarks. However, if they succeed in making a successful parry of the thrust and then a successful riposte, the instigator of the play must not only face the disparagement with which the others have answered him but also accept the fact that his assumption of superiority in footwork has proven false. He is made to look foolish; he loses face. Hence it is always a gamble to "make a remark." The tables can be turned and the aggressor can lose more than he could have gained had his move won the point. Successful ripostes or comebacks in our society are sometimes called squelches or toppers; theoretically it would be possible for a squelch to be squelched, a topper to be topped, and a riposte to be parried with a counterriposte, but except in staged interchanges this third level of successful action seems rare.[17]

THE CHOICE OF APPROPRIATE FACE-WORK

When an incident occurs, the person whose face is threatened may attempt to reinstate the ritual order by means of one kind of strategy, while the other participants may desire or expect a practice of a different type to be employed. When, for example, a minor mishap occurs, momentarily revealing a person in wrong face or out of face, the others are often more willing and able to act blind to the discrepancy than is the threatened person himself. Often they would prefer him to exercise poise,[18] while he feels that he cannot afford to overlook what has happened to his face and so becomes apologetic and

[17] In board and card games the player regularly takes into consideration the possible responses of his adversaries to a play that he is about to make, and even considers the possibility that his adversaries will know that he is taking such precautions. Conversational play is by comparison surprisingly impulsive; people regularly make remarks about others present without carefully designing their remarks to prevent a successful comeback. Similarly, while feinting and sandbagging are theoretical possibilities during talk, they seem to be little exploited.

[18] Folklore imputes a great deal of poise to the upper classes. If there is truth in this belief it may lie in the fact that the upper-class person tends to find himself in encounters in which he outranks the other participants in ways additional to class. The ranking participant is often somewhat independent of the good opinion of the others and finds it practical to be arrogant, sticking to a face regardless of whether the encounter supports it. On the other hand, those who are in the power of a fellow-participant tend to be very much concerned with the valuation he makes of them or witnesses being made of them, and so find it difficult to maintain a slightly wrong face without becoming embarrassed and apologetic. It may be added that people who lack awareness of the symbolism in minor events may keep cool in difficult situations, showing poise that they do not really possess.

shamefaced, if he is the creator of the incident, or destructively assertive, if the others are responsible for it.[19] Yet on the other hand, a person may manifest poise when the others feel that he ought to have broken down into embarrassed apology—that he is taking undue advantage of their helpfulness by his attempts to brazen it out. Sometimes a person may himself be undecided as to which practice to employ, leaving the others in the embarrassing position of not knowing which tack they are going to have to follow. Thus when a person makes a slight *gaffe*, he and the others may become embarrassed not because of inability to handle such difficulties, but because for a moment no one knows whether the offender is going to act blind to the incident, or give it joking recognition, or employ some other face-saving practice.

COOPERATION IN FACE-WORK

When a face has been threatened, face-work must be done, but whether this is initiated and primarily carried through by the person whose face is threatened, or by the offender, or by a mere witness,[20] is often of secondary importance. Lack of effort on the part of one person induces compensative effort from others; a contribution by one person relieves the others of the task. In fact, there are many minor incidents in which the offender and the

[19] Thus, in our society, when a person feels that others expect him to measure up to approved standards of cleanliness, tidiness, fairness, hospitality, generosity, affluence, and so on, or when he sees himself as someone who ought to maintain such standards, he may burden an encounter with extended apologies for his failings, while all along the other participants do not care about the standard, or do not believe the person is really lacking in it, or are convinced that he is lacking in it and see the apology itself as a vain effort at self-elevation.

[20] Thus one function of seconds in actual duels, as well as in figurative ones, is to provide an excuse for not fighting that both contestants can afford to accept.

offended simultaneously attempt to initiate an apology.[21] Resolution of the situation to everyone's apparent satisfaction is the first requirement; correct apportionment of blame is typically a secondary consideration. Hence terms such as tact and *savoir-faire* fail to distinguish whether it is the person's own face that his diplomacy saves or the face of the others. Similarly, terms such as *gaffe* and *faux pas* fail to specify whether it is the actor's own face he has threatened or the face of other participants. And it is understandable that if one person finds he is powerless to save his own face, the others seem especially bound to protect him. For example, in polite society, a handshake that perhaps should not have been extended becomes one that cannot be declined. Thus one accounts for the *noblesse oblige* through which those of high status are expected to curb their power of embarrassing their lessers,[22] as

[21] See, for instance, Jackson Toby, "Some Variables in Role Conflict Analysis," *Social Forces* (1952) 30:323–37: "With adults there is less likelihood for essentially trivial issues to produce conflict. The automatic apology of two strangers who accidentally collide on a busy street illustrates the integrative function of etiquette. In effect, each of the parties to the collision says, 'I don't know whether I am responsible for this situation, but *if* I am, you have a right to be angry with me, a right that I pray you will not exercise.' By defining the situation as one in which both parties must abase themselves, society enables each to keep his self-respect. Each may feel in his heart of hearts, 'Why can't that stupid ass watch where he's going?' But overtly *each plays the role of the guilty party* whether he feels he has been miscast or not" (p. 325).

[22] Regardless of the person's relative social position, in one sense he has power over the other participants and they must rely upon his considerateness. When the others act toward him in some way, they presume upon a social relationship to him, since one of the things expressed by interaction is the relationship of the interactants. Thus they compromise themselves, for they place him in a position to discredit the claims they express as to his attitude toward them. Hence in response to claimed social relationships every person, of high estate or low, will be expected to exercise *noblesse oblige* and refrain from exploiting the compromised position of the others.

Since social relationships are defined partly in terms of vol-

well as the fact that the handicapped often accept courtesies that they can manage better without.

Since each participant in an undertaking is concerned, albeit for differing reasons, with saving his own face and the face of the others, then tacit cooperation will naturally arise so that the participants together can attain their shared but differently motivated objectives.

One common type of tacit cooperation in face-saving is the tact exerted in regard to face-work itself. The person not only defends his own face and protects the face of the others, but also acts so as to make it possible and even easy for the others to employ face-work for themselves and him. He helps them to help themselves and him. Social etiquette, for example, warns men against asking for New Year's Eve dates too early in the season, lest the girl find it difficult to provide a gentle excuse for refusing. This second-order tact can be further illustrated by the widespread practice of negative-attribute etiquette. The person who has an unapparent negatively valued attribute often finds it expedient to begin an encounter with an unobtrusive admission of his failing, especially with persons who are uninformed about him. The others are thus warned in advance against making disparaging remarks about his kind of person and are saved from the contradiction of

---

untary mutual aid, refusal of a request for assistance becomes a delicate matter, potentially destructive of the asker's face. Chester Holcombe, *The Real Chinaman* (New York, Dodd, Mead, 1895), provides a Chinese instance: "Much of the falsehood to which the Chinese as a nation are said to be addicted is a result of the demands of etiquette. A plain, frank 'no' is the height of discourtesy. Refusal or denial of any sort must be softened and toned down into an expression of regretted inability. Unwillingness to grant a favor is never shown. In place of it there is seen a chastened feeling of sorrow that unavoidable but quite imaginary circumstances render it wholly impossible. Centuries of practice in this form of evasion have made the Chinese matchlessly fertile in the invention and development of excuses. It is rare, indeed, that one is caught at a loss for a bit of artfully embroidered fiction with which to hide an unwelcome truth" (pp. 274–75).

acting in a friendly fashion to a person toward whom they are unwittingly being hostile. This strategy also prevents the others from automatically making assumptions about him which place him in a false position and saves him from painful forbearance or embarrassing remonstrances.

Tact in regard to face-work often relies for its operation on a tacit agreement to do business through the language of hint—the language of innuendo, ambiguities, well-placed pauses, carefully worded jokes, and so on.[23] The rule regarding this unofficial kind of communication is that the sender ought not to act as if he had officially conveyed the message he has hinted at, while the recipients have the right and the obligation to act as if they have not officially received the message contained in the hint. Hinted communication, then, is deniable communication; it need not be faced up to. It provides a means by which the person can be warned that his current line or the current situation is leading to loss of face, without this warning itself becoming an incident.

Another form of tacit cooperation, and one that seems to be much used in many societies, is reciprocal self-denial. Often the person does not have a clear idea of what would be a just or acceptable apportionment of judgments during the occasion, and so he voluntarily deprives or depreciates himself while indulging and complimenting the others, in both cases carrying the judgments safely past what is likely to be just. The favorable judgments about himself he allows to come from the others; the unfavorable judgments of himself are his own contributions. This "after you, Alphonse" technique works, of course, because in depriving himself he can reliably anticipate that the others will compliment or indulge him. Whatever allocation of favors is eventually established, all participants are first

[23] Useful comments on some of the structural roles played by unofficial communication can be found in a discussion of irony and banter in Tom Burns, "Friends, Enemies, and the Polite Fiction," *Amer. Sociol. Rev.* (1953), 18:654–62.

given a chance to show that they are not bound or constrained by their own desires and expectations, that they
have a properly modest view of themselves, and that they
can be counted upon to support the ritual code. Negative
bargaining, through which each participant tries to make
the terms of trade more favorable to the other side, is
another instance; as a form of exchange perhaps it is more
widespread than the economist's kind.

A person's performance of face-work, extended by his
tacit agreement to help others perform theirs, represents
his willingness to abide by the ground rules of social interaction. Here is the hallmark of his socialization as an
interactant. If he and the others were not socialized in
this way, interaction in most societies and most situations
would be a much more hazardous thing for feelings and
faces. The person would find it impractical to be oriented
to symbolically conveyed appraisals of social worth, or
to be possessed of feelings—that is, it would be impractical
for him to be a ritually delicate object. And as I shall suggest, if the person were not a ritually delicate object, occasions of talk could not be organized in the way they
usually are. It is no wonder that trouble is caused by a
person who cannot be relied upon to play the face-saving
game.

The Ritual Roles of the Self

So far I have implicitly been using a double definition
of self: the self as an image pieced together from the expressive implications of the full flow of events in an undertaking; and the self as a kind of player in a ritual game
who copes honorably or dishonorably, diplomatically or
undiplomatically, with the judgmental contingencies of the
situation. A double mandate is involved. As sacred objects,
men are subject to slights and profanation; hence as
players of the ritual game they have had to lead themselves into duels, and wait for a round of shots to go wide

of the mark before embracing their opponents. Here is an echo of the distinction between the value of a hand drawn at cards and the capacity of the person who plays it. This distinction must be kept in mind, even though it appears that once a person has gotten a reputation for good or bad play this reputation may become part of the face he must later play at maintaining.

Once the two roles of the self have been separated, one can look to the ritual code implicit in face-work to learn how the two roles are related. When a person is responsible for introducing a threat to another's face, he apparently has a right, within limits, to wriggle out of the difficulty by means of self-abasement. When performed voluntarily these indignities do not seem to profane his own image. It is as if he had the right of insulation and could castigate himself qua actor without injuring himself qua object of ultimate worth. By token of the same insulation he can belittle himself and modestly underplay his positive qualities, with the understanding that no one will take his statements as a fair representation of his sacred self. On the other hand, if he is forced against his will to treat himself in these ways, his face, his pride, and his honor will be seriously threatened. Thus, in terms of the ritual code, the person seems to have a special license to accept mistreatment at his own hands that he does not have the right to accept from others. Perhaps this is a safe arrangement because he is not likely to carry this license too far, whereas the others, were they given this privilege, might be more likely to abuse it.

Further, within limits the person has a right to forgive other participants for affronts to his sacred image. He can forbearantly overlook minor slurs upon his face, and in regard to somewhat greater injuries he is the one person who is in a position to accept apologies on behalf of his sacred self. This is a relatively safe prerogative for the person to have in regard to himself, for it is one that is exercised in the interests of the others or of the undertaking. Interestingly enough, when the person commits a *gaffe* against himself, it is not he who has the license to forgive the event; only the others have that prerogative, and it is a safe prerogative for them to have because they can exercise it only in his interests or in the interests of the undertaking. One finds, then, a system of checks and balances by which each participant tends to be given the right to handle only those matters which he will have little motivation for mishandling. In short, the rights and obligations of an interactant are designed to prevent him from abusing his role as an object of sacred value.

Spoken Interaction

Most of what has been said so far applies to encounters of both an immediate and mediated kind, although in the latter the interaction is likely to be more attenuated, with each participant's line being gleaned from such things as written statements and work records. During direct personal contacts, however, unique informational conditions prevail and the significance of face becomes especially clear. The human tendency to use signs and symbols means that evidence of social worth and of mutual evaluations will be conveyed by very minor things, and these things will be witnessed, as will the fact that they have been witnessed. An unguarded glance, a momentary change in tone of voice, an ecological position taken or not taken, can drench a talk with judgmental significance. Therefore, just as there is no occasion of talk in which improper impressions could not intentionally or unintentionally arise, so there is no occasion of talk so trivial as not to require each participant to show serious concern with the way in which he handles himself and the others present. Ritual factors which are present in mediated contacts are here present in an extreme form.

In any society, whenever the physical possibility of spoken interaction arises, it seems that a system of practices, conventions, and procedural rules comes into play which functions as a means of guiding and organizing the flow of messages. An understanding will prevail as to when and where it will be permissible to initiate talk, among whom, and by means of what topics of conversation. A set of significant gestures is employed to initiate a spate of communication and as a means for the persons concerned to accredit each other as legitimate participants.[24] When this process of reciprocal ratification occurs, the persons so ratified are in what might be called a *state of talk*—that is, they have declared themselves officially open to one another for purposes of spoken communication and guarantee together to maintain a flow of words. A set of significant gestures is also employed by which one or more new participants can officially join the talk, by which one or more accredited participants can officially withdraw, and by which the state of talk can be terminated.

A single focus of thought and visual attention, and a single flow of talk, tends to be maintained and to be legitimated as officially representative of the encounter. The concerted and official visual attention of the participants tends to be transferred smoothly by means of formal

[24] The meaning of this status can be appreciated by looking at the kinds of unlegitimated or unratified participation that can occur in spoken interaction. A person may overhear others unbeknownst to them; he can overhear them when they know this to be the case and when they choose either to act as if he were not overhearing them or to signal to him informally that they know he is overhearing them. In all of these cases, the outsider is officially held at bay as someone who is not formally participating in the occasion. Ritual codes, of course, require a ratified participant to be treated quite differently from an unratified one. Thus, for example, only a certain amount of insult from a ratified participant can be ignored without this avoidance practice causing loss of face to the insulted persons; after a point they must challenge the offender and demand redress. However, in many societies apparently, many kinds of verbal abuse from unratified participants can be ignored, without this failure to challenge constituting a loss of face.

or informal clearance cues, by which the current speaker signals that he is about to relinquish the floor and the prospective speaker signals a desire to be given the floor. An understanding will prevail as to how long and how frequently each participant is to hold the floor. The recipients convey to the speaker, by appropriate gestures, that they are according him their attention. Participants restrict their involvement in matters external to the encounter and observe a limit to involvement in any one message of the encounter, in this way ensuring that they will be able to follow along whatever direction the topic of conversation takes them. Interruptions and lulls are regulated so as not to disrupt the flow of messages. Messages that are not part of the officially accredited flow are modulated so as not to interfere seriously with the accredited messages. Nearby persons who are not participants visibly desist in some way from exploiting their communication position and also modify their own communication, if any, so as not to provide difficult interference. A particular ethos or emotional atmosphere is allowed to prevail. A polite accord is typically maintained, and participants who may be in real disagreement with one another give temporary lip service to views that bring them into agreement on matters of fact and principle. Rules are followed for smoothing out the transition, if any, from one topic of conversation to another.[25]

These rules of talk pertain not to spoken interaction considered as an ongoing process, but to *an* occasion of talk or episode of interaction as a naturally bounded unit. This unit consists of the total activity that occurs during the time that a given set of participants have accredited one another for talk and maintain a single moving focus of attention.[26]

[25] For a further treatment of the structure of spoken interaction see Goffman, footnote 14.

[26] I mean to include formal talks where rules of procedure are explicitly prescribed and officially enforced, and where only

The conventions regarding the structure of occasions of talk represent an effective solution to the problem of organizing a flow of spoken messages. In attempting to discover how it is that these conventions are maintained in force as guides to action, one finds evidence to suggest a functional relationship between the structure of the self and the structure of spoken interaction.

The socialized interactant comes to handle spoken interaction as he would any other kind, as something that must be pursued with ritual care. By automatically appealing to face, he knows how to conduct himself in regard to talk. By repeatedly and automatically asking himself the question, "If I do or do not act in this way, will I or others lose face?" he decides at each moment, consciously or unconsciously, how to behave. For example, entrance into an occasion of spoken interaction may be taken as a symbol of intimacy or legitimate purpose, and so the person must, to save his face, desist from entering into talk with a given set of others unless his circumstances justify what is expressed about him by his entrance. Once approached for talk, he must accede to the others in order to save their face. Once engaged in conversation, he must demand only the amount of attention that is an appropriate expression of his relative social worth. Undue lulls come to be potential signs of having nothing in common, or of being insufficiently self-possessed to create something to say, and hence must be avoided. Similarly, interruptions and inattentiveness may convey disrespect and must be avoided unless the implied disrespect is an accepted part of the relationship. A surface of agreement must be maintained by means of discretion and white lies, so that the assumption of mutual approval will not be discredited. Withdrawal must be handled so that it will not

certain categories of participants may be allowed to hold the floor—as well as chats and sociable talks where rules are not explicit and the role of speaker passes back and forth among the participants.

convey an improper evaluation.[27] The person must restrain his emotional involvement so as not to present an image of someone with no self-control or dignity who does not rise above his feelings.

The relation between the self and spoken interaction is further displayed when one examines the ritual interchange. In a conversational encounter, interaction tends to proceed in spurts, an interchange at a time, and the flow of information and business is parcelled out into these relatively closed ritual units.[28] The lull between interchanges tends to be greater than the lull between turns at talking in an interchange, and there tends to be a less meaningful relationship between two sequential interchanges than between two sequential speeches in an interchange.

This structural aspect of talk arises from the fact that when a person volunteers a statement or message, however trivial or commonplace, he commits himself and those he addresses, and in a sense places everyone present in jeopardy. By saying something, the speaker opens himself up to the possibility that the intended recipients will affront him by not listening or will think him forward, foolish, or offensive in what he has said. And should he meet with such a reception, he will find himself committed to the necessity of taking face-saving action against them. Fur-

[27] Among people who have had some experience in interacting with one another, conversational encounters are often terminated in such a way as to give the appearance that all participants have independently hit upon the same moment to withdraw. The disbandment is general, and no one may be conscious of the exchange of cues that has been required to make such a happy simultaneity of action possible. Each participant is thus saved from the compromising position of showing readiness to spend further time with someone who is not as ready to spend time with him.

[28] The empirical discreteness of the interchange unit is sometimes obscured when the same person who provides the terminating turn at talking in one interchange initiates the first turn at talking in the next. However, the analytical utility of the interchange as a unit remains.

thermore, by saying something the speaker opens his intended recipients up to the possibility that the message will be self-approving, presumptuous, demanding, insulting, and generally an affront to them or to their conception of him, so that they will find themselves obliged to take action against him in defense of the ritual code. And should the speaker praise the recipients, they will be obliged to make suitable denials, showing that they do not hold too favorable an opinion of themselves and are not so eager to secure indulgences as to endanger their reliability and flexibility as interactants.

Thus when one person volunteers a message, thereby contributing what might easily be a threat to the ritual equilibrium, someone else present is obliged to show that the message has been received and that its content is acceptable to all concerned or can be acceptably countered. This acknowledging reply, of course, may contain a tactful rejection of the original communication, along with a request for modification. In such cases, several exchanges of messages may be required before the interchange is terminated on the basis of modified lines. The interchange comes to a close when it is possible to allow it to do so—that is, when everyone present has signified that he has been ritually appeased to a degree satisfactory to him.[29] A momentary lull between interchanges is possible, for it comes at a time when it will not be taken as a sign of something untoward.

In general, then, a person determines how he ought to conduct himself during an occasion of talk by testing the potentially symbolic meaning of his acts against the self-

[29] The occurrence of the interchange unit is an empirical fact. In addition to the ritual explanation for it, others may be suggested. For example, when the person makes a statement and receives a reply at once, this provides him with a way of learning that his statement has been received and correctly received. Such "metacommunication" would be necessary on functional grounds even were it unnecessary on ritual ones.

images that are being sustained. In doing this, however, he incidentally subjects his behavior to the expressive order that prevails and contributes to the orderly flow of messages. His aim is to save face; his effect is to save the situation. From the point of view of saving face, then, it is a good thing that spoken interaction has the conventional organization given it; from the point of view of sustaining an orderly flow of spoken messages, it is a good thing that the self has the ritual structure given it.

I do not mean, however, to claim that another kind of person related to another kind of message organization would not do as well. More important, I do not claim that the present system is without weaknesses or drawbacks; these must be expected, for everywhere in social life a mechanism or functional relation which solves one set of problems necessarily creates a set of potential difficulties and abuses all its own. For example, a characteristic problem in the ritual organization of personal contacts is that while a person can save his face by quarreling or by indignantly withdrawing from the encounter, he does this at the cost of the interaction. Furthermore, the person's attachment to face gives others something to aim at; they can not only make an effort to wound him unofficially, but may even make an official attempt utterly to destroy his face. Also, fear over possible loss of his face often prevents the person from initiating contacts in which important information can be transmitted and important relationships re-established; he may be led to seek the safety of solitude rather than the danger of social encounters. He may do this even though others feel that he is motivated by "false pride"—a pride which suggests that the ritual code is getting the better of those whose conduct is regulated by it. Further, the "after you, Alphonse" complex can make the termination of an interchange difficult. So, too, where each participant feels that he must sacrifice a little more than has been sacrificed for him, a kind of vicious indulgence cycle may occur—much like the hostility cycle that can lead to open quarrels—with each person receiving things he does not want and giving in return things he would rather keep. Again, when people are on formal terms, much energy may be spent in ensuring that events do not occur which might effectively carry an improper expression. And on the other hand, when a set of persons are on familiar terms and feel that they need not stand on ceremony with one another, then inattentiveness and interruptions are likely to become rife, and talk may degenerate into a happy babble of disorganized sound.

The ritual code itself requires a delicate balance, and can be easily upset by anyone who upholds it too eagerly or not eagerly enough, in terms of the standards and expectations of his group. Too little perceptiveness, too little *savoir-faire*, too little pride and considerateness, and the person ceases to be someone who can be trusted to take a hint about himself or give a hint that will save others embarrassment. Such a person comes to be a real threat to society; there is nothing much that can be done with him, and often he gets his way. Too much perceptiveness or too much pride, and the person becomes someone who is thin-skinned, who must be treated with kid gloves, requiring more care on the part of others than he may be worth to them. Too much *savoir-faire* or too much considerateness, and he becomes someone who is too socialized, who leaves the others with the feeling that they do not know how they really stand with him, nor what they should do to make an effective long-term adjustment to him.

In spite of these inherent "pathologies" in the organization of talk, the functional fitness between the socialized person and spoken interaction is a viable and practical one. The person's orientation to face, especially his own, is the point of leverage that the ritual order has in regard to him; yet a promise to take ritual care of his face is built into the very structure of talk.

FACE AND SOCIAL RELATIONSHIPS

When a person begins a mediated or immediate encounter, he already stands in some kind of social relationship to the others concerned, and expects to stand in a given relationship to them after the particular encounter ends. This, of course, is one of the ways in which social contacts are geared into the wider society. Much of the activity occurring during an encounter can be understood as an effort on everyone's part to get through the occasion and all the unanticipated and unintentional events that can cast participants in an undesirable light, without disrupting the relationships of the participants. And if relationships are in the process of change, the object will be to bring the encounter to a satisfactory close without altering the expected course of development. This perspective nicely accounts, for example, for the little ceremonies of greeting and farewell which occur when people begin a conversational encounter or depart from one. Greetings provide a way of showing that a relationship is still what it was at the termination of the previous coparticipation, and, typically, that this relationship involves sufficient suppression of hostility for the participants temporarily to drop their guards and talk. Farewells sum up the effect of the encounter upon the relationship and show what the participants may expect of one another when they next meet. The enthusiasm of greetings compensates for the weakening of the relationship caused by the absence just terminated, while the enthusiasm of farewells compensates the relationship for the harm that is about to be done to it by separation.[30]

[30] Greetings, of course, serve to clarify and fix the roles that the participants will take during the occasion of talk and to commit participants to these roles, while farewells provide a way of unambiguously terminating the encounter. Greetings and farewells may also be used to state, and apologize for, extenuat-

It seems to be a characteristic obligation of many social relationships that each of the members guarantees to support a given face for the other members in given situations. To prevent disruption of these relationships, it is therefore necessary for each member to avoid destroying the others' face. At the same time, it is often the person's social relationship with others that leads him to participate in certain encounters with them, where incidentally he will be dependent upon them for supporting his face. Furthermore, in many relationships, the members come to share a face, so that in the presence of third parties an improper act on the part of one member becomes a source of acute embarrassment to the other members. A social relationship, then, can be seen as a way in which the person is more than ordinarily forced to trust his self-image and face to the tact and good conduct of others.

The Nature of the Ritual Order

The ritual order seems to be organized basically on accommodative lines, so that the imagery used in thinking about other types of social order is not quite suitable for it. For the other types of social order a kind of schoolboy model seems to be employed: if a person wishes to sustain a particular image of himself and trust his feelings to it, he must work hard for the credits that will buy this self-enhancement for him; should he try to obtain ends by improper means, by cheating or theft, he will be punished,

---

ing circumstances—in the case of greetings for circumstances that have kept the participants from interacting until now, and in the case of farewells for circumstances that prevent the participants from continuing their display of solidarity. These apologies allow the impression to be maintained that the participants are more warmly related socially than may be the case. This positive stress, in turn, assures that they will act more ready to enter into contacts than they perhaps really feel inclined to do, thus guaranteeing that diffuse channels for potential communication will be kept open in the society.

disqualified from the race, or at least made to start all over again from the beginning. This is the imagery of a hard, dull game. In fact, society and the individual join in one that is easier on both of them, yet one that has dangers of its own.

Whatever his position in society, the person insulates himself by blindnesses, half-truths, illusions, and rationalizations. He makes an "adjustment" by convincing himself, with the tactful support of his intimate circle, that he is what he wants to be and that he would not do to gain his ends what the others have done to gain theirs. And as for society, if the person is willing to be subject to informal social control—if he is willing to find out from hints and glances and tactful cues what his place is, and keep it— then there will be no objection to his furnishing this place at his own discretion, with all the comfort, elegance, and nobility that his wit can muster for him. To protect this shelter he does not have to work hard, or join a group, or compete with anybody; he need only be careful about the expressed judgments he places himself in a position to witness. Some situations and acts and persons will have to be avoided; others, less threatening, must not be pressed too far. Social life is an uncluttered, orderly thing because the person voluntarily stays away from the places and topics and times where he is not wanted and where he might be disparaged for going. He cooperates to save his face, finding that there is much to be gained from venturing nothing.

Facts are of the schoolboy's world—they can be altered by diligent effort but they cannot be avoided. But what the person protects and defends and invests his feelings in is an idea about himself, and ideas are vulnerable not to facts and things but to communications. Communications belong to a less punitive scheme than do facts, for communications can be by-passed, withdrawn from, disbelieved, conveniently misunderstood, and tactfully conveyed. And even should the person misbehave and break the truce he has made with society, punishment need not be the consequence. If the offense is one that the offended persons can let go by without losing too much face, then they are likely to act forbearantly, telling themselves that they will get even with the offender in another way at another time, even though such an occasion may never arise and might not be exploited if it did. If the offense is great, the offended persons may withdraw from the encounter, or from future similar ones, allowing their withdrawal to be reinforced by the awe they may feel toward someone who breaks the ritual code. Or they may have the offender withdrawn, so that no further communication can occur. But since the offender can salvage a good deal of face from such operations, withdrawal is often not so much an informal punishment for an offense as it is merely a means of terminating it. Perhaps the main principle of the ritual order is not justice but face, and what any offender receives is not what he deserves but what will sustain for the moment the line to which he has committed himself, and through this the line to which he has committed the interaction.

Throughout this paper it has been implied that underneath their differences in culture, people everywhere are the same. If persons have a universal human nature, they themselves are not to be looked to for an explanation of it. One must look rather to the fact that societies everywhere, if they are to be societies, must mobilize their members as self-regulating participants in social encounters. One way of mobilizing the individual for this purpose is through ritual; he is taught to be perceptive, to have feelings attached to self and a self expressed through face, to have pride, honor, and dignity, to have considerateness, to have tact and a certain amount of poise. These are some of the elements of behavior which must be built into the person if practical use is to be made of him as an interactant, and

44

it is these elements that are referred to in part when one speaks of universal human nature.

Universal human nature is not a very human thing. By acquiring it, the person becomes a kind of construct, built up not from inner psychic propensities but from moral rules that are impressed upon him from without. These rules, when followed, determine the evaluation he will make of himself and of his fellow-participants in the encounter, the distribution of his feelings, and the kinds of practices he will employ to maintain a specified and obligatory kind of ritual equilibrium. The general capacity to be bound by moral rules may well belong to the individual, but the particular set of rules which transforms him into a human being derives from requirements established in the ritual organization of social encounters. And if a particular person or group or society seems to have a unique character all its own, it is because its standard set of human-nature elements is pitched and combined in a particular way. Instead of much pride, there may be little. Instead of abiding by the rules, there may be much effort to break them safely. But if an encounter or undertaking is to be sustained as a viable system of interaction organized on ritual principles, then these variations must be held within certain bounds and nicely counterbalanced by corresponding modifications in some of the other rules and understandings. Similarly, the human nature of a particular set of persons may be specially designed for the special kind of undertakings in which they participate, but still each of these persons must have within him something of the balance of characteristics required of a usable participant in any ritually organized system of social activity.

THE NATURE OF
DEFERENCE AND DEMEANOR

Under the influence of Durkheim and Radcliffe-Brown, some students of modern society have learned to look for the symbolic meaning of any given social practice and for the contribution of the practice to the integrity and solidarity of the group that employs it. However, in directing their attention away from the individual to the group, these students seem to have neglected a theme that is presented in Durkheim's chapter on the soul.[1] There he suggests that the individual's personality can be seen as one apportionment of the collective *mana,* and that (as he implies in later chapters), the rites performed to representations of the social collectivity will sometimes be performed to the individual himself.

In this paper I want to explore some of the senses in which the person in our urban secular world is allotted a kind of sacredness that is displayed and confirmed by symbolic acts. An attempt will be made to build a conceptual scaffold by stretching and twisting some common anthropological terms. This will be used to support two concepts which I think are central to this area: deference and demeanor. Through these reformulations I will try to show that a version of Durkheim's social psychology can be effective in modern dress.

Data for the paper are drawn chiefly from a brief observational study of mental patients in a modern research

[1] Emile Durkheim, *The Elementary Forms of the Religious Life,* tr. J. W. Swain (Free Press, Glencoe, Ill., 1954), pp. 240–72.

hospital.[2] I use these data on the assumption that a logical place to learn about personal proprieties is among persons who have been locked up for spectacularly failing to maintain them. Their infractions of propriety occur in the confines of a ward, but the rules broken are quite general ones, leading us outward from the ward to a general study of our Anglo-American society.

INTRODUCTION

A rule of conduct may be defined as a guide for action, recommended not because it is pleasant, cheap, or effective, but because it is suitable or just. Infractions characteristically lead to feelings of uneasiness and to negative social sanctions. Rules of conduct infuse all areas of activ-

[2] Ward A was formally given over to pharmacological research and contained two normal controls, both nineteen-year-old Mennonite conscientious objectors, two hypertensive women in their fifties, and two women in their thirties diagnosed as schizophrenic and in fair degree of remission. For two months the writer participated in the social life of the ward in the official capacity of a normal control, eating and socializing with the patients during the day and sleeping overnight occasionally in a patient's room. Ward B was one given over to the study of schizophrenic girls and their so-called schizophrenogenic mothers: a seventeen-year-old girl, Betty, and her mother, Mrs. Baum; Grace, fifteen years old, and Mary, thirty-one years old, whose mothers visited the ward most days of the week. The writer spent some of the weekday on Ward B in the capacity of staff sociologist. Within limits, it is possible to treat Ward A as an example of an orderly nonmental ward and Ward B as an example of a ward with somewhat disturbed mental patients. It should be made quite clear that only one aspect of the data will be considered, and that for every event cited additional interpretations would be in order, for instance, psychoanalytical ones.

I am grateful to the administrators of these wards, Dr. Seymour Perlin and Dr. Murray Bowen, and to their staffs, for co-operation and assistance, and to Dr. John A. Clausen and Charlotte Green Schwartz then of the National Institute of Mental Health for critical suggestions.

ity and are upheld in the name and honor of almost everything. Always, however, a grouping of adherents will be involved—if not a corporate social life—providing through this a common sociological theme. Attachment to rules leads to a constancy and patterning of behavior; while this is not the only source of regularity in human affairs it is certainly an important one. Of course, approved guides to conduct tend to be covertly broken, side-stepped, or followed for unapproved reasons, but these alternatives merely add to the occasions in which rules constrain at least the surface of conduct.

Rules of conduct impinge upon the individual in two general ways: directly, as *obligations*, establishing how he is morally constrained to conduct himself; indirectly, as *expectations*, establishing how others are morally bound to act in regard to him. A nurse, for example, has an obligation to follow medical orders in regard to her patients; she has the expectation, on the other hand, that her patients will pliantly co-operate in allowing her to perform these actions upon them. This pliancy, in turn, can be seen as an obligation of the patients in regard to their nurse, and points up the interpersonal, actor-recipient character of many rules: what is one man's obligation will often be another's expectation.

Because obligations involve a constraint to act in a particular way, we sometimes picture them as burdensome or irksome things, to be fulfilled, if at all, by gritting one's teeth in conscious determination. In fact, most actions which are guided by rules of conduct are performed unthinkingly, the questioned actor saying he performs "for no reason" or because he "felt like doing so." Only when his routines are blocked may he discover that his neutral little actions have all along been consonant with the proprieties of his group and that his failure to perform them can become a matter of shame and humiliation. Similarly, he may so take for granted his expectations regarding others that only when things go unexpectedly wrong will he suddenly discover that he has grounds for indignation.

Once it is clear that a person may meet an obligation without feeling it, we can go on to see that an obligation which *is* felt as something that *ought* to be done may strike the obligated person either as a desired thing or as an onerous one, in short, as a pleasant or unpleasant duty. In fact, the same obligation may appear to be a desirable duty at one point and an undesirable one at another, as when a nurse, obliged to administer medication to patients, may be glad of this when attempting to establish social distance from attendants (who in some sense may be considered by nurses to be not "good enough" to engage in such activity), yet burdened by it on occasions when she finds that dosage must be determined on the basis of illegibly written medical orders. Similarly, an expectation may be perceived by the expectant person as a wanted or unwanted thing, as when one person feels he will deservedly be promoted and another feels he will deservedly be fired. In ordinary usage, a rule that strikes the actor or recipient as a personally desirable thing, apart from its propriety, is sometimes called a right or privilege, as it will be here, but these terms have additional implications, suggesting that special class of rules which an individual may invoke but is not required to do so. It should also be noted that an actor's pleasant obligation may constitute a recipient's pleasant expectation, as with the kiss a husband owes his wife when he returns from the office, but that, as the illustration suggests, all kinds of combinations are possible.

When an individual becomes involved in the mainte-nance of a rule, he tends also to become committed to a particular image of self. In the case of his obligations, he becomes to himself and others the sort of person who follows this particular rule, the sort of person who would naturally be expected to do so. In the case of his expecta-tions, he becomes dependent upon the assumption that others will properly perform such of their obligations as affect him, for their treatment of him will express a conception of him. In establishing himself as the sort of person who treats others in a particular way and is treated by them in a particular way, he must make sure that it will be possible for him to act and be this kind of person. For example, with certain psychiatrists there seems to be a point where the obligation of giving psychotherapy to patients, *their* patients, is transformed into something they must do if they are to retain the image they have come to have of themselves. The effect of this transformation can be seen in the squirming some of them may do in the early phases of their careers when they may find themselves employed to do research, or administer a ward, or give therapy to those who would rather be left alone.

In general then, when a rule of conduct is broken we find that two individuals run the risk of becoming discredited: one with an obligation, who should have governed himself by the rule; the other with an expectation, who should have been treated in a particular way because of this governance. Both actor and recipient are threatened.

An act that is subject to a rule of conduct is, then, a communication, for it represents a way in which selves are confirmed—both the self for which the rule is an obligation and the self for which it is an expectation. An act that is subject to rules of conduct but does not conform to them is also a communication—often even more so—for infractions make news and often in such a way as to disconfirm the selves of the participants. Thus rules of conduct transform both action and inaction into expression, and whether the individual abides by the rules or breaks them, something significant is likely to be communicated. For example, in the wards under study, each research psychiatrist tended to expect his patients to come regularly for their therapeutic hours. When patients fulfilled this obligation, they showed that they appreciated their need for

51

treatment and that their psychiatrist was the sort of person who could establish a "good relation" with patients. When a patient declined to attend his therapeutic hour, others on the ward tended to feel that he was "too sick" to know what was good for him, and that perhaps his psychiatrist was not the sort of person who was good at establishing relationships. Whether patients did or did not attend their hours, something of importance about them and their psychiatrist tended to be communicated to the staff and to other patients on the ward.

In considering the individual's participation in social action, we must understand that in a sense he does not participate as a total person but rather in terms of a special capacity or status; in short, in terms of a special self. For example, patients who happen to be female may be obliged to act shamelessly before doctors who happen to be male, since the medical relation, not the sexual one, is defined as officially relevant. In the research hospital studied, there were both patients and staff who were Negro, but this minority-group status was not one in which these individuals were officially (or even, in the main, unofficially) active. Of course, during face-to-face encounters individuals may participate officially in more than one capacity. Further, some unofficial weight is almost always given to capacities defined as officially irrelevant, and the reputation earned in one capacity will flow over and to a degree determine the reputation the individual earns in his other capacities. But these are questions for more refined analysis.

In dealing with rules of conduct it is convenient to distinguish two classes, symmetrical and asymmetrical.[3] A symmetrical rule is one which leads an individual to have obligations or expectations regarding others that these others have in regard to him. For example, in the two

[3] R. H. Thouless, *General and Social Psychology* (University Tutorial Press, London, 1951), pp. 272–73.

hospital wards, as in most other places in our society, there was an understanding that each individual was not to steal from any other individual, regardless of their respective statuses, and that each individual could similarly expect not to be stolen from by anyone. What we call common courtesies and rules of public order tend to be symmetrical, as are such biblical admonitions as the rule about not coveting one's neighbor's wife. An asymmetrical rule is one that leads others to treat and be treated by an individual differently from the way he treats and is treated by them. For example, doctors give medical orders to nurses, but nurses do not give medical orders to doctors. Similarly, in some hospitals in America nurses stand up when a doctor enters the room, but doctors do not ordinarily stand up when a nurse enters the room.

Students of society have distinguished in several ways among types of rules, as for example, between formal and informal rules; for this paper, however, the important distinction is that between substance and ceremony.[4] A substantive rule is one which guides conduct in regard to matters felt to have significance in their own right, apart from what the infraction or maintenance of the rule expresses about the selves of the persons involved. Thus, when an individual refrains from stealing from others, he upholds a substantive rule which primarily serves to protect the property of these others and only incidentally functions to protect the image they have of themselves as persons with proprietary rights. The expressive implications of substantive rules are officially considered to be

[4] I take this distinction from Durkheim (Emile Durkheim, "The Determination of Moral Facts," *Sociology and Philosophy*, tr. D. F. Pocock, Free Press, Glencoe, Ill., 1953, especially pp. 42–43); see also A. R. Radcliffe-Brown, "Taboo," *Structure and Function in Primitive Society* (Free Press, Glencoe, Ill., 1952, pp. 143–44), and Talcott Parsons, *The Structure of Social Action* (McGraw-Hill, New York, 1937, pp. 430–33); sometimes the dichotomy is phrased in terms of "intrinsic" or "instrumental" versus "expressive" or "ritual."

secondary; this appearance must be maintained, even though in some special situations everyone may sense that the participants were primarily concerned with expression.

A ceremonial rule is one which guides conduct in matters felt to have secondary or even no significance in their own right, having their primary importance—officially anyway—as a conventionalized means of communication by which the individual expresses his character or conveys his appreciation of the other participants in the situation.[5]

[5] While the substantive value of ceremonial acts is felt to be quite secondary it may yet be quite appreciable. Wedding gifts in American society provide an example. It is even possible to say in some cases that if a sentiment of a given kind is to be conveyed ceremonially it will be necessary to employ a sign-vehicle which has a given amount of substantive value. Thus in the American lower-middle class, it is understood that a small investment in an engagement ring, as such investments go, may mean that the man places a small value on his fiancee as these things go, even though no one may believe that women and rings are commensurate things. In those cases where it becomes too clear that the substantive value of a ceremonial act is the only concern of the participants, as when a girl or an official receives a substantial gift from someone not interested in proper relations, then the community may respond with a feeling that their symbol system has been abused.

An interesting limiting case of the ceremonial component of activity can be found in the phenomenon of "gallantry," as when a man calmly steps aside to let a strange lady precede him into a lifeboat, or when a swordsman, fighting a duel, courteously picks up his opponent's fallen weapon and proffers it to him. Here an act that is usually a ceremonial gesture of insignificant substantive value is performed under conditions where it is known to have unexpectedly great substantive value. Here, as it were, the forms of ceremony are maintained above and beyond the call of duty.

In general, then, we can say that all ceremonial gestures differ in the degree to which they have substantive value, and that this substantive value may be systematically used as part of the communication value of the act, but that still the ceremonial order is different from the substantive one and is so understood.

This usage departs from the everyday one, where "ceremony" tends to imply a highly specified, extended sequence of symbolic action performed by august actors on solemn occasions when religious sentiments are likely to be invoked. In my attempt to stress what is common to such practices as tipping one's hat and coronations, I will perforce ignore the differences among them to an extent that many anthropologists might perhaps consider impracticable.

In all societies, rules of conduct tend to be organized into codes which guarantee that everyone acts appropriately and receives his due. In our society the code which governs substantive rules and substantive expressions comprises our law, morality, and ethics, while the code which governs ceremonial rules and ceremonial expressions is incorporated in what we call etiquette. All of our institutions have both kinds of codes, but in this paper attention will be restricted to the ceremonial one.

The acts or events, that is, the sign-vehicles or tokens which carry ceremonial messages, are remarkably various in character. They may be linguistic, as when an individual makes a statement of praise or depreciation regarding self or other, and does so in a particular language and intonation;[6] gestural, as when the physical bearing of an individual conveys insolence or obsequiousness; spatial, as when an individual precedes another through the door, or sits on his right instead of his left; task-embedded, as when an individual accepts a task graciously and performs it in the presence of others with aplomb and dexterity; part of the communication structure, as when an individual speaks more frequently than the others, or receives more attentiveness than they do. The important point is that ceremonial activity, like substantive activity, is an analytical element referring to a component or function of ac-

[6] P. L. Garvin and S. H. Riesenberg, "Respect Behavior on Pronape: An Ethnolinguistic Study," *American Anthropologist,* 54 (1952), 201–20.

tion, not to concrete empirical action itself. While some activity that has a ceremonial component does not seem to have an appreciable substantive one, we find that all activity that is primarily substantive in significance will nevertheless carry some ceremonial meaning, provided that its performance is perceived in some way by others. The manner in which the activity is performed, or the momentary interruptions that are allowed so as to exchange minor niceties, will infuse the instrumentally-oriented situation with ceremonial significance.

All of the tokens employed by a given social group for ceremonial purposes may be referred to as its ceremonial idiom. We usually distinguish societies according to the amount of ceremonial that is injected into a given period and kind of interaction, or according to the expansiveness of the forms and the minuteness of their specification; it might be better to distinguish societies according to whether required ceremony is performed as an unpleasant duty or, spontaneously, as an unfelt or pleasant one.

Ceremonial activity seems to contain certain basic components. As suggested, a main object of this paper will be to delineate two of these components, deference and demeanor, and to clarify the distinction between them.

DEFERENCE

By deference I shall refer to that component of activity which functions as a symbolic means by which appreciation is regularly conveyed *to* a recipient *of* this recipient, or of something of which this recipient is taken as a symbol, extension, or agent.[7] These marks of devotion represent

[7] Some of the conceptual material on deference used in this paper derives from a study supported by a Ford Foundation grant for a propositional inventory of social stratification directed by Professor E. A. Shils of the University of Chicago. I am very grateful to Mr. Shils for orienting me to the study of deference behavior. He is not responsible for any misuse I may have made of his conception.

ways in which an actor celebrates and confirms his relation to a recipient. In some cases, both actor and recipient
may not really be individuals at all, as when two ships
greet each other with four short whistle blasts when passing. In some cases, the actor is an individual but the recipient is some object or idol, as when a sailor salutes the
quarterdeck upon boarding ship, or when a Catholic
genuflects to the altar. I shall only be concerned, however, with the kind of deference that occurs when both
actor and recipient are individuals, whether or not they
are acting on behalf of something other than themselves.
Such ceremonial activity is perhaps seen most clearly in
the little salutations, compliments, and apologies which
punctuate social intercourse, and may be referred to as
"status rituals" or "interpersonal rituals."[8] I use the term
"ritual" because this activity, however informal and secular,
represents a way in which the individual must guard and
design the symbolic implications of his acts while in the
immediate presence of an object that has a special value
for him.[9]

There appear to be two main directions in which the
study of deference rituals may go. One is to settle on a
given ritual and attempt to discover factors common to
all of the social situations in which it is performed, for it
is through such an analysis that we can get at the "meaning" of the ritual. The other is to collect all of the rituals
that are performed to a given recipient, from whomever
the ritual comes. Each of these rituals can then be interpreted for the symbolically expressed meaning that is

[8] Techniques for handling these ceremonial obligations are
considered in "On Face-Work."
[9] This definition follows Radcliffe-Brown's (op. cit., p. 123)
except that I have widened his term "respect" to include other
kinds of regard: "There exists a ritual relation whenever a society imposes on its members a certain attitude towards an
object, which attitude involves some measure of respect expressed in a traditional mode of behavior with reference to that
object."

embodied in it. By piecing together these meanings we can arrive at the conception of the recipient that others are obliged to maintain of him to him.

The individual may desire, earn, and deserve deference, but by and large he is not allowed to give it to himself, being forced to seek it from others. In seeking it from others, he finds he has added reason for seeking them out, and in turn society is given added assurance that its members will enter into interaction and relationships with one another. If the individual could give himself the deference he desired there might be a tendency for society to disintegrate into islands inhabited by solitary cultish men, each in continuous worship at his own shrine.

The appreciation carried by an act of deference implies that the actor possesses a sentiment of regard for the recipient, often involving a general evaluation of the recipient. Regard is something the individual constantly has for others, and knows enough about to feign on occasion; yet in having regard for someone, the individual is unable to specify in detail what in fact he has in mind.

Those who render deference to an individual may feel, of course, that they are doing this merely because he is an instance of a category, or a representative of something, and that they are giving him his due not because of what they think of him "personally" but in spite of it. Some organizations, such as the military, explicitly stress this sort of rationale for according deference, leading to an impersonal bestowal of something that is specifically directed toward the person. By easily showing a regard that he does not have, the actor can feel that he is preserving a kind of inner autonomy, holding off the ceremonial order by the very act of upholding it. And of course in scrupulously observing the proper forms he may find that he is free to insinuate all kinds of disregard by carefully modifying intonation, pronunciation, pacing, and so forth.

In thinking about deference it is common to use as a model the rituals of obeisance, submission, and propitiation that someone under authority gives to someone in authority. Deference comes to be conceived as something a subordinate owes to his superordinate. This is an extremely limiting view of deference on two grounds. First, there are a great many forms of symmetrical deference which social equals owe to one another; in some societies, Tibetan for example, salutations between high-placed equals can become prolonged displays of ritual conduct, exceeding in duration and expansiveness the kind of obeisance a subject may owe his ruler in less ritualized societies. Similarly, there are deference obligations that superordinates owe their subordinates; high priests all over the world seem obliged to respond to offerings with some equivalent of "Bless you, my son." Secondly, the regard in which the actor holds the recipient need not be one of respectful awe; there are other kinds of regard that are regularly expressed through interpersonal rituals also, such as trust, as when an individual welcomes sudden strangers into his house, or capacity-esteem, as when the individual defers to another's technical advice. A sentiment of regard that plays an important role in deference is that of affection and belongingness. We see this in the extreme in the obligation of a newly married man in our society to treat his bride with affectional deference whenever it is possible to twist ordinary behavior into a display of this kind. We find it more commonly, for example, as a component in many farewells where, as in our middle-class society, the actor will be obliged to infuse his voice with sadness and regret, paying deference in this way to the recipient's status as someone whom others can hold dearly. In "progressive" psychiatric establishments, a deferential show of acceptance, affection, and concern may form a constant and significant aspect of the stance taken by staff members when contacting patients. On Ward B, in fact, the two youngest patients seemed to have become so experienced in receiving such offerings, and so doubtful of them, that they would sometimes reply in a mocking way, apparently in an effort to re-establish the interaction on what seemed to these patients to be a more sincere level.

It appears that deference behavior on the whole tends to be honorific and politely toned, conveying appreciation of the recipient that is in many ways more complimentary to the recipient than the actor's true sentiments might warrant. The actor typically gives the recipient the benefit of the doubt, and may even conceal low regard by extra punctiliousness. Thus acts of deference often attest to ideal guide lines to which the actual activity between actor and recipient can now and then be referred. As a last resort, the recipient has a right to make a direct appeal to these honorific definitions of the situation, to press his theoretic claims, but should he be rash enough to do so, it is likely that his relationship to the actor will be modified thereafter. People sense that the recipient ought not to take the actor literally or force his hand, and ought to rest content with the show of appreciation as opposed to a more substantive expression of it. Hence one finds that many automatic acts of deference contain a vestigial meaning, having to do with activity in which no one is any longer engaged and implying an appreciation long since not expected—and yet we know these antique tributes cannot be neglected with impunity.

In addition to a sentiment of regard, acts of deference typically contain a kind of promise, expressing in truncated form the actor's avowal and pledge to treat the recipient in a particular way in the on-coming activity. The pledge affirms that the expectations and obligations of the recipient, both substantive and ceremonial, will be allowed and supported by the actor. Actors thus promise to maintain the conception of self that the recipient has built up from the rules he is involved in. (Perhaps the prototype here is the public act of allegiance by which a subject officially acknowledges his subservience in certain matters to his lord.) Deferential pledges are frequently conveyed through spoken terms of address involving status-identifiers, as when a nurse responds to a rebuke in the operating room with the phrase, "yes, Doctor," signifying by term of address and tone of voice that the criticism has been understood and that, however unpalatable, it has not caused her to rebel. When a putative recipient fails to receive anticipated acts of deference, or when an actor makes clear that he is giving homage with bad grace, the recipient may feel that the state of affairs which he has been taking for granted has become unstable, and that an insubordinate effort may be made by the actor to re-allocate tasks, relations, and power. To elicit an established act of deference, even if the actor must first be reminded of his obligations and warned about the consequence of discourtesy, is evidence that if rebellion comes it will come slyly; to be pointedly refused an expected act of deference is often a way of being told that open insurrection has begun.

A further complication must be mentioned. A particular act of deference is something an actor, acting in a given capacity, owes a recipient, acting in a given capacity. But these two individuals are likely to be related to one another through more than one pair of capacities, and these additional relationships are likely to receive ceremonial expression too. Hence the same act of deference may show signs of different kinds of regard, as when a doctor by a paternal gesture shows authority over a nurse in her capacity as subordinate technician but affection for her as a young female who is dependent on him in his capacity as a supportive older male. Similarly, an attendant in cheerfully addressing a doctor as "Doc" may sometimes show respect for the medical role and yet male-solidarity with the person who fills it. Throughout this paper we must therefore keep in mind that a spate of deferential behavior is not a single note expressing a single relationship between two individuals active in a single pair of capacities, but rather a medley of voices answering to the fact that actor and recipient are in many different relations to one another, no one of which can usually be given exclusive and continuous determinacy of ceremonial conduct. An interesting example of this complexity in regard to master-servant relations may be cited from a nineteenth-century book of etiquette:

"Issue your commands with gravity and gentleness, and in a reserved manner. Let your voice be composed, but avoid a tone of familiarity or sympathy with them. It is better in addressing them to use a higher key of voice, and not to suffer it to fall at the end of a sentence. The best-bred man whom we ever had the pleasure of meeting always employed, in addressing servants, such forms of speech as these— 'I'll thank you for so and so,'—'Such a thing if you please.'—with a gentle tone, but very elevated key. The perfection of manner, in this particular, is, to indicate by your language, that the performance is a favour, and by your tone that it is a matter of course."[10]

Deference can take many forms, of which I shall consider only two broad groupings, avoidance rituals and presentational rituals.

Avoidance rituals, as a term, may be employed to refer to those forms of deference which lead the actor to keep at a distance from the recipient and not violate what Simmel has called the "ideal sphere" that lies around the recipient:

"Although differing in size in various directions and differing according to the person with whom one entertains relations, this sphere cannot be penetrated, unless the personality value of the individual is thereby destroyed. A sphere of this sort is placed around man by his honor. Language poignantly designates an insult to one's honor as 'coming too close;' the radius of this sphere marks, as it were, the dis-

[10] Anonymous, *The Laws of Etiquette* (Carey, Lee, and Blanchard, Philadelphia, 1836), p. 188.

tance whose trespassing by another person insults one's honor."[11]

Any society could be profitably studied as a system of deferential stand-off arrangements, and most studies give us some evidence of this.[12] Avoidance of other's personal name is perhaps the most common example from anthropology, and should be as common in sociology.

Here, it should be said, is one of the important differences between social classes in our society: not only are some of the tokens different through which consideration for the privacy of others is expressed, but also, apparently, the higher the class the more extensive and elaborate are the taboos against contact. For example, in a study of a Shetlandic community the writer found that as one moves from middle-class urban centers in Britain to the rural lower-class islands, the distance between chairs at table decreases, so that in the outermost Shetland Islands actual bodily contact during meals and similar social occasions is not considered an invasion of separateness and no effort need be made to excuse it. And yet, whatever the rank of the participants in an action, the actor is likely to feel that the recipient has some warranted expectation of inviolability.

Where an actor need show no concern about penetrating the recipient's usual personal reserve, and need have no fear of contaminating him by any penetration into his privacy, we say that the actor is on terms of familiarity with the recipient. (The mother who feels at liberty to pick her child's nose is an extreme example.) Where the actor must show circumspection in his approach to the recipient, we speak of nonfamiliarity or respect. Rules governing conduct between two individuals may, but need

[11] Georg Simmel, *The Sociology of Georg Simmel*, tr., ed. by Kurt Wolff (Free Press, Glencoe, Ill., 1950), p. 321.
[12] *E.g.* F. W. Hodge, *Etiquette: Handbook of American Indians* (Government Printing House, Washington, D.C., 1907), p. 442.

not, be symmetrical in regard to either familiarity or respect.

There appear to be some typical relations between ceremonial distance and other kinds of sociological distance. Between status equals we may expect to find interaction guided by symmetrical familiarity. Between superordinate and subordinate we may expect to find asymmetrical relations, the superordinate having the right to exercise certain familiarities which the subordinate is not allowed to reciprocate. Thus, in the research hospital, doctors tended to call nurses by their first names, while nurses responded with "polite" or "formal" address. Similarly, in American business organizations the boss may thoughtfully ask the elevator man how his children are, but this entrance into another's life may be blocked to the elevator man, who can appreciate the concern but not return it. Perhaps the clearest form of this is found in the psychiatrist-patient relation, where the psychiatrist has a right to touch on aspects of the patient's life that the patient might not even allow himself to touch upon, while of course this privilege is not reciprocated. (There are some psychoanalysts who believe it desirable to "analyze the counter-transference with the patient" but this or any other familiarity on the part of the patient is strongly condemned by official psychoanalytical bodies.) Patients, especially mental ones, may not even have the right to question their doctor about his opinion of their own case; for one thing, this would bring them into too intimate a contact with an area of knowledge in which doctors invest their special apartness from the lay public which they serve.

While these correlations between ceremonial distance and other kinds of distance are typical, we must be quite clear about the fact that other relationships are often found. Thus, status equals who are not well acquainted may be on terms of reciprocal respect, not familiarity. Further, there are many organizations in America where differences in rank are seen as so great a threat to the

equilibrium of the system that the ceremonial aspect of behavior functions not as a way of iconically expressing
these differences but as a way of carefully counterbalanc-
ing them. In the research hospital under study, psychiatrists, psychologists, and sociologists were part of a single
ceremonial group as regards first-naming, and this symmetrical familiarity apparently served to allay some feeling
on the part of psychologists and sociologists that they
were not equal members of the team, as indeed they
were not. Similarly, in a study of small business managers,
the writer[13] found that filling-station attendants had the
right to interrupt their boss, slap him on the back, rib him,
use his phone, and take other liberties, and that this ritual
license seemed to provide a way in which the manager
could maintain morale and keep his employees honest.
We must realize that organizations that are quite similar
structurally may have quite different deference styles, and
that deference patterns are partly a matter of changing
fashion.

In our society, rules regarding the keeping of one's distance are multitudinous and strong. They tend to focus
around certain matters, such as physical places and properties defined as the recipient's "own," the body's sexual
equipment, etc. An important focus of deferential avoidance consists in the verbal care that actors are obliged
to exercise so as not to bring into discussion matters that
might be painful, embarrassing, or humiliating to the recipient. In Simmel's words:

"The same sort of circle which surrounds man—although it is value-accentuated in a very different
sense—is filled out by his affairs and by his characteristics. To penetrate this circle by taking notice,
constitutes a violation of his personality. Just as material property is, so to speak, an extension of the

[13] Unpublished paper prepared for Social Research, Inc.,
1952.

ego, and any interference with our property is, for this reason, felt to be a violation of the person, there also is an intellectual private-property, whose violation effects a lesion of the ego in its very center. Discretion is nothing but the feeling that there exists a right in regard to the sphere of the immediate life contents. Discretion, of course, differs in its extension with different personalities just as the positions of honor and of property have different radii with respect to 'close' individuals, and to strangers, and indifferent persons."[14]

Referential avoidance may be illustrated from Ward A, where rules in this regard were well institutionalized.[15] The fact that two of the female patients had had experience in a state-type mental hospital was not raised either in serious conversation or in jest, except when initiated by these women themselves; nor was a question of the age of these patients (who were in their middle thirties) raised. The fact that the two male patients were conscientious objectors was never raised, even by the CO's themselves. The fact that one of the patients was blind and that another was colored was never raised by the others in their presence. When a poor patient declined to participate in an outing on a claim of indifference, her rationalization for not going was accepted at face-value and her fiction respected, even though others knew that she wanted to go but was ashamed to because she did not have a suitable coat. Patients about to be given drugs experimentally, or who had just been given drugs, were not questioned about their feelings, unless they themselves raised the topic. Unmarried women, whether patients or nurses, were not directly questioned about

14 Simmel, *op. cit.*, p. 322.
15 I am grateful to Dr. Seymour Perlin for bringing my attention to some of these avoidances and for pointing out the significance of them.

boy friends. Information about religious affiliations was volunteered but rarely requested.

Violation of rules regarding privacy and separateness is a phenomenon that can be closely studied on mental wards because ordinarily there is so much of it done by patients and staff. Sometimes it arises from what are felt to be the substantive or instrumental requirements of the situation. When a mental patient checks into a hospital, an itemized account is usually made of every one of his belongings; this requires his giving himself up to others in a way that he may have learned to define as a humiliation. Periodically his effects may have to be searched in a general effort to clear the ward of "sharps," liquor, narcotics, and other contraband. The presence of a microphone known to be concealed in each patient's room and connected with a speaker in the nurses' station is an additional invasion (but one provided only in the newest hospitals); the censoring of outgoing mail is another. Psychotherapy, especially when the patient appreciates that other staff members will learn about his progress and even receive a detailed report of the case, is another such invasion; so too is the practice of having nurses and attendants "chart" the course of the patient's daily feelings and activity. Efforts of staff to "form relations" with patients, to break down periods of withdrawal in the interest of therapy, is another example. Classic forms of "nonperson treatment" are found, with staff members so little observing referential avoidance that they discuss intimacies about a patient in his presence as if he were not there at all. There will be no door to the toilet, or one that the patient cannot lock; dormitory sleeping, especially in the case of middle-class patients, is a similar encroachment on privacy. The care that is given to "very disturbed" patients in many large public hospitals leads in a similar direction, as with forced medication, cold packs applied to the naked body, or confinement while naked in an empty strongroom into which staff and patients may look. Another instance is forced feeding, whereby a frightened mute patient who may want to keep certain food out of his mouth is matched against an attendant who must see that patients are fed.

Invasions of privacy which have an instrumental technical rationale can be paralleled with others of a more purely ceremonial nature. Thus "acting out" and "psychopathic" patients are ones who can be counted on to overreach polite bounds and ask embarrassing questions of fellow-patients and staff, or proffer compliments which would not ordinarily be in their province to give, or proffer physical gestures of appreciation such as hugging or kissing, which are felt to be inappropriate. Thus, on Ward B, male staff members were plagued by such statements as "Why did you cut yourself shaving like that," "Why do you always wear the same pants, I'm getting sick of them," "Look at all the dandruff you've got." If seated by one of the patients, a male staff member might have to edge continuously away so as to keep a seemly safe distance between himself and the patient.

Some of the ways in which individuals on Ward A kept their distance were made clear in contrast to the failure of Ward B's patients to do so. On Ward A the rule that patients were to remain outside the nurses' station was observed. Patients would wait for an invitation or, as was commonly the case, stay in the doorway so that they could talk with those in the station and yet not presume upon them. It was therefore not necessary for the staff to lock the station door when a nurse was in the station. On Ward B it was not possible to keep three of the patients out of the station by request alone, and so the door had to be kept locked if privacy was to be maintained. Even then, the walls of the station were effectively battered down by continuous banging and shouting. In other words, on Ward A the protective ring that nurses and attendants drew around themselves by retreating into the station was respected by the patients, whereas on Ward B it was not.

A second illustration may be cited. Patients on Ward A had mixed feelings about some of their doctors, but each patient knew of one or two doctors that he or she liked. Thus, while at table, when a favorite doctor passed by, there would be an exchange of greetings but, ceremonially speaking, nothing more. No one would have felt it right to chase after the doctors, pester them, and in general invade their right of separateness. On Ward B, however, the entrance of a doctor was very often a signal for some of the patients to rush up to him, affectionally presume on him by grasping his hand or putting an arm around him, and then to walk with him down the corridor, engaging in a kidding affectionate conversation. And often when a doctor had retired behind a ward office door, a patient would bang on the door and look through its glass window, and in other ways refuse to keep expected distance.

One patient on Ward B, Mrs. Baum, seemed especially talented in divining what would be an invasion of other people's privacy. On a shopping expedition, for example, she had been known to go behind the counter or examine the contents of a stranger's shopping bag. At other times she would enter a stranger's car at an intersection and ask for a lift. In general she could provide the student with a constant reminder of the vast number of different acts and objects that are employed as markers by which the borders of privacy are staked out, suggesting that in the case of some "mental disorders" symptomatology is specifically and not merely incidentally an improper keeping of social distance.

Analysis of deferential avoidance has sometimes been held back because there is another kind of ceremonial avoidance, a self-protective kind, that may resemble deferential restraint but is analytically quite different from it. Just as the individual may avoid an object so as not to pollute or defile it, so he may avoid an object so as not to be polluted or defiled by it. For example, in Ward B, when Mrs. Baum was in a paranoid state she refused to allow her daughter to accept a match from a Negro attendant, appearing to feel that contact with a member of a group against which she was prejudiced would be polluting; so, too, while kissing the doctors and nurses in an expansive birthday mood, she gave the appearance that she was trying but could not bring herself to kiss the attendant. In general, it would seem, one avoids a person of high status out of deference to him and avoids a person of lower status than one's own out of a self-protective concern. Perhaps the social distance sometimes carefully maintained between equals may entail both kinds of avoidance on both their parts. In any case, the similarity in the two kinds of avoidance is not deep. A nurse who keeps away from a patient out of sympathetic appreciation that he wants to be alone wears one expression on her face and body; when she maintains the same physical distance from a patient because he has been incontinent and smells, she is likely to wear a different expression. In addition, the distances an actor keeps out of deference to others decline when he rises in status, but the self-protective ones increase.[16]

Avoidance rituals have been suggested as one main type

[16] Research on social distance scales has often most surprisingly overlooked the fact that an individual may keep his distance from others because they are too sacred for him, as well as because they are not sacred enough. The reason for this persistent error constitutes a problem in the sociology of knowledge. In general, following the students of Radcliffe-Brown, we must distinguish between "good-sacredness," which represents something too pure to make contact with, and "bad-sacredness," which represents something too impure to make contact with, contrasting both these sacred states and objects to ritually neutral matters. (See M. M. Srinivas, *Religion and Society Among the Coorgs of South India* [Oxford University Press, 1952], pp. 106–7.) Radcliffe-Brown (*op. cit.*) does not introduce the caution that in some societies the distinction between good and bad sacred is much less clearcut than in our own.

of deference. A second type, termed *presentational rituals*, encompasses acts through which the individual makes specific attestations to recipients concerning how he regards them and how he will treat them in the on-coming interaction. Rules regarding these ritual practices involve specific prescriptions, not specific proscriptions; while avoidance rituals specify what is not to be done, presentational rituals specify what is to be done. Some illustrations may be taken from social life on Ward A as maintained by the group consisting of patients, attendants, and nurses. These presentational rituals will not, I think, be much different from those found in many other organizations in our society.

When members of the ward passed by each other, salutations would ordinarily be exchanged, the length of the salutation depending on the period that had elapsed since the last salutation and the period that seemed likely before the next. At table, when eyes met a brief smile of recognition would be exchanged; when someone left for the weekend, a farewell involving a pause in on-going activity and a brief exchange of words would be involved. In any case, there was the understanding that when members of the ward were in a physical position to enter into eye-to-eye contact of some kind, this contact would be effected. It seemed that anything less would not have shown proper respect for the state of relatedness that existed among the members of the ward.

Associated with salutations were practices regarding the "noticing" of any change in appearance, status, or repute, as if these changes represented a commitment on the part of the changed individual which had to be underwritten by the group. New clothes, new hairdos, occasions of being "dressed up" would call forth a round of compliments, whatever the group felt about the improvement. Similarly, any effort on the part of a patient to make something in the occupational therapy room or to perform in other ways was likely to be commended by others. Staff members who

71

participated in the hospital amateur theatricals were complimented, and when one of the nurses was to be married, pictures of her fiancé and his family were viewed by all and approved. In these ways a member of the ward tended to be saved from the embarrassment of presenting himself to others as someone who had risen in value, while receiving a response as someone who had declined, or remained the same.

Another form of presentational deference was the practice of staff and patients pointedly requesting each and every patient to participate in outings, occupational therapy, concert-going, meal-time conversation, and other forms of group activity. Refusals were accepted but no patient was not asked.

Another standard form of presentational deference on Ward A was that of extending small services and aid. Nurses would make minor purchases for patients in the local town; patients coming back from home visits would pick up other patients by car to save them having to come back by public transportation; male patients would fix the things that males are good at fixing and female patients would return the service. Food came from the kitchen already allocated to individual trays, but at each meal a brisk business was done in exchanging food, and outright donations occurred whereby those who did not care for certain foods gave them to those who did. Most members of the ward took a turn at conveying the food trays from the kitchen cart to the table, as they did in bringing toast and coffee for the others from the sidetable. These services were not exchanged in terms of a formal schedule worked out to ensure fairness, but rather as an unplanned thing, whereby the actor was able to demonstrate that the private objectives of the recipient were something in which others present sympathetically participated.

I have mentioned four very common forms of presentational deference: salutations, invitations, compliments, and minor services. Through all of these the recipient is told that he is not an island unto himself and that others are, or seek to be, involved with him and with his personal private concerns. Taken together, these rituals provide a continuous symbolic tracing of the extent to which the recipient's ego has not been bounded and barricaded in regard to others.

Two main types of deference have been illustrated: presentational rituals through which the actor concretely depicts his appreciation of the recipient; and avoidance rituals, taking the form of proscriptions, interdictions, and taboos, which imply acts the actor must refrain from doing lest he violate the right of the recipient to keep him at a distance. We are familiar with this distinction from Durkheim's classification of ritual into positive and negative rites.[17]

In suggesting that there are things that must be said and done to a recipient, and things that must not be said and done, it should be plain that there is an inherent opposition and conflict between these two forms of deference. To ask after an individual's health, his family's well-being, or the state of his affairs, is to present him with a sign of sympathetic concern; but in a certain way to make this presentation is to invade the individual's personal reserve, as will be made clear if an actor of wrong status asks him these questions, or if a recent event has made such a question painful to answer. As Durkheim suggested, "The human personality is a sacred thing; one dare not violate it nor infringe its bounds, while at the same time the greatest good is in communion with others."[18] I would like to cite two ward illustrations of this inherent opposition between the two forms of deference.

On Ward A, as in other wards in the hospital, there was

17 Durkheim, *The Elementary Forms,* p. 299.
18 Emile Durkheim, "The Determination of Moral Facts," p. 37.

a "touch system."[19] Certain categories of personnel had the privilege of expressing their affection and closeness to others by the ritual of bodily contact with them. The actor places his arms around the waist of the recipient, rubs a hand down the back of the recipient's neck, strokes the recipient's hair and forehead, or holds the recipient's hand. Sexual connotation is of course officially excluded. The most frequent form that the ritual took was for a nurse to extend such a touch-confirmation to a patient. Nonetheless, attendants, patients, and nurses formed one group in regard to touch rights, the rights being symmetrical. Any one of these individuals had a right to touch any member of his own category or any member of the other categories. (In fact some forms of touch, as in playful fighting or elbow-strength games, were intrinsically symmetrical.) Of course some members of the ward disliked the system, but this did not alter the rights of others to incorporate them into it. The familiarity implicit in such exchanges was affirmed in other ways, such as symmetrical first-naming. It may be added that in many mental hospitals, patients, attendants, and nurses do not form one group for ceremonial purposes, and the obligation of patients to accept friendly physical contact from staff is not reciprocated.

In addition to these symmetrical touch relations on the ward, there were also asymmetrical ones. The doctors touched other ranks as a means of conveying friendly support and comfort, but other ranks tended to feel that it would be presumptuous for them to reciprocate a doctor's touch, let alone initiate such a contact with a doctor.[20]

[19] The only source I know on touch systems is the very interesting work by Edward Gross ("Informal Relations and the Social Organization of Work," Unpublished Ph.D. Dissertation, Department of Sociology, University of Chicago, 1949) on rights regarding pinching of females of private secretarial rank in a commercial business office.

[20] The then head nurse, a male, initiated arm embraces

Now it should be plain that if a touch system is to be maintained, as it is in many hospitals in America, and if members of the ward are to receive the confirmation and support this ritual system provides, then persons other than doctors coming to live or work on the ward must make themselves intimately available to the others present. Rights of apartness and inviolability which are demanded and accorded in many other establishments in our society must here be forgone, in this particular. The touch system, in short, is only possible to the degree that individuals forego the right to keep others at a physical distance.

A second illustration of the sense in which the two forms of deference act in opposition to each other turns upon the point of social participation. On Ward A there was a strong feeling of in-group solidarity among all non-medical ranks—nurses, attendants, and patients. One way in which this was expressed was through joint participation in meals, card-games, room-visits, TV parties, occupational therapy, and outings. Ordinarily individuals were ready not only to participate in these activities but also to do so with visible pleasure and enthusiasm. One gave oneself to these occasions and through this giving the group flourished.

In the context of this participation pattern, and in spite of its importance for the group, it was understood that patients had the right of disaffection. Although it was felt to be an affront to group solidarity to come late for break-

---

with the physician acting as ward administrator. This seemed to create a false note and was felt to be forward. The nurse, interestingly enough, has left the service. It should be added that on one ward in the hospital, a ward given over to the close study of a small number of highly delinquent boys, patients and staff of all ranks, including doctors, apparently formed a single ceremonial group. Members of the group were linked by symmetrical rules of familiarity, so that it was permissible for an eight-year-old to call the ward administrator by his first name, joke with him, and swear in his presence.

fast, late-comers were only mildly chided for doing so. Once at table, a patient was obliged to return the greetings offered him, but after this if his mood and manner patently expressed his desire to be left alone, no effort would be made to draw him into the meal-time conversation. If a patient took his food from the table and retired to his room or to the empty TV lounge, no one chased after him. If a patient refused to come on an outing, a little joke was made of it, warning the individual what he would miss, and the matter would be dropped. If a patient refused to play cards at a time when this would deny the others a necessary fourth, joking remonstrances would be made but not continued. And on any occasion, if the patient appeared depressed, moody, or even somewhat disarrayed, an effort was made not to notice this or to attribute it to a need for physical care and rest. These kinds of delicacy and restriction of demands seemed to serve the social function of keeping informal life free from the contamination of being a "treatment" or a prescription, and meant that in certain matters the patient had a right to prevent intrusion when, where, and how he wanted to do so. It is apparent, however, that the right to withdraw into privacy was a right that was accorded at the expense of those kinds of acts through which the individual was expected to display his relatedness to the others on the ward. There is an inescapable opposition between showing a desire to include an individual and showing respect for his privacy.

As an implication of this dilemma, we must see that social intercourse involves a constant dialectic between presentational rituals and avoidance rituals. A peculiar tension must be maintained, for these opposing requirements of conduct must somehow be held apart from one another and yet realized together in the same interaction: the gestures which carry an actor to a recipient must also signify that things will not be carried too far.

DEMEANOR

It was suggested that the ceremonial component of concrete behavior has at least two basic elements, deference and demeanor. Deference, defined as the appreciation an individual shows of another to that other, whether through avoidance rituals or presentational rituals, has been discussed and demeanor may now be considered.

By demeanor I shall refer to that element of the individual's ceremonial behavior typically conveyed through deportment, dress, and bearing, which serves to express to those in his immediate presence that he is a person of certain desirable or undesirable qualities. In our society, the "well" or "properly" demeaned individual displays such attributes as: discretion and sincerity; modesty in claims regarding self; sportsmanship; command of speech and physical movements; self-control over his emotions, his appetites, and his desires; poise under pressure; and so forth.

When we attempt to analyze the qualities conveyed through demeanor, certain themes become apparent. The well-demeaned individual possesses the attributes popularly associated with "character training" or "socialization," these being implanted when a neophyte of any kind is housebroken. Rightly or wrongly, others tend to use such qualities diagnostically, as evidence of what the actor is generally like at other times and as a performer of other activities. In addition, the properly demeaned individual is someone who has closed off many avenues of perception and penetration that others might take to him, and is therefore unlikely to be contaminated by them. Most importantly, perhaps, good demeanor is what is required of an actor if he is to be transformed into someone who can be relied upon to maintain himself as an interactant, poised for communication, and to act so that others do not endanger themselves by presenting themselves as interactants to him.

It should be noted once again that demeanor involves attributes derived from interpretations others make of the way in which the individual handles himself during social intercourse. The individual cannot establish these attributes for his own by verbally avowing that he possesses them, though sometimes he may rashly try to do this. (He can, however, contrive to conduct himself in such a way that others, through their interpretation of his conduct, will impute the kinds of attributes to him he would like others to see in him.) In general, then, through demeanor the individual creates an image of himself, but properly speaking this is not an image that is meant for his own eyes. Of course this should not prevent us from seeing that the individual who acts with good demeanor may do so because he places an appreciable value upon himself, and that he who fails to demean himself properly may be accused of having "no self-respect" or of holding himself too cheaply in his own eyes.

As in the case of deference, an object in the study of demeanor is to collect all the ceremonially relevant acts that a particular individual performs in the presence of each of the several persons with whom he comes in contact, tô interpret these acts for the demeanor that is symbolically expressed through them, and then to piece these meanings together into an image of the individual, an image of him in others' eyes.

Rules of demeanor, like rules of deference, can be symmetrical or asymmetrical. Between social equals, symmetrical rules of demeanor seem often to be prescribed. Between unequals many variations can be found. For example, at staff meetings on the psychiatric units of the hospital, medical doctors had the privilege of swearing, changing the topic of conversation, and sitting in undignified positions; attendants, on the other hand, had the right to attend staff meetings and to ask questions during them (in line with the milieu-therapy orientation of these research units) but were implicitly expected to conduct themelves with greater circumspection than was required of doctors. (This was pointed out by a perceptive occupational therapist who claimed she was always reminded that a mild young female psychiatrist was really an M.D. by the fact that this psychiatrist exercised these prerogatives of informal demeanor.) The extreme here perhaps is the master-servant relation as seen in cases where valets and maids are required to perform in a dignified manner services of an undignified kind. Similarly, doctors had the right to saunter into the nurses' station, lounge on the station's dispensing counter, and engage in joking with the nurses; other ranks participated in this informal interaction with doctors, but only after doctors had initiated it.

On Ward A, standards of demeanor were maintained that seem to be typical in American middle-class society. The eating pace maintained at table suggested that no one present was so over-eager to eat, so little in control of impulses, so jealous of his rights, as to wolf down his food or take more than his share. At pinochle, the favorite card game, each player would coax spectators to take his hand and spectators would considerately decline the offer, expressing in this way that a passion for play had in no way overwhelmed them. Occasionally a patient appeared in the day-room or at meals with bathrobe (a practice permitted of patients throughout the hospital) but ordinarily neat street wear was maintained, illustrating that the individual was not making his appearance before others in a lax manner or presenting too much of himself too freely. Little profanity was employed and no open sexual remarks.

On Ward B, bad demeanor (by middle-class standards) was quite common. This may be illustrated from meal-time behavior. A patient would often lunge at an extra piece of food or at least eye an extra piece covetously. Even when each individual at table was allowed to receive an equal share, over-eagerness was shown by the practice of taking all of one's share at once instead of waiting until one serving had been eaten. Occasionally a patient would come to table half-dressed. One patient frequently belched loudly at meals and was occasionally flatulent. Messy manipulation of food sometimes occurred. Swearing and cursing were common. Patients would occasionally push their chairs back from the table precipitously and bolt for another room, coming back to the table in the same violent manner. Loud sounds were sometimes made by sucking on straws in empty pop bottles. Through these activities, patients expressed to the staff and to one another that their selves were not properly demeaned ones.

These forms of misconduct are worth study because they make us aware of some aspects of good demeanor we usually take for granted; for aspects even more usually taken for granted, we must study "back" wards in typical mental hospitals. There patients are denudative, incontinent, and they openly masturbate; they scratch themselves violently; drooling occurs and a nose may run unchecked; sudden hostilities may flare up and "paranoid" immodesties be projected; speech or motor activity may occur at a manic or depressed pace, either too fast or too slow for propriety; males and females may comport themselves as if they were of the other sex or hardly old enough to have any. Such wards are of course the classic settings of bad demeanor.

A final point about demeanor may be mentioned. Whatever his motives for making a well demeaned appearance before others, it is assumed that the individual will exert his own will to do so, or that he will pliantly co-operate should it fall to someone else's lot to help him in this matter. In our society, a man combs his own hair until it gets too long, then he goes to a barber and follows instructions while it is being cut. This voluntary submission is crucial, for personal services of such a kind are done close to the very center of the individual's inviolability and can easily result in transgressions; server and served must co-operate closely if these are not to occur. If, however, an individual fails to maintain what others see as proper personal appearance, and if he refuses to co-operate with those who are charged with maintaining it for him, then the task of making him presentable against his will is likely to cost him at the moment a great deal of dignity and deference, and this in turn may create complex feelings in those who find they must cause him to pay this price. This is one of the occupational dilemmas of those employed to make children and mental patients presentable. It is easy to order attendants to "dress up" and shave male patients on visitors' day, and no doubt when this is done patients make a more favorable appearance, but while this appearance is in the process of being achieved—in the showers or the barbershop, for example—the patients may be subjected to extreme indignities.

DEFERENCE AND DEMEANOR

Deference and demeanor are analytical terms; empirically there is much overlapping of the activities to which they refer. An act through which the individual gives or withholds deference to others typically provides means by which he expresses the fact that he is a well or badly demeaned individual. Some aspects of this overlapping may be cited. First, in performing a given act of presentational deference, as in offering a guest a chair, the actor finds himself doing something that can be done with smoothness and aplomb, expressing self-control and poise, or with clumsiness and uncertainty, expressing an irresolute character. This is, as it were, an incidental and adventitious connection between deference and demeanor. It may be illustrated from recent material on doctor-patient relationships, where it is suggested that one complaint a doctor may have against some of his patients is that they do not bathe before coming for an examination;[21] while bathing

21 Ernest Dichter, *A Psychological Study of the Doctor-*

is a way of paying deference to the doctor it is at the same time a way for the patient to present himself as a clean, well demeaned person. A further illustration is found in acts such as loud talking, shouting, or singing, for these acts encroach upon the right of others to be let alone, while at the same time they illustrate a badly demeaned lack of control over one's feelings.

The same connection between deference and demeanor has had a bearing on the ceremonial difficulties associated with intergroup interaction: the gestures of deference expected by members of one society have sometimes been incompatible with the standards of demeanor maintained by members of another. For example, during the nineteenth century, diplomatic relations between Britain and China were embarrassed by the fact that the *Kot'ow* demanded of visiting ambassadors by the Chinese Emperor was felt by some British ambassadors to be incompatible with their self-respect.[22]

A second connection between deference and demeanor turns upon the fact that a willingness to give others their deferential due is one of the qualities which the individual owes it to others to express through his conduct, just as a willingness to conduct oneself with good demeanor is in general a way of showing deference to those present.

In spite of these connections between deference and demeanor, the analytical relation between them is one of "complementarity," not identity. The image the individual owes to others to maintain of himself is not the same type of image these others are obliged to maintain of him. Deference images tend to point to the wider society outside the interaction, to the place the individual has achieved in the hierarchy of this society. Demeanor images tend to point to qualities which any social position gives its incum-

---

Patient Relationship (California Medical Association, Alameda County Medical Association, 1950), pp. 5–6.

[22] R. K. Douglas, *Society in China* (Innes, London, 1895), pp. 291–96.

bents a chance to display during interaction, for these qualities pertain more to the way in which the individual handles his position than to the rank and place of that position relative to those possessed by others.

Further, the image of himself the individual owes it to others to maintain through his conduct is a kind of justification and compensation for the image of him that others are obliged to express through their deference to him. Each of the two images in fact may act as a guarantee and check upon the other. In an interchange that can be found in many cultures, the individual defers to guests to show how welcome they are and how highly he regards them; they in turn decline the offering at least once, showing through their demeanor that they are not presumptuous, immodest, or over-eager to receive favor. Similarly, a man starts to rise for a lady, showing respect for her sex; she interrupts and halts his gesture, showing she is not greedy of her rights in this capacity but is ready to define the situation as one between equals. In general, then, by treating others deferentially one gives them an opportunity to handle the indulgence with good demeanor. Through this differentiation in symbolizing function the world tends to be bathed in better images than anyone deserves, for it is practical to signify great appreciation of others by offering them deferential indulgences, knowing that some of these indulgences will be declined as an expression of good demeanor.

There are still other complementary relations between deference and demeanor. If an individual feels he ought to show proper demeanor in order to warrant deferential treatment, then he must be in a position to do so. He must, for example, be able to conceal from others aspects of himself which would make him unworthy in their eyes, and to conceal himself from them when he is in an indignified state, whether of dress, mind, posture, or action. The avoidance rituals which others perform in regard to him give him room to maneuver, enabling him to present only a self that is worthy of deference; at the same time, this avoidance makes it easier for them to assure themselves that the deference they have to show him is warranted.

To show the difference between deference and demeanor, I have pointed out the complementary relation between them, but even this kind of relatedness can be overstressed. The failure of an individual to show proper deference to others does not necessarily free them from the obligation to act with good demeanor in his presence, however disgruntled they may be at having to do this. Similarly, the failure of an individual to conduct himself with proper demeanor does not always relieve those in his presence from treating him with proper deference. It is by separating deference and demeanor that we can appreciate many things about ceremonial life, such as that a group may be noted for excellence in one of these areas while having a bad reputation in the other. Hence we can find a place for arguments such as De Quincey's,[23] that an Englishman shows great self-respect but little respect for others while a Frenchman shows great respect for others but little respect for himself.

We are to see, then, that there are many occasions when it would be improper for an individual to convey about himself what others are ready to convey about him to him, since each of these two images is a warrant and justification for the other, and not a mirror image of it. The Meadian notion that the individual takes toward himself the attitude others take to him seems very much an oversimplification. Rather the individual must rely on others to complete the picture of him of which he himself is allowed to paint only certain parts. Each individual is responsible for the demeanor image of himself and the deference image of others, so that for a complete man to be ex-

[23] Thomas De Quincey, "French and English Manners," *Collected Writings of Thomas De Quincey*, David Mason, ed. (Adams and Charles Black, Edinburgh, 1890), vol. XIV, 327–34.

pressed, individuals must hold hands in a chain of ceremony, each giving deferentially with proper demeanor to the one on the right what will be received deferentially from the one on the left. While it may be true that the individual has a unique self all his own, evidence of this possession is thoroughly a product of joint ceremonial labor, the part expressed through the individual's demeanor being no more significant than the part conveyed by others through their deferential behavior toward him.

CEREMONIAL PROFANATIONS

There are many situations and many ways in which the justice of ceremony can fail to be maintained. There are occasions when the individual finds that he is accorded deference of a misidentifying kind, whether the misidentification places him in a higher or lower position than he thinks right. There are other occasions when he finds that he is being treated more impersonally and unceremonially than he thinks proper and feels that his treatment ought to be more punctuated with acts of deference, even though these may draw attention to his subordinate status. A frequent occasion for ceremonial difficulty occurs at moments of intergroup contact, since different societies and subcultures have different ways of conveying deference and demeanor, different ceremonial meanings for the same act, and different amounts of concern over such things as poise and privacy. Travel books such as Mrs. Trollope's[24] are full of autobiographical material on these misunderstandings, and sometimes seem to have been written chiefly to publicize them.

Of the many kinds of ceremonial transgressions there is one which a preliminary paper on ceremony is obliged to consider: it is the kind that appears to have been per-

---

[24] Mrs. Trollope, *Domestic Manners of the Americans* (Whittaker, Treacher; London, 1832).

petrated on purpose and to employ consciously the very language of ceremony to say what is forbidden. The idiom through which modes of proper ceremonial conduct are established necessarily creates ideally effective forms of desecration, for it is only in reference to specified proprieties that one can learn to appreciate what will be the worst possible form of behavior. Profanations are to be expected, for every religious ceremony creates the possibility of a black mass.[25]

When we study individuals who are on familiar terms with one another and need stand on little ceremony, we often find occasions when standard ceremonial forms that are inapplicable to the situation are employed in what is felt to be a facetious way, apparently as a means of poking fun at social circles where the ritual is seriously employed. When among themselves, nurses at the research hospital sometimes addressed one another humorously as Miss ——; doctors under similar conditions sometimes called one another "Doctor" with the same joking tone of voice. Similarly, elaborate offering of a chair or precedence through a door was sometimes made between an actor and recipient who were actually on terms of symmetrical familiarity. In Britain, where speech and social style are clearly stratified, a great amount of this unserious profanation of rituals can be found, with upper class people mocking lower class ceremonial gestures, and lower class people when among themselves fully returning the compliment. The practice perhaps reaches its highest expression in music hall revues, where lower class performers beautifully mimic upper class ceremonial conduct for an audience whose status falls somewhere in between.

[25] A kind of ceremonial profanation also seems to exist with respect to substantive rules. In law what are sometimes called "spite actions" provide illustrations, as does the phenomenon of vandalism. But, as previously suggested, these represent ways in which the substantive order is abused for ceremonial purposes.

Some playful profanation seems to be directed not so much at outsiders as at the recipient himself, by way of lightly teasing him or testing ritual limits in regard to him. It should be said that in our society this kind of play is directed by adults to those of lesser ceremonial breed—to children, old people, servants, and so forth—as when an attendant affectionately ruffles a patient's hair or indulges in more drastic types of teasing.[26] Anthropologists have described this kind of license in an extreme form in the case of "siblings-in-law who are potential secondary spouses."[27] However apparent the aggressive overtones of this form of conduct may be, the recipient is given the opportunity of acting as if no serious affront to his honor has occurred, or at least an affront no more serious than that of being defined as someone with whom it is permissible to joke. On Ward B, when Mrs. Baum was given a sheet too small for her bed she used it to playfully bag one of the staff members. Her daughter occasionally jokingly employed the practice of bursting large bubblegum bubbles as close to the face of a staff person as possible without touching him, or stroking the arm and hand of a male staff member in parody of affectional gestures, gleefully proposing sexual intercourse with him.

A less playful kind of ritual profanation is found in the practice of defiling the recipient but in such a way and from such an angle that he retains the right to act as if he has not received the profaning message. On Ward B, where staff members had the occupational obligation of "relating to" the patients and responding to them with friendliness, nurses would sometimes mutter *sotto voce*

[26] *Cf.* Harold Taxel, "Authority Structure in a Mental Hospital Ward," Unpublished Master's Thesis, Department of Sociology, University of Chicago, 1953, p. 68; and Robert H. Willoughby, "The Attendant in the State Mental Hospital," Unpublished Master's Thesis, Department of Sociology, University of Chicago, 1953, p. 90.

[27] George P. Murdock, *Social Structure* (Macmillan, New York, 1949), p. 282.

vituperations when patients were trying and difficult. Patients, in turn, employed the same device. When a nurse's back was turned, patients would sometimes stick their tongues out, thumb their noses, or grimace at her. These are of course standard forms of ritual contempt in our Anglo-American society, constituting a kind of negative deference. Other instances may be cited. On one occasion Mrs. Baum, to the amusement of others present, turned her back on the station window, bent down, and flipped her skirt up, in an act of ritual contempt which was apparently once more prevalent as a standard insult than it is today. In all these cases we see that although ceremonial liberties are taken with the recipient, he is not held in sufficiently low regard to be insulted "to his face." This line between what can be conveyed about the recipient while in a state of talk with him, and what can only be conveyed about him when not in talk with him, is a basic ceremonial institution in our society, ensuring that face-to-face interaction is likely to be mutually approving. An appreciation of how deep this line is can be obtained on mental wards, where severely disturbed patients can be observed co-operating with staff members to maintain a thin fiction that the line is being kept.

But of course there are situations where an actor conveys ritual profanation of a recipient while officially engaged in talk with him or in such a way that the affront cannot easily be overlooked. Instead of recording and classifying these ritual affronts, students have tended to cover them all with a psychological tent, labelling them as "aggressions" or "hostile outbursts," while passing on to other matters of study.

In some psychiatric wards, face-to-face ritual profanation is a constant phenomenon. Patients may profane a staff member or a fellow-patient by spitting at him, slapping his face, throwing feces at him, tearing off his clothes, pushing him off the chair, taking food from his grasp, screaming into his face, sexually molesting him, etc. On

Ward B, on occasion, Betty would slap and punch her mother's face and tramp on her mother's bare feet with heavy shoes; and abuse her, at table, with those four-letter words that middle-class children ordinarily avoid in reference to their parents, let alone their presence. It should be repeated that while from the point of view of the actor these profanations may be a product of blind impulse, or have a special symbolic meaning,[28] from the point of view of the society at large and its ceremonial idiom these are not random impulsive infractions. Rather, these acts are exactly those calculated to convey complete disrespect and contempt through symbolic means. Whatever is in the patient's mind, the throwing of feces at an attendant is a use of our ceremonial idiom that is as exquisite in its way as is a bow from the waist done with grace and a flourish. Whether he knows it or not, the patient speaks the same ritual language as his captors; he merely says what they do not wish to hear, for patient behavior which does not carry ritual meaning in terms of the daily ceremonial discourse of the staff will not be perceived by the staff at all.

In addition to profanation of others, individuals for varieties of reasons and in varieties of situations give the appearance of profaning themselves, acting in a way that seems purposely designed to destroy the image others have of them as persons worthy of deference. Ceremonial mortification of the flesh has been a theme in many social movements. What seems to be involved is not merely bad demeanor but rather the concerted efforts of an individual sensitive to high standards of demeanor to act against his own interests and exploit ceremonial arrangements by presenting himself in the worst possible light.

In many psychiatric wards, what appears to staff and other patients as self-profanation is a common occurrence.

[28] Morris S. Schwartz and Alfred H. Stanton, "A Social Psychological Study of Incontinence," *Psychiatry*, 13 (1950), 319–416.

For example, female patients can be found who have systematically pulled out all the hair from their head, presenting themselves thereafter with a countenance that is guaranteed to be grotesque. Perhaps the extreme for our society is found in patients who smear themselves with and eat their own feces.[29]

Self-profanation also occurs of course at the verbal level. Thus, on Ward A, the high standards of demeanor were broken by the blind patient who at table would sometimes thrust a consideration of her infirmity upon the others present by talking in a self-pitying fashion about how little use she was to anybody and how no matter how you looked at it she was still blind. Similarly, on Ward B, Betty was wont to comment on how ugly she was, how fat, and how no one would want to have someone like her for a girl-friend. In both cases, these self-derogations, carried past the limits of polite self-depreciation, were considered a tax upon the others: they were willing to exert protective referential avoidance regarding the individual's shortcomings and felt it was unfair to be forced into contaminating intimacy with the individual's problems.

Conclusions

The rules of conduct which bind the actor and the recipient together are the bindings of society. But many of the acts which are guided by these rules occur infrequently or take a long time for their consummation. Opportunities to affirm the moral order and the society could therefore be rare. It is here that ceremonial rules play their social function, for many of the acts which are guided by these rules last but a brief moment, involve no substantive outlay, and can be performed in every social inter-

[29] E. D. Wittkower and J. D. La Tendresse, "Rehabilitation of Chronic Schizophrenics by a New Method of Occupational Therapy," *British Journal of Medical Psychology*, 28 (1955), 42–47.

action. Whatever the activity and however profanely instrumental, it can afford many opportunities for minor ceremonies as long as other persons are present. Through these observances, guided by ceremonial obligations and expectations, a constant flow of indulgences is spread through society, with others who are present constantly reminding the individual that he must keep himself together as a well demeaned person and affirm the sacred quality of these others. The gestures which we sometimes call empty are perhaps in fact the fullest things of all.

It is therefore important to see that the self is in part a ceremonial thing, a sacred object which must be treated with proper ritual care and in turn must be presented in a proper light to others. As a means through which this self is established, the individual acts with proper demeanor while in contact with others and is treated by others with deference. It is just as important to see that if the individual is to play this kind of sacred game, then the field must be suited to it. The environment must ensure that the individual will not pay too high a price for acting with good demeanor and that deference will be accorded him. Deference and demeanor practices must be institutionalized so that the individual will be able to project a viable, sacred self and stay in the game on a proper ritual basis.

An environment, then, in terms of the ceremonial component of activity, is a place where it is easy or difficult to play the ritual game of having a self. Where ceremonial practices are thoroughly institutionalized, as they were on Ward A, it would appear easy to be a person. Where these practices are not established, as to a degree they were not in Ward B, it would appear difficult to be a person. Why one ward comes to be a place in which it is easy to have a self and another ward comes to be a place where this is difficult depends in part on the type of patient that is recruited and the type of regime the staff attempts to maintain.

One of the bases upon which mental hospitals throughout the world segregate their patients is degree of easily apparent "mental illness." By and large this means that patients are graded according to the degree to which they violate ceremonial rules of social intercourse. There are very good practical reasons for sorting patients into different wards in this way, and in fact that institution is backward where no one bothers to do so. This grading very often means, however, that individuals who are desperately uncivil in some areas of behavior are placed in the intimate company of those who are desperately uncivil in others. Thus, individuals who are the least ready to project a sustainable self are lodged in a milieu where it is practically impossible to do so.

It is in this context that we can reconsider some interesting aspects of the effect of coercion and constraint upon the individual. If an individual is to act with proper demeanor and show proper deference, then it will be necessary for him to have areas of self-determination. He must have an expendable supply of the small indulgences which his society employs in its idiom of regard—such as cigarettes to give, chairs to proffer, food to provide, and so forth. He must have freedom of bodily movement so that it will be possible for him to assume a stance that conveys appropriate respect for others and appropriate demeanor on his own part; a patient strapped to a bed may find it impractical not to befoul himself, let alone to stand in the presence of a lady. He must have a supply of appropriate clean clothing if he is to make the sort of appearance that is expected of a well demeaned person. To look seemly may require a tie, a belt, shoe laces, a mirror, and razor blades—all of which the authorities may deem unwise to give him. He must have access to the eating utensils which his society defines as appropriate ones for use, and may find that meat cannot be circumspectly eaten with a cardboard spoon. And finally, without too much cost to himself he must be able to decline certain kinds of work, now sometimes classified as "industrial therapy," which his social group considers *infra dignitatem*.

When the individual is subject to extreme constraint he is automatically forced from the circle of the proper. The sign vehicles or physical tokens through which the customary ceremonies are performed are unavailable to him. Others may show ceremonial regard for him, but it becomes impossible for him to reciprocate the show or to act in such a way as to make himself worthy of receiving it. The only ceremonial statements that are possible for him are improper ones.

The history of the care of mental cases is the history of constricting devices: constraining gloves, camisoles, floor and seat chains, handcuffs, "biter's mask," wet-packs, supervised toileting, hosing down, institutional clothing, forkless and knifeless eating, and so forth.[30] The use of these devices provides significant data on the ways in which the ceremonial grounds of selfhood can be taken away. By implication we can obtain information from this history about the conditions that must be satisfied if individuals are to have selves. Unfortunately, today there are still mental institutions where the past of other hospitals can be empirically studied now. Students of interpersonal ceremony should seek these institutions out almost as urgently as students of kinship have sought out disappearing cultures.

Throughout this paper I have assumed we can learn about ceremony by studying a contemporary secular situation—that of the individual who has declined to employ the ceremonial idiom of his group in an acceptable manner and has been hospitalized. In a crosscultural view it is convenient to see this as a product of our complex division of labor which brings patients together instead of leaving

[30] See W. R. Thomas, "The Unwilling Patient," *Journal of Medical Science*, 99 (1953), especially p. 193; and Alexander Walk, "Some Aspects of the 'Moral Treatment' of the Insane up to 1854," *Journal of Medical Science*, 100 (1954), 191–201.

each in his local circle. Further, this division of labor also brings together those who have the task of caring for these patients.

We are thus led to the special dilemma of the hospital worker: as a member of the wider society he ought to take action against mental patients, who have transgressed the rules of ceremonial order; but his occupational role obliges him to care for and protect these very people. When "milieu therapy" is stressed, these obligations further require him to convey warmth in response to hostility; relatedness in response to alienation.

We have seen that hospital workers must witness improper conduct without applying usual negative sanctions, and yet that they must exercise disrespectful coercion over their patients. A third peculiarity is that staff members may be obliged to render to patients services such as changing socks, tying shoelaces or trimming fingernails, which outside the hospital generally convey elaborate deference. In the hospital setting, such acts are likely to convey something inappropriate since the attendant at the same time exerts certain kinds of power and moral superiority over his charges. A final peculiarity in the ceremonial life of mental hospitals is that individuals collapse as units of minimal ceremonial substance and others learn that what had been taken for granted as ultimate entities are really held together by rules that can be broken with some kind of impunity. Such understanding, like one gained at war or at a kinsman's funeral, is not much talked about but it tends, perhaps, to draw staff and patients together into an unwilling group sharing undesired knowledge.

In summary, then, modern society brings transgressors of the ceremonial order to a single place, along with some ordinary members of society who make their living there. These dwell in a place of unholy acts and unholy understandings, yet some of them retain allegiance to the ceremonial order outside the hospital setting. Somehow ceremonial people must work out mechanisms and techniques for living without certain kinds of ceremony.

In this paper I have suggested that Durkheimian notions about primitive religion can be translated into concepts of deference and demeanor, and that these concepts help us to grasp some aspects of urban secular living. The implication is that in one sense this secular world is not so irreligious as we might think. Many gods have been done away with, but the individual himself stubbornly remains as a deity of considerable importance. He walks with some dignity and is the recipient of many little offerings. He is jealous of the worship due him, yet, approached in the right spirit, he is ready to forgive those who may have offended him. Because of their status relative to his, some persons will find him contaminating while others will find they contaminate him, in either case finding that they must treat him with ritual care. Perhaps the individual is so viable a god because he can actually understand the ceremonial significance of the way he is treated, and quite on his own can respond dramatically to what is proffered him. In contacts between such deities there is no need for middlemen; each of these gods is able to serve as his own priest.

EMBARRASSMENT
AND SOCIAL ORGANIZATION

An individual may recognize extreme embarrassment in
others and even in himself by the objective signs of emotional disturbance: blushing, fumbling, stuttering, an un-
usually low- or high-pitched voice, quavering speech or
breaking of the voice, sweating, blanching, blinking, tremor
of the hand, hesitating or vacillating movement, absent-
mindedness, and malapropisms. As Mark Baldwin remarked about shyness, there may be "a lowering of the
eyes, bowing of the head, putting of hands behind the
back, nervous fingering of the clothing or twisting of the
fingers together, and stammering, with some incoherence
of idea as expressed in speech."[1] There are also symptoms
of a subjective kind: constriction of the diaphragm, a feeling of wobbliness, consciousness of strained and unnatural
gestures, a dazed sensation, dryness of the mouth, and
tenseness of the muscles. In cases of mild discomfiture
these visible and invisible flusterings occur but in less per-
ceptible form.

In the popular view it is only natural to be at ease
during interaction, embarrassment being a regrettable de-
viation from the normal state. The individual, in fact, might
say he felt "natural" or "unnatural" in the situation, meaning that he felt comfortable in the interaction or embarrassed in it. He who frequently becomes embarrassed in
the presence of others is regarded as suffering from a fool-

[1] James Mark Baldwin, *Social and Ethical Interpretations in
Mental Development* (London, 1902), p. 212.

ish unjustified sense of inferiority and in need of therapy.[2]

To utilize the flustering syndrome in analyzing embarrassment, the two kinds of circumstance in which it occurs must first be distinguished. First, the individual may become flustered while engaged in a task of no particular value to him in itself, except that his long-range interests require him to perform it with safety, competence, or dispatch, and he fears he is inadequate to the task. Discomfort will be felt *in* the situation but in a sense not *for* it; in fact, often the individual will not be able to cope with it just because he is so anxiously taken up with the eventualities lying beyond it. Significantly, the individual may become "rattled" although no others are present.

This paper will not be concerned with these occasions of instrumental chagrin but rather with the kind that occurs in clear-cut relation to the real or imagined presence of others. Whatever else, embarrassment has to do with the figure the individual cuts before others felt to be there at the time. The crucial concern is the impression one makes on others in the present—whatever the long-range or unconscious basis of this concern may be. This fluctuating configuration of those present is a most important reference group.

---

[2] A sophisticated version is the psychoanalytical view that uneasiness in social interaction is a result of impossible expectations of attention based on unresolved expectations regarding parental support. Presumably an object of therapy is to bring the individual to see his symptoms in their true psychodynamic light, on the assumption that thereafter perhaps he will not need them (see Paul Schilder, "The Social Neurosis," *Psycho-Analytical Review*, XXV (1938), 1–19; Gerhart Piers and Milton Singer, *Shame and Guilt: A Psychoanalytical and a Cultural Study* (Springfield, Ill., Charles C. Thomas, 1953), esp. p. 26; Leo Rangell, "The Psychology of Poise," *International Journal of Psychoanalysis*, XXXV (1954), 313–32; Sandor Ferenczi, "Embarrassed Hands," in *Further Contributions to the Theory and Technique of Psychoanalysis* (London, Hogarth Press, 1950), pp. 315–16).

VOCABULARY OF EMBARRASSMENT

A social encounter is an occasion of face-to-face inter-action, beginning when individuals recognize that they have moved into one another's immediate presence and ending by an appreciated withdrawal from mutual participation. Encounters differ markedly from one another in purpose, social function, kind and number of personnel, setting, etc., and, while only conversational encounters will be considered here, obviously there are those in which no word is spoken. And yet, in our Anglo-American society, at least, there seems to be no social encounter which cannot become embarrassing to one or more of its participants, giving rise to what is sometimes called an incident or false note. By listening for this dissonance, the sociologist can generalize about the ways in which interaction can go awry and, by implication, the conditions necessary for interaction to be right. At the same time he is given good evidence that all encounters are members of a single natural class, amenable to a single framework of analysis.

By whom is the embarrassing incident caused? *To* whom is it embarrassing? *For* whom is this embarrassment felt? It is not always an individual for whose plight participants feel embarrassment; it may be for pairs of participants who are together having difficulties and even for an encounter as a whole. Further, if the individual for whom embarrassment is felt happens to be perceived as a responsible representative of some faction or subgroup (as is very often the case in three-or-more-person interaction), then the members of this faction are likely to feel embarrassed and to feel it for themselves. But, while a *gaffe* or *faux pas* can mean that a single individual is at one and the same time the cause of an incident, the one who feels embarrassed by it, and the one for whom he feels embarrassment, this is not, perhaps, the typical case, for in these matters ego boundaries seem especially weak. When an individual finds himself in a situation which ought to make him blush, others present usually will blush with and for him, though he may not have sufficient sense of shame or appreciation of the circumstances to blush on his own account.

The words "embarrassment," "discomfiture," and "uneasiness" are used here in a continuum of meanings. Some occasions of embarrassment seem to have an abrupt orgasmic character; a sudden introduction of the disturbing event is followed by an immediate peak in the experience of embarrassment and then by a slow return to the preceding ease, all phases being encompassed in the same encounter. A bad moment thus mars an otherwise euphoric situation.

At the other extreme we find that some occasions of embarrassment are sustained at the same level throughout the encounter, beginning when the interaction begins and lasting until the encounter is terminated. The participants speak of an uncomfortable or uneasy situation, not of an embarrassing incident. In such case, of course, the whole encounter becomes for one or more of the parties an incident that causes embarrassment. Abrupt embarrassment may often be intense, while sustained uneasiness is more commonly mild, involving barely apparent flusterings. An encounter which seems likely to occasion abrupt embarrassment may, because of this, cast a shadow of sustained uneasiness upon the participants, transforming the entire encounter into an incident itself.

In forming a picture of the embarrassed individual, one relies on imagery from mechanics: equilibrium or self-control can be lost, balance can be overthrown. No doubt the physical character of flustering in part evokes this imagery. In any case, a completely flustered individual is one who cannot for the time being mobilize his muscular and intellectual resources for the task at hand, although he would like to; he cannot volunteer a response to those around him that will allow them to sustain the conversation smoothly. He and his flustered actions block the line of activity the others have been pursuing. He is present with them, but he is not "in play." The others may be forced to stop and turn their attention to the impediment; the topic of conversation is neglected, and energies are directed to the task of re-establishing the flustered individual, of studiously ignoring him, or of withdrawing from his presence.

To conduct one's self comfortably in interaction and to be flustered are directly opposed. The more of one, the less, on the whole, of the other; hence through contrast each mode of behavior can throw light upon the characteristics of the other. Face-to-face interaction in *any* culture seems to require just those capacities that flustering seems guaranteed to destroy. Therefore, events which lead to embarrassment and the methods for avoiding and dispelling it may provide a cross-cultural framework of sociological analysis.

The pleasure or displeasure that a social encounter affords an individual, and the affection or hostility that he feels for the participants, can have more than one relation to his composure or lack of it. Compliments, acclaim, and sudden reward may throw the recipient into a state of joyful confusion, while a heated quarrel can be provoked and sustained, although throughout the individual feels composed and in full command of himself. More important, there is a kind of comfort which seems a formal property of the situation and which has to do with the coherence and decisiveness with which the individual assumes a well-integrated role and pursues momentary objectives having nothing to do with the content of the actions themselves. A feeling of discomfiture per se seems always to be unpleasant, but the circumstances that arouse it may have immediate pleasant consequences for the one who is discomfited.

In spite of this variable relation between displeasure and discomfiture, to appear flustered, in our society at least, is considered evidence of weakness, inferiority, low status, moral guilt, defeat, and other unenviable attributes. And, as previously suggested, flustering threatens the encounter itself by disrupting the smooth transmission and reception by which encounters are sustained. When discomfiture arises from any of these sources, understandably the flustered individual will make some effort to conceal his state from the others present. The fixed smile, the nervous hollow laugh, the busy hands, the downward glance that conceals the expression of the eyes, have become famous as signs of attempting to conceal embarrassment. As Lord Chesterfield puts it:

> They are ashamed in company, and so disconcerted that they do not know what they do, and try a thousand tricks to keep themselves in countenance; which tricks afterwards grow habitual to them. Some put their fingers to their nose, others scratch their head, others twirl their hats; in short, every awkward, ill-bred body has his tricks.[3]

These gestures provide the individual with screens to hide behind while he tries to bring his feelings back into tempo and himself back into play.

Given the individual's desire to conceal his embarrassment, given the setting and his skill at handling himself, he may seem poised according to some obvious signs yet prove to be embarrassed according to less apparent ones. Thus, while making a public speech, he may succeed in controlling his voice and give an impression of ease, yet those who sit beside him on the platform may see that his hands are shaking or that facial tics are giving the lie to his composed front.

Since the individual dislikes to feel or appear embarrassed, tactful persons will avoid placing him in this position. In addition, they will often pretend not to know that he has lost composure or has grounds for losing it. They may try to suppress signs of having recognized his state or

[3] *Letters of Lord Chesterfield to His Son* (Everyman's ed., New York, E. P. Dutton & Co., 1929), p. 80.

hide them behind the same kind of covering gesture that he might employ. Thus they protect his face and his feelings and presumably make it easier for him to regain composure or at least hold on to what he still has. However, just as the flustered individual may fail to conceal his embarrassment, those who perceive his discomfort may fail in their attempt to hide their knowledge, whereupon they all will realize that his embarrassment has been seen and that the seeing of it was something to conceal. When this point is reached, ordinary involvement in the interaction may meet a painful end. In all this dance between the concealer and the concealed-from, embarrassment presents the same problem and is handled in the same ways as any other offense against propriety.

There seems to be a critical point at which the flustered individual gives up trying to conceal or play down his uneasiness: he collapses into tears or paroxysms of laughter, has a temper tantrum, flies into a blind rage, faints, dashes to the nearest exit, or becomes rigidly immobile as when in panic. After that it is very difficult for him to recover composure. He answers to a new set of rhythms, characteristic of deep emotional experience, and can hardly give even a faint impression that he is at one with the others in interaction. In short, he abdicates his role as someone who sustains encounters. The moment of crisis is of course socially determined: the individual's breaking point is that of the group to whose affective standards he adheres. On rare occasions all the participants in an encounter may pass this point and together fail to maintain even a semblance of ordinary interaction. The little social system they created in interaction collapses; they draw apart or hurriedly try to assume a new set of roles.

The terms "poise," "*sang-froid*," and "aplomb," referring to the capacity to maintain one's own composure, are to be distinguished from what is called "graciousness," "tact," or "social skill," namely, the capacity to avoid causing oneself or others embarrassment. Poise plays an important role in communication, for it guarantees that those present will not fail to play their parts in interaction but will continue as long as they are in one another's presence to receive and transmit disciplined communications. It is no wonder that trial by taunting is a test that every young person passes through until he develops a capacity to maintain composure.[4] Nor should it come as a surprise that many of our games and sports commemorate the themes of composure and embarrassment: in poker, a dubious claim may win money for the player who can present it calmly; in judo, the maintenance and loss of composure are specifically fought over; in cricket, self-command or "style" is supposed to be kept up under tension.

The individual is likely to know that certain special situations always make him uncomfortable and that he has certain "faulty" relationships which always cause him uneasiness. His daily round of social encounters is largely determined, no doubt, by his major social obligations, but he goes a little out of his way to find situations that will not be embarrassing and to by-pass those that will. An individual who firmly believes that he has little poise, perhaps even exaggerating his failing, is shy and bashful; dreading all encounters, he seeks always to shorten them or avoid them altogether. The stutterer is a painful instance of this, showing us the price the individual may be willing to pay for his social life.[5]

[4] One interesting form in which this trial has been institutionalized in America, especially in lower-class Negro society, is "playing the dozens" (see John Dollard, "Dialectic of Insult," *American Imago*, I [1939], 3–25; R. F. B. Berdie, "Playing the Dozens," *Journal of Abnormal and Social Psychology*, XLII [1947], 120–21). On teasing in general see S. J. Sperling, "On the Psychodynamics of Teasing," *Journal of the American Psycho-analytical Association*, I (1953), 458–83.

[5] Cf. H. J. Heltman, "Psycho-social Phenomena of Stuttering and Their Etiological and Therapeutic Implications," *Journal of Social Psychology*, IX (1938), 79–96.

CAUSES OF EMBARRASSMENT

Embarrassment has to do with unfulfilled expectations (but not with those of a statistical kind). Given their social identities and the setting, the participants will sense what sort of conduct *ought* to be maintained as the appropriate thing, however much they may despair of its actually occurring. An individual may firmly expect that certain others will make him ill at ease, and yet this knowledge may increase his discomfiture instead of lessening it. An entirely unexpected flash of social engineering may save a situation, all the more effective for their being unanticipated.

The expectations relevant to embarrassment are moral, then, but embarrassment does not arise from the breach of *any* moral expectation, for some infractions give rise to resolute moral indignation and no uneasiness at all. Rather we should look to those moral obligations which surround the individual in only one of his capacities, that of someone who carries on social encounters. The individual, of course, is obliged to remain composed, but this tells us that things are going well, not why. And things go well or badly because of what is perceived about the social identities of those present.

During interaction the individual is expected to possess certain attributes, capacities, and information which, taken together, fit together into a self that is at once coherently unified and appropriate for the occasion. Through the expressive implications of his stream of conduct, through mere participation itself, the individual effectively projects this acceptable self into the interaction, although he may not be aware of it, and the others may not be aware of having so interpreted his conduct. At the same time he must accept and honor the selves projected by the other participants. The elements of a social encounter, then, consist of effectively projected claims to an acceptable self and the confirmation of like claims on the part of the others. The contributions of all are oriented to these and built up on the basis of them.

When an event throws doubt upon or discredits these claims, then the encounter finds itself lodged in assumptions which no longer hold. The responses the parties have made ready are now out of place and must be choked back, and the interaction must be reconstructed. At such times the individual whose self has been threatened (the individual *for* whom embarrassment is felt) and the individual who threatened him may both feel ashamed of what together they have brought about, sharing this sentiment just when they have reason to feel apart. And this joint responsibility is only right. By the standards of the wider society, perhaps only the discredited individual ought to feel ashamed; but, by the standards of the little social system maintained through the interaction, the discreditor is just as guilty as the person he discredits—sometimes more so, for, if he has been posing as a tactful man, in destroying another's image he destroys his own.

But of course the trouble does not stop with the guilty pair or with those who have identified themselves sympathetically with them. Having no settled and legitimate object to which to play out their own unity, the others find themselves unfixed and discomfited. This is why embarrassment seems to be contagious, spreading, once started, in ever widening circles of discomfiture.

There are many classic circumstances under which the self projected by an individual may be discredited, causing him shame and embarrassment over what he has or appears to have done to himself and to the interaction. To experience a sudden change in status, as by marriage or promotion, is to acquire a self that other individuals will not fully admit because of their lingering attachment to the old self. To ask for a job, a loan of money, or a hand in marriage is to project an image of self as worthy, under conditions where the one who can discredit the assumption may have good reason to do so. To affect the style of one's occupational or social betters is to make claims that may well be discredited by one's lack of familiarity with the role.

The physical structure of an encounter itself is usually accorded certain symbolic implications, sometimes leading a participant against his will to project claims about himself that are false and embarrassing. Physical closeness easily implies social closeness, as anyone knows who has happened upon an intimate gathering not meant for him or who has found it necessary to carry on fraternal "small talk" with someone too high or low or strange to ever be a brother. Similarly, if there is to be talk, someone must initiate it, feed it, and terminate it; and these acts may awkwardly suggest rankings and power which are out of line with the facts.

Various kinds of recurrent encounters in a given society may share the assumption that participants have attained certain moral, mental, and physiognomic standards. The person who falls short may everywhere find himself inadvertently trapped into making implicit identity-claims which he cannot fulfil. Compromised in every encounter which he enters, he truly wears the leper's bell. The individual who most isolates himself from social contacts may then be the least insulated from the demands of society. And, if he only imagines that he possesses a disqualifying attribute, his judgment of himself may be in error, but in the light of it his withdrawal from contact is reasonable. In any case, in deciding whether an individual's grounds for shyness are real or imaginary, one should seek not for "justifiable" disqualifications but for the much larger range of characteristics which actually embarrass encounters.

In all these settings the same fundamental thing occurs: the expressive facts at hand threaten or discredit the assumptions a participant finds he has projected about his identity.[6] Thereafter those present find they can neither do without the assumptions nor base their own responses upon them. The inhabitable reality shrinks until everyone feels "small" or out of place.

An additional complication must be noted. Often important everyday occasions of embarrassment arise when the self projected is somehow confronted with another self which, though valid in other contexts, cannot be here sustained in harmony with the first. Embarrassment, then, leads us to the matter of "role segregation." Each individual has more than one role, but he is saved from role dilemma by "audience segregation," for, ordinarily, those before whom he plays out one of his roles will not be the individuals before whom he plays out another, allowing him to be a different person in each role without discrediting either.

In every social system, however, there are times and places where audience segregation regularly breaks down and where individuals confront one another with selves incompatible with the ones they extend to each other on other occasions. At such times, embarrassment, especially the mild kind, clearly shows itself to be located not in the individual but in the social system wherein he has his several selves.

[6] In addition to his other troubles, he has discredited his implicit claim to poise. He will feel he has cause, then, to become embarrassed over his embarrassment, even though no one present may have perceived the earlier stages of his discomfiture. But a qualification must be made. When an individual, receiving a compliment, blushes from modesty, he may lose his reputation for poise but confirm a more important one, that of being modest. Feeling that his chagrin is nothing to be ashamed of, his embarrassment will not lead him to be embarrassed. On the other hand, when embarrassment is clearly expected as a reasonable response, he who fails to become embarrassed may appear insensitive and thereupon become embarrassed because of this appearance.

DOMAIN OF EMBARRASSMENT

Having started with psychological considerations, we have come by stages to a structural sociological point of view. Precedent comes from social anthropologists and their analyses of joking and avoidance. One assumes that embarrassment is a normal part of normal social life, the individual becoming uneasy not because he is personally maladjusted but rather because he is not; presumably anyone with his combination of statuses would do likewise. In an empirical study of a particular social system, the first object would be to learn what categories of persons become embarrassed in what recurrent situations. And the second object would be to discover what would happen to the social system and the framework of obligations if embarrassment had not come to be systematically built into it.

An illustration may be taken from the social life of large social establishments—office buildings, schools, hospitals, etc. Here, in elevators, halls, and cafeterias, at newsstands, vending machines, snack counters, and entrances, all members are often formally on an equal if distant footing.[7] In Benoit-Smullyan's terms, situs, not status or locus, is expressed.[8] Cutting across these relationships of equality and distance is another set of relation-

[7] This equal and joint membership in a large organization is often celebrated annually at the office party and in amateur dramatic skits, this being accomplished by pointedly excluding outsiders and scrambling the rank of insiders.

[8] Émile Benoit-Smullyan, "Status, Status Types, and Status Interrelations," *American Sociological Review*, IX (1944), 151–61. In a certain way the claim of equal institutional membership is reinforced by the ruling in our society that males ought to show certain minor courtesies to females; all other principles, such as distinctions between racial groups and occupational categories, must be suppressed. The effect is to stress situs and equality.

ships, arising in work teams whose members are ranked by such things as prestige and authority and yet drawn together by joint enterprise and personal knowledge of one another.

In many large establishments, staggered work hours, segregated cafeterias, and the like help to insure that those who are ranked and close in one set of relations will not have to find themselves in physically intimate situations where they are expected to maintain equality and distance. The democratic orientation of some of our newer establishments, however, tends to throw differently placed members of the same work team together at places such as the cafeteria, causing them uneasiness. There is no way for them to act that does not disturb one of the two basic sets of relations in which they stand to each other. These difficulties are especially likely to occur in elevators, for there individuals who are not quite on chatting terms must remain for a time too close together to ignore the opportunity for informal talk—a problem solved, of course, for some, by special executive elevators. Embarrassment, then, is built into the establishment ecologically.

Because of possessing multiple selves the individual may find he is required both to be present and to not be present on certain occasions. Embarrassment ensues: the individual finds himself being torn apart, however gently. Corresponding to the oscillation of his conduct is the oscillation of his self.

Social Function of Embarrassment

When an individual's projected self is threatened during interaction, he may with poise suppress all signs of shame and embarrassment. No flusterings, or efforts to conceal having seen them, obtrude upon the smooth flow of the encounter; participants can proceed as if no incident has occurred.

When situations are saved, however, something important may be lost. By showing embarrassment when he can be neither of two people, the individual leaves open the possibility that in the future he may effectively be either.[9] His role in the current interaction may be sacrificed, and even the encounter itself, but he demonstrates that, while he cannot present a substainable and coherent self on this occasion, he is at least disturbed by the fact and may prove worthy at another time. To this extent, embarrassment is not an irrational impulse breaking through socially prescribed behavior but part of this orderly behavior itself. Flusterings are an extreme example of that important class of acts which are usually quite spontaneous and yet no less required and obligatory than ones self-consciously performed.

Behind a conflict in identity lies a more fundamental conflict, one of organizational principle, since the self, for many purposes, consists merely of the application of legitimate organizational principles to one's self. One builds one's identity out of claims which, if denied, give one the right to feel righteously indignant. Behind the apprentice's claims for a full share in the use of certain plant facilities there is the organizational principle: all members of the establishment are equal in certain ways *qua* members. Behind the specialist's demand for suitable financial recognition there is the principle that the type of work, not mere work, determines status. The fumblings of the apprentice and the specialist when they

[9] A similar argument was presented by Samuel Johnson in his piece "Of Bashfulness," *The Rambler*, (1751), No. 139: "It generally happens that assurance keeps an even pace with ability; and the fear of miscarriage, which hinders our first attempts, is gradually dissipated as our skill advances towards certainty of success. The bashfulness, therefore, which prevents disgrace, that short temporary shame which secures us from the danger of lasting reproach, cannot be properly counted among our misfortunes."

reach the Coca-Cola machine at the same time express an incompatibility of organizational principles.[10]

The principles of organization of any social system are likely to come in conflict at certain points. Instead of permitting the conflict to be expressed in an encounter, the individual places himself between the opposing principles. He sacrifices his identity for a moment, and sometimes the encounter, but the principles are preserved. He may be ground between opposing assumptions, thereby preventing direct friction between them, or he may be almost pulled apart, so that principles with little relation to one another may operate together. Social structure gains elasticity; the individual merely loses composure.

[10] At such moments "joshing" sometimes occurs. It is said to be a means of releasing the tension caused either by embarrassment or by whatever caused embarrassment. But in many cases this kind of banter is a way of saying that what occurs now is not serious or real. The exaggeration, the mock insult, the mock claims—all these reduce the seriousness of conflict by denying reality to the situation. And this, of course, in another way, is what embarrassment does. It is natural, then, to find embarrassment and joking together, for both help in denying the same reality.

ALIENATION FROM INTERACTION

I. Introduction

When the individual in our Anglo-American society engages in a conversational encounter with others he may become spontaneously involved in it. He can become unthinkingly and impulsively immersed in the talk and carried away by it, oblivious to other things, including himself. Whether his involvement is intense and not easily disrupted, or meager and easily distracted, the topic of talk can form the main focus of his cognitive attention and the current talker can form the main focus of his visual attention. The binding and hypnotic effect of such involvement is illustrated by the fact that while thus involved the individual can simultaneously engage in other goal-directed activities (chewing gum, smoking, finding a comfortable sitting position, performing repetitive tasks, etc.) yet manage such side-involvements in an abstracted, fugue-like fashion so as not to be distracted from his main focus of attention by them.

The individual, like an infant or an animal, can of course become spontaneously involved in unsociable solitary tasks. When this occurs the task takes on at once a weight and a lightness, affording the performer a firm sense of reality. As a main focus of attention talk is unique, however, for talk creates for the participant a world and a reality that has other participants in it. Joint spontaneous involvement is a *unio mystico*, a socialized trance. We must also see that a conversation has a life of its own and makes demands on its own behalf. It is a little social system with its own boundary-maintaining tendencies; it is a little patch of commitment and loyalty with its own heroes[1] and its own villains.

Taking joint spontaneous involvement as a point of reference, I want to discuss how this involvement can fail to occur and the consequence of this failure. I want to consider the ways in which the individual can become alienated from a conversational encounter, the uneasiness that arises with this, and the consequence of this alienation and uneasiness upon the interaction. Since alienation can occur in regard to any imaginable talk, we may be able to learn from it something about the generic properties of spoken interaction.

II. INVOLVEMENT OBLIGATIONS

When individuals are in one another's immediate presence, a multitude of words, gestures, acts, and minor events become available, whether desired or not, through which one who is present can intentionally or unintentionally symbolize his character and his attitudes. In our society a system of etiquette obtains that enjoins the individual to handle these expressive events fittingly, projecting through them a proper image of himself, an appropriate respect for the others present, and a suitable regard for the setting. When the individual intentionally or unintentionally breaks a rule of etiquette, others present may mobilize themselves to restore the ceremonial order, somewhat as they do when other types of social order are transgressed.

Through the ceremonial order that is maintained by a system of etiquette, the capacity of the individual to be

[1] One of its heroes is the wit who can introduce references to wider, important matters in a way that is ineffably suited to the current moment of talk. Since the witticism will never again be as telling, a sacrifice has been offered up to the conversation, and respect paid to its unique reality by an act that shows how thoroughly the actor is alive to the interaction.

carried away by a talk become socialized, taking on a burden of ritual value and social function. Choice of main focus of attention, choice of side-involvements and of intensity of involvement, become hedged in with social constraints, so that some allocations of attention become socially proper and other allocations improper.

There are many occasions when the individual participant in a conversation finds that he and the others are locked together by involvement obligations with respect to it. He comes to feel it is defined as appropriate (and hence either desirable in itself or prudent) to give his main focus of attention to the talk, and to become spontaneously involved in it, while at the same time he feels that each of the other participants has the same obligation. Due to the ceremonial order in which his actions are embedded, he may find that any alternate allocation of involvement on his part will be taken as a discourtesy and cast an uncalled-for reflection upon the others, the setting, or himself. And he will find that his offense has been committed in the very presence of those who are offended by it. Those who break the rules of interaction commit their crimes in jail.

The task of becoming spontaneously involved in something, when it is a duty to oneself or others to do so, is a ticklish thing, as we all know from experience with dull chores or threatening ones. The individual's actions must happen to satisfy his involvement obligations, but in a certain sense he cannot act *in order* to satisfy these obligations, for such an effort would require him to shift his attention from the topic of conversation to the problem of being spontaneously involved in it. Here, in a component of non-rational impulsiveness—not only tolerated but actually demanded—we find an important way in which the interactional order differs from other kinds of social order.

The individual's obligation to maintain spontaneous involvement in the conversation and the difficulty of doing so place him in a delicate position. He is rescued by his co-participants, who control their own actions so that he will not be forced from appropriate involvement. But the moment he is rescued he will have to rescue someone else, and so his job as interactant is only complicated the more. Here, then, is one of the fundamental aspects of social control in conversation: the individual must not only maintain proper involvement himself but also act so as to ensure that others will maintain theirs. This is what the individual owes the others in their capacity as interactants, regardless of what is owed them in whatever other capacities they participate, and it is this obligation that tells us that, whatever social role the individual plays during a conversational encounter, he will in addition have to fill the role of interactant.

The individual will have approved and unapproved reasons for fulfilling his obligation *qua* interactant, but in all cases to do so he must be able rapidly and delicately to take the role of the others and sense the qualifications their situation ought to bring to his conduct if they are not to be brought up short by it. He must be sympathetically aware of the kinds of things in which the others present can become spontaneously and properly involved, and then attempt to modulate his expression of attitudes, feelings, and opinions according to the company.

Thus, as Adam Smith argued in his *Theory of the Moral Sentiments,* the individual must phrase his own concerns and feelings and interests in such a way as to make these maximally usable by the others as a source of appropriate involvement; and this major obligation of the individual *qua* interactant is balanced by his right to expect that others present will make some effort to stir up their sympathies and place them at his command. These two tendencies, that of the speaker to scale down his expressions and that of the listeners to scale up their interests, each in the light of the other's capacities and demands, form the bridge that people build to one another, allowing them to meet for a moment of talk in a communion of reciprocally sustained involvement. It is this spark, not the more obvious kinds of love, that lights up the world.

III. The Forms of Alienation

If we take conjoint spontaneous involvement in a topic of conversation as a point of reference, we shall find that alienation from it is common indeed. Joint involvement appears to be a fragile thing, with standard points of weakness and decay, a precarious unsteady state that is likely at any time to lead the individual into some form of alienation. Since we are dealing with obligatory involvement, forms of alienation will constitute misbehavior of a kind that can be called "misinvolvement." Some of the standard forms of alienative misinvolvement may be considered now.

1. External Preoccupation. The individual may neglect the prescribed focus of attention and give his main concern to something that is unconnected with what is being talked about at the time and even unconnected with the other persons present, at least in their capacity as fellow-participants. The object of the individual's preoccupation may be one that he ought to have ceased considering upon entering the interaction, or one that is to be appropriately considered only later in the encounter or after the encounter has terminated. The preoccupation may also take the form of furtive by-play between the individual and one or two other participants. The individual may even be preoccupied with a vague standard of work-activity, which he cannot maintain because of his obligation to participate in the interaction.

The offensiveness of the individual's preoccupation varies according to the kind of excuse the others feel he has for it. At one extreme there is preoccupation that is felt to be quite voluntary, the offender giving the impression that he could easily give his attention to the conversation but is wilfully refusing to do so. At the other extreme there is "involuntary" preoccupation, a consequence of the offender's understandably deep involvement in vital matters outside the interaction.

Individuals who could excusably withdraw involvement from a conversation often remain loyal and decline to do so. Through this they show a nice respect for fellow-participants and affirm the moral rules that transform socially responsible people into people who are interactively responsible as well. It is of course through such rules, and through such reaffirming gestures, that society is made safe for the little worlds sustained in face-to-face encounters. No culture, in fact, seems to be without exemplary tales for illustrating the dignity and weight that might be given to these passing realities; everywhere we find enshrined a Drake who gallantly finishes some kind of game before going out to battle some kind of Armada, and everywhere an outlaw who is engagingly civil to those he robs and to those who later hang him for it.[2]

2. *Self-consciousness.* At the cost of his involvement in the prescribed focus of attention, the individual may focus his attention more than he ought upon himself—himself as someone who is faring well or badly, as someone calling forth a desirable or undesirable response from others. It is possible, of course, for the individual to dwell upon himself as a topic of conversation—to be self-centered in this way—and yet not to be self-conscious. Self-consciousness for the individual does not, it seems, result from his deep interest in the topic of conversation, which may happen to be himself, but rather from his giving attention to himself as an interactant at a time when he ought to be free to involve himself in the content of the conversation.

A general statement about sources of self-consciousness

[2] Yet different strata in the same society can be unequally concerned that members learn to project themselves into encounters; the tendency to keep conversations alive and lively may be a way in which some strata, not necessarily adjacent, are characteristically different from others.

ought to be added. During interaction the individual is often accorded by others and by impersonal events in the situation an image and appraisal of self that is at least temporarily acceptable to him. He is then free to turn his attention to matters less close to home. When this definition of self is threatened, the individual typically withdraws attention from the interaction in a hurried effort to correct for the incident that has occurred. If the incident threatens to raise his standing in the interaction, his flight into self-consciousness may be a way of rejoicing; if the incident threatens to lower his standing and damage or discredit his self-image in some way, then flight into self-consciousness may be a way of protecting the self and licking its wounds. As a source of self-consciousness, threat of loss seems more common and important than threat of gain.

Whatever the cause of self-consciousness, we are all familiar with the vacillation of action and the flusterings through which self-consciousness is expressed; we are all familiar with the phenomenon of embarrassment.

Self-consciousness can be thought of as a kind of preoccupation with matters internal to the interactive social system, and as such has received more common-sense consideration than other kinds of internal preoccupation. In fact we do not have common-sense words to refer to these other kinds of improper involvement. Two forms of these I shall refer to as "interaction-consciousness" and "other-consciousness" to emphasize a similarity to self-consciousness.

3. *Interaction-consciousness.* A participant in talk may become consciously concerned to an improper degree with the way in which the interaction, *qua* interaction, is proceeding, instead of becoming spontaneously involved in the official topic of conversation. Since interaction-consciousness is not as famous as self-consciousness, some sources of it may be cited by way of illustration.

A common source of interaction-consciousness is related

to the special responsibility that an individual may have for the interaction "going well," i.e. calling forth the proper kind of involvement from those present. Thus, at a small social gathering the hostess may be expected to join in with her guests and become spontaneously involved in the conversation they are maintaining, and yet at the same time if the occasion does not go well she, more than others, will be held responsible for the failure. In consequence, she sometimes becomes so much concerned with the social machinery of the occasion and with how the evening is going as a whole that she finds it impossible to give herself up to her own party.

Another common source of interaction-consciousness may be mentioned. Once individuals enter a conversation they are obliged to continue it until they have the kind of basis for withdrawing that will neutralize the potentially offensive implications of taking leave of others. While engaged in the interaction it will be necessary for them to have subjects at hand to talk about that fit the occasion and yet provide content enough to keep the talk going; in other words, safe supplies are needed.[3] What we call "small talk" serves this purpose. When individuals use up their small talk, they find themselves officially lodged in a state of talk but with nothing to talk about; interaction-consciousness experienced as a "painful silence" is the typical consequence.

4. *Other-consciousness.* During interaction, the individual may become distracted by another participant as an object of attention—exactly as in the case of self-consciousness he can become distracted by concern over himself.[4]

[3] The problem of safe supplies is further considered in my "Communication Conduct in an Island Community," Unpublished Ph.D. Dissertation, Department of Sociology, University of Chicago, 1953, ch. XV.

[4] Other-consciousness is briefly but explicitly considered in James Baldwin, *Social and Ethical Interpretations in Mental Development* (London, 1902), pp. 213–14.

If the individual finds that whenever he is in the conversational presence of specific others they cause him to be overly conscious of them at the expense of the prescribed involvement in the topic of conversation, then they may acquire the reputation in his eyes of being faulty interactants, especially if he feels he is not alone in the trouble he has with them. He is then likely to impute certain characteristics to those who are thus perceived, doing so in order to explain and account for the distraction they cause him. It will be useful to our understanding of interaction to list a few of the attributes imputed in this way.

By the terms "affectation" and "insincerity" the individual tends to identify those who seem to feign through gestures what they expect him to accept as an uncontrived expressive overflow of their behavior. Affectation, as Cooley suggests, ". . . exists when the passion to influence others seems to overbalance the established character and give it an obvious twist or pose." . . . "Thus there are persons who in the simplest conversation do not seem to forget themselves, and enter frankly and disinterestedly into the subject, but are felt to be always preoccupied with the thought of the impression they are making, imagining praise or depreciation, and usually posing a little to avoid the one or gain the other."[5] Affected individuals seem chiefly concerned with controlling the evaluation an observer will make of them, and seem partly taken in by their own pose; insincere individuals seem chiefly concerned with controlling the impression the observer will form of their attitude toward certain things or persons, especially toward him, and seem not to be taken in by their own pose. It may be added that while those who are felt to be self-conscious give the impression of being overly concerned with what will happen or has happened to them, those who are felt to be insincere or affected give the impression that

[5] Charles H. Cooley, *Human Nature and the Social Order* (Charles Scribner's Sons, New York, 1922), pp. 196, 215.

they are overly concerned with what they can achieve in what is to follow and are willing to put on an act in order to achieve it. When the individual senses that others are insincere or affected he tends to feel they have taken unfair advantage of their communication position to promote their own interests; he feels they have broken the ground rules of interaction. His hostility to their unfair play leads him to focus his attention upon them and their misdemeanor at the price of his own involvement in the conversation.

In considering the attributes imputed to those who cause another to be conscious of them, we must give importance to the factor of immodesty. On analytical grounds overmodesty should equally count as a source of other-consciousness, but, empirically, immodesty seems much the more important of the two. What the individual takes to be immodesty in others may present itself in many forms: immodest individuals may seem to praise themselves verbally; they may talk about themselves and their activity in a way that assumes greater interest in and familiarity with their personal life than the individual actually possesses; they may speak more frequently and at greater length than the individual feels is fitting; they may take a more prominent "ecological" position than he thinks they warrant, etc.

One interesting source of other-consciousness is to be found in the phenomenon of "over-involvement." During any conversation, standards are established as to how much the individual is to allow himself to be carried away by the talk, how thoroughly he is to permit himself to be caught up in it. He will be obliged to prevent himself from becoming so swollen with feelings and a readiness to act that he threatens the bounds regarding affect that have been established for him in the interaction. He will be obliged to express a margin of disinvolvement, although of course this margin will differ in extent according to the socially recognized importance of the occasion and his official role in it. When the individual does become over-involved in the topic of conversation, and gives others the impression that he does not have a necessary measure of self-control over his feelings and actions, when, in short, the interactive world becomes too real for him, then the others are likely to be drawn from involvement in the talk to an involvement in the talker. What is one man's over-eagerness will become another's alienation. In any case we are to see that over-involvement has the effect of momentarily incapacitating the individual as an interactant; others have to adjust to his state while he becomes incapable of adjusting to theirs. Interestingly enough, when the impulse of the over-involved individual has ebbed a little, he may come to sense his impropriety and become self-conscious, illustrating again the fact that the alienative effect the individual has on others is usually one he cannot escape having upon himself. Regardless of this, we must see that a readiness to become over-involved is a form of tyranny practised by children, *prima donnas,* and lords of all kinds, who momentarily put their own feelings above the moral rules that ought to have made society safe for interaction.

A final source of other-consciousness may be mentioned. If the individual is to become involved in a topic of conversation, then, as a listener, he will have to give his aural and usually his visual attention to the source of communication, that is, to the speaker, and especially to the speaker's voice and face. (This physical requirement is underlined by social rules that often define inattention to the speaker as an affront to him.) If the speaker's communication apparatus itself conveys additional information all during the time that transmission is occurring, then the listener is likely to be distracted by competing sources of stimuli, becoming over-aware of the speaker at the expense of what is being said. The sources of this distraction are well known: the speaker may be very ugly or very beautiful; he may have a speech defect such as a lisp or a stutter; he may have inadequate familiarity with the language, dialect, or jargon that the listeners expect to hear; he may have a slight facial peculiarity, such as a hare lip, eye twitch, crossed or wall eyes; he may have temporary communication difficulties such as a stiff neck, a hoarse voice, etc. Apparently the closer the defect is to the communication equipment upon which the listener must focus his attention, the smaller the defect need be to throw the listener off balance. (It should be added that in so far as a speaker is required to direct his attention to his listener and yet not be overly conscious of him, defects in the appearance of the listener can cause the speaker to be uneasy.) These minor defects in the apparatus of communication tend to shut off the afflicted individual from the stream of daily contacts, transforming him into a faulty interactant, either in his own eyes or in the eyes of others.

In concluding this discussion of sources of alienating distraction, I should like to state an obvious caution. When the individual senses that others are unsuitably involved, it will always be relative to the standards of his group that he will sense the others have behaved improperly. Similarly, an individual who would cause certain others to be unduly conscious of him because of his apparent insincerity, affectation, or immodesty would pass unnoticed in a subculture where conversational discipline was less strict. Hence, when members of different groups interact with one another, it is quite likely that at least one of the participants will be distracted from spontaneous involvement in the topic of conversation because of what appears to him to be unsuitable behavior on the part of the others.[6] It is to these differences in expressive customs

[6] For example, in social intercourse among traditional Shetlanders, the pronoun "I" tends to be little used; its greater use by individuals from the mainland of Great Britain, and especially its relatively frequent use by Americans, leads the Shetlander to feel that these non-Shetlandic people are immod-

that we ought to look first in trying to account for the improper behavior of those with whom we happen to be participating and not try, initially at least, to find some source of blame within the personalities of the offenders.

IV. ON THE REPERCUSSIVE CHARACTER OF INVOLVEMENT OFFENSES

I have suggested that disenchantment with an interaction may take the form of preoccupation, self-consciousness, other-consciousness, and interaction-consciousness. These forms of alienation have been separated for purposes of identification. In actual conversation, when one kind occurs the others will not be far behind.

When the individual senses that he or other participants are failing to allocate their involvement according to standards that he approves, and in consequence that they are conveying an improper attitude toward the interaction and the participants, then his sentiments are likely to be roused by the impropriety—much as they would be were any other obligations of the ceremonial order broken. But matters do not stop here. The witnessing of an offense against involvement obligations, as against other ceremonial obligations, causes the witness to turn his attention from the conversation at hand to the offense that has occurred during it. If the individual feels responsible for the offense that has occurred, he is likely to be led to feel shamefully self-conscious. If others seem responsible for the offense, then he is likely to be led to feel indignantly other-conscious in regard to them. But to be self-conscious or other-conscious is in itself an offense against involvement obligations. The mere witnessing of an involvement offense, let alone its punishment, can cause a crime against the interaction, the victim of the first

---

est and gross. Shetlandic tact, it might be added, frequently prevents non-islanders from learning that their manner causes Shetlanders to be uneasy.

crime himself being made a criminal. Thus, during spoken interaction, when one individual is stricken with uneasiness, others often come down with the disease.

A note of qualification should be added. The individual may become misinvolved and yet neither he nor others may become aware that this is the case, let alone become improperly involved because of this awareness. He commits a latent offense that only awaits someone's perception of it to make it manifest. When others come to see that he is misinvolved, and convey the fact of this judgment to him, he may become self-consciously flustered in consequence, as he may also do when he discovers this fact for himself. Thus an individual may "come to" from a brown study and embarrassingly find himself in the midst of an interaction but patently alienated from it.

V. The Affectation of Involvement

When a conversation fails to capture the spontaneous involvement of an individual who is obliged to participate in it, he is likely to contrive an appearance of being really involved. This he must do to save the feelings of the other participants and their good opinion of him, regardless of his motives for wanting to effect this saving. In doing so he has a damping effect upon the repercussive consequences of misinvolvement, ensuring that while he may be disaffected his disaffection will not contaminate others. At the same time, however, he drives a wedge between himself and the world that could become real for him. And the gap that is created in this way he fills with that special kind of uneasiness that is characteristically found during conversation; the kind of uneasiness that occurs when involvement obligations can neither be laid aside nor spontaneously realized; the kind that occurs when the individual is separated from the reality of interaction, yet at a time when interaction is all around him.

As a form of contrivance, affected involvement will be

differently judged according to the motive the alienated individual has for contriving it. Some shows of involvement are felt to be cynical because the individual seems to be interested ultimately not in the feelings of the others but rather in what can be gained by deluding the others into a belief that they have captured his attention. He gives the impression that he is occupied with the talk but proves to be really occupied with the task of giving this impression.

On the other hand, if the alienated individual is genuinely concerned with the feelings of the others, as important matters in their own right, then any act that protects these feelings may be considered a form of tact and approved on this ground.

It should be noted that often the show of involvement given by the tactful interactant is not as good a show as he is capable of giving. Some power that is almost beyond him will force him to demonstrate to others and to himself that this kind of interaction with these participants is not the sort of thing that can capture his attention; someone must see that he is perhaps above or beyond it. Here we find a form of insubordination carried on by those who may not really be in a position to rebel.

The ways of not quite concealing tactfully concealed misinvolvement constitute, then, the symptoms of boredom. Some symptoms of boredom suggest that the individual will make no effort to terminate the encounter or his official participation in it but that he will no longer give as much to it. The initiation of side-involvements, such as leafing through a magazine or lighting a cigarette, are instances. Other symptoms of boredom suggest that the individual is about to terminate official participation and function as a tactful warning of this.[7]

[7] There is in fact a small literature in "applied human relations" detailing ways in which the superordinate can imply that an interview is over, allowing the actual leave-taking to be initiated, in a face-saving way, by the other.

To manifest signs of boredom is an inconsiderate thing. But in a certain way he who does so assures the others that he is not affecting something that is not felt; they at least know where they stand with him. To suppress these signs completely is suspect, for this prevents others from obtaining the benefit of feed-back cues that might tell them what the situation really is. Thus, while there is one obligation to affect involvement, there is another one inducing the individual not to affect it too well. It is an interesting fact that when the self of the boring individual is deeply committed to the proceedings, as it may be, for example, during leave-takings and avowals of affection, then the bored individual is likely to feel a strong compunction to conceal signs of alienation and thoroughly affect involvement. It is thus at the most poignant and crucial moments of life that the individual is often forced to be the most contriving; these, too, will be the times when the boring individual will be in greatest need of candor from others and least able to bear receiving it.

I have suggested that a show of involvement may be affected by cynical participants and by tactful ones; the same show may also be affected by those who feel self-consciously embarrassed. They may even add to their production by affecting signs of boredom. A condition that casts doubt upon the individual himself is thus exchanged, he hopes, for one that casts doubt upon the others. There is a psychological doctrine that carries this observation one step further and argues that when the individual is himself convinced that he is bored, he may be trying to conceal from himself that he is actually embarrassed.[8]

[8] For psychoanalytic versions of this theme see Ralph Greenson ("On Boredom," *Journal of the American Psychoanalytical Association*, vol. I: 7–21) and Otto Fenichel ("The Psychology of Boredom," no. 26 in the *Collected Papers of Otto Fenichel*, First Series [Norton, New York, 1953]). Some interesting observations on the cult of boredom and the place of this cult in the world of an adolescent can be found in J. D. Salinger's novel, *The Catcher in the Rye* (Little, Brown, Boston, 1951).

Conversational encounters in which participants feel obliged to maintain spontaneous involvement and yet cannot manage to do so are ones in which they feel uneasy, and ones in which they may well generate uneasiness in others. The individual recognizes that certain situations will produce this alienation in him and others, and that other situations are quite unlikely to do so. He recognizes that certain individuals are faulty interactants because they are never ready to become spontaneously involved in social encounters and he will have folk-terms such as "cold fish," "kill-joy," "drag," "wet blanket" to refer to these refractory participants. Those who fail to support conversations with their social betters he may call gauche; while those who disdain involvement with their inferiors he may call snobs; in either case condemning these persons for putting rank before interaction. As previously suggested, the individual will also know some persons who are faulty because their manner and social attributes make it difficult for others to become properly involved. It is apparent, too, that in any interaction a role-function develops which ensures that everyone becomes and remains spontaneously involved. This sparking function may be fulfilled by different participants at different times in the interaction. Should one participant fail to help keep the interaction going, other participants will have to do his share of work. An individual may acquire a reputation for this kind of labor, creating gratitude or resentment as one who is always the life of the encounter.

VI. Generalizing the Framework

1. The Context of Involvement Obligations. One limitation we have set ourselves is to deal with situations where all those present to one another are officially obliged to maintain themselves as participants in conversation and to maintain spontaneous involvement in the conversation. This is a frequent enough condition to serve as a reference point, but there is no need to be ultimately bound by it. Involvement obligations are in fact defined in terms of the total context in which the individual finds himself. Thus there will be some situations where the main involvement of those present is supposed to be invested in a physical task; conversation, if carried on at all, will have to be treated as a side-involvement to be picked up or dropped, depending on the current demands of the task at hand. There will be other situations where the role and status of a particular participant will be nicely expressed by his right to treat a conversation in a cavalier fashion, participating in it or not, depending on his inclination at the moment. A father sometimes has this right regarding the mealtime conversation maintained by lesser members of the family, while they do not.

I should like to cite another way in which the individual may accept a different allocation of involvement for himself from that expected of others. In the teasing that the young receive from the old, or in the interrogations that employees receive from employers, loss of composure on the subordinate's part may be accepted by the superordinate as an expected and proper part of the involvement pattern. At such times the subordinate may feel he would like to be spontaneously involved in the talk but is in too much of a panic to do so, while the superordinate may feel that for him the appropriate focus of attention, and one he can sustain with comfort, is not the actual talk but the wider situation created by the humorous plight of the inferior as he struggles in the conversation.[9] In fact, if

[9] The plight of the self-conscious person is in fact so good a stimulus for calling forth spontaneous involvement on the part of those who witness it, that during conversations where there may be difficulty in capturing the involvement of those present, individuals may take turns both at committing minor infractions against propriety and at becoming embarrassed, thus ensuring involvement. Hence the paradox that if all the rules of correct social behavior are exactly followed, the interaction may become flaccid, stale, and flat.

the subordinate shows composure on these occasions, the superior may feel affronted and embarrassed. Similarly there will be occasions when we feel an individual ought, out of respect for the difficulties he is in, to be preoccupied or over-involved. This misinvolvement may somewhat disrupt the interaction, but perfect poise on his part might so scandalize those present as to disrupt the interaction even more. Thus while it is true that sometimes an individual will be thought an interaction hero if he remains involved in a conversation under difficult conditions, at other times such loyalty will be thought foolhardy.

Differential obligations regarding the same spoken interaction may be seen most clearly in large-scale interactions, such as public speeches, where we are likely to find specialization and segregation of involvement roles, with a division between full participants, who are expected to talk or listen, and non-participating specialists, whose job is to move unobtrusively about and look after some of the mechanics of the occasion. Examples of these non-participants are domestics, ushers, doormen, stenographers, and microphone men. The special alignment these officials have to the interaction is their particular right and obligation; it is accepted openly by them and for them, and they would in fact cause uneasiness were they to become manifestly involved in the content of the talk. They show respect for the occasion by treating it as a side-involvement.

Participants, themselves, in large-scale interaction can have a license in regard to involvement that could not be afforded them in two- or three-person talk, perhaps because the more participants there are to sustain the proceedings, the less dependent the occasion will be on any one participant. In any case, we often find in large-scale interaction that it is permissible for a few participants to enter for a moment into by-plays and side-discussions, providing they modulate their voice and manner to show respect for the official proceedings. In fact, a participant may even leave the room for a moment and do this in such a way as to convey the impression that his main focus of attention is still held by the talk, even though his body is not present. On such occasions, main involvement and side-involvements may become fictions maintained officially in form while alternate involvement patterns are actually maintained in practice.

2. *Pseudo-conversations.* We have so far restricted our attention to interactions that have as their constituent communicative acts the turns at talking taken by participants. We can extend our view and consider conversation-like interactions in which the token exchanged is not speeches but stylized gestures, as in the interchange of non-verbal greetings,[10] or moves of some kind, as in card games. These unspoken yet conversation-like interactions seem to be similar, structurally, to spoken interaction, except that the capacities that must be mobilized in order to carry on such interaction seem to have more to do with muscular control of limbs than in the case of spoken interaction.

3. *Unfocused Interaction.* I have suggested that speech-, gesture-, and game-interactions are characterized by a sin-

[10] The following is an instance of psychiatrist-patient interaction that is verbal on one side only: ". . . in the course of an analysis of a very disturbed schizophrenic with depressive features the patient hid herself within her only garment, a blanket, so that only the eyebrow showed; nothing daunted I continued the conversation from where we left off last time and noted changes in that eloquent but only visible member, which changes—a frown, scowl, surprise, a flicker of amusement, a softening of the curve—indicated the changes in her mood and thought. My surmises proved correct for when next she displayed her face and used her voice she corroborated the general trend of my guesses as to what had gone on in her mind. That session was no verbal *interchange*—it might even be called an eyebrow analysis—but there was an endeavour to verbalize, to conceptualize and make concrete 'in the here and now' what was occurring concurrently in her mind." (John Richman, "The Role and Future of Psychotherapy with Psychiatry," *Journal of Mental Science,* 96 [1950], 189)

gle official focus of cognitive and visual attention that all full-fledged participants help to sustain. (The focus of visual attention may move, of course, from one participant to another as one speaker gives up his speaking-role and returns to the role of listener.) With this focused kind of interaction we must contrast the unfocused kind, where individuals in one another's visual and aural range go on about their respective business unconnected by a shared focus of attention. Street behavior and conduct at a large social party are instances.

When we examine unfocused interactions we find that involvement obligations are defined not in relation to a conjoint focus of cognitive and visual attention but in relation to a role that can be suggested by the phrase "decorous individual noninterferingly going about his proper business." Once we shift to this point of reference, however, we find that all the kinds of misinvolvement that occur during focused interaction also occur during unfocused interaction, though sometimes under a different name. Just as an adolescent may become self-consciously uneasy when talking to his teacher, so, in walking into a full classroom, he may feel that he is being critically observed and that his way of walking, which he feels is stiff and wooden, reveals his social anxiety. Just as we can have preoccupied persons in conversational interaction, so in unfocused interaction we can have "absent-minded" participants, who by their posture, facial expression, and physical movements suggest that they are momentarily "away," that they have momentarily let fall the expressive costume that individuals are expected to wear whenever they are in the immediate presence of others. And, of course, boredom, too, can occur during unfocused interaction, as we may observe in almost any queue of individuals waiting to buy a ticket. And just as agencies such as alcohol and marijuana may be employed to transform a conversation into something that is not embarrassing or boring, so these may function to put individuals at ease in the wider scene provided by unfocused interaction. Just as a witticism may do honor to the conversational moment, so the wearing of new or special clothing, the serving of rare or costly food, and the use of perishable flowers can draw attention to the unique value of a wider social occasion. Clearly, then, there are ways in which the perspective employed in this paper can be used for studying unfocused interaction.

We must not, however, expect the similarity between the two kinds of interaction to be complete. For example, it appears that individuals are more frequently unself-conscious in their capacity as participants in unfocused interaction than they are as participants in focused interaction, especially focused interaction of the spoken kind. In fact, in spoken interaction, spontaneous "normal" involvement seems to be the exception and alienation of some kind the statistical rule. That is understandable. On the one hand, participants are required to be spontaneously carried away by the topic of conversation; on the other hand, they are obliged to control themselves so that they will always be ready to stay within the role of communicator and stay alive to the touchy issues that might cause the others to become ill at ease. On the one hand they are obliged to adhere to all applicable rules of conduct, and on the other they are obliged to take enough liberties to ensure a minimum level of involving excitement. These obligations seem to be in opposition to each other, requiring a balance of conduct that is so delicate and precarious that alienation and uneasiness for someone in the interaction are the typical result. Unfocused interaction does not seem to require the same delicacy of adjustment.

VII. Conclusion

Many social encounters of the conversational type seem to share a fundamental requirement: the spontaneous involvement of the participants in an official focus of attention must be called forth and sustained. When this requirement exists and is fulfilled, the interaction "comes off" or is euphoric as an interaction. When the encounter fails to capture the attention of the participants, but does not release them from the obligation of involving themselves in it, then persons present are likely to feel uneasy; for them the interaction fails to come off. A person who chronically makes himself or others uneasy in conversation and perpetually kills encounters is a faulty interactant; he is likely to have such a baleful effect upon the social life around him that he may just as well be called a faulty person.

Of any individual, then, it will be significant to know whether his status and manner tend to hinder the maintenance of spontaneous involvement in the interaction, or to help it along. It should be noted that this information pertains to the individual in his capacity as interactant, and that, regardless of the other capacities in which he may be active at the time, the role of interactant is something he will be obliged to maintain.

Social encounters differ a great deal in the importance that participants give to them but, whether crucial or picayune, all encounters represent occasions when the individual can become spontaneously involved in the proceedings and derive from this a firm sense of reality. And this kind of feeling is not a trivial thing, regardless of the package in which it comes. When an incident occurs and spontaneous involvement is threatened, then reality is threatened. Unless the disturbance is checked, unless the interactants regain their proper involvement, the illusion of reality will be shattered, the minute social system that is brought into being with each encounter will be disorganized, and the participants will feel unruled, unreal, and anomic.

Aside from the sense of reality it offers, a particular encounter may be of little consequence, yet we must see that the rules of conduct that oblige individuals to be able and ready to give themselves up to such moments are of transcendent importance. Men who are held by these rules are held ready for spoken interaction, and spoken interaction between many kinds of people on many kinds of occasion is necessary if society's work is to be done.

The sense of reality that has been discussed in this paper takes its form in opposition to modes of alienation, to states like preoccupation, self-consciousness, and boredom. In turn, these modes of disengagement are to be understood by reference to the central issue of spontaneous involvement. When we have seen the way in which a spoken encounter can succeed or fail in bringing its participants to it, and have seen that unfocused interaction can be looked at in the same way, we have a lead to follow in the understanding of other kinds of commitments—the individual's occupational career, his political involvements, his family membership—for there will be a sense in which these wider matters consist in recurrent occasions of focused and unfocused interaction. By looking at the ways in which the individual can be thrown out of step with the sociable moment, perhaps we can learn something about the way in which he can become alienated from things that take much more of his time.

MENTAL SYMPTOMS
AND PUBLIC ORDER*

Persons who come to the attention of a psychiatrist typically come to the attention of their lay associates first. What psychiatrists see as mental illness, the lay public usually first sees as offensive behavior—behavior worthy of scorn, hostility and other negative social sanctions. The objective of psychiatry all along has been to interpose a technical perspective: understanding and treatment is to replace retribution; a concern for the interests of the offender is to replace a concern for the social circle he has offended. I refrain from enlarging here on how unfortunate it has been for many offenders to have been granted this medical good fortune.

Freudian psychiatry introduced an important twist in this medical line. In little classics of analysis, Freudians have shown that particular delicts, now called symptoms, can be interpreted or read as part of the offender's system of communication and defense, in particular a reversion to infantile modes of conduct. The final triumph of this psychological, technical perspective is the implication that socially improper behavior can be psychologically normal (as when a man shows strength enough to terminate an unhealthy marital relationship), and a socially proper behavior can be truly sick (as illustrated by the obsessive concerns and sexual withdrawal of some research chem-

* Reprinted with permission from *Disorders of Communication*, Research Publications, A.R.N.M.D., vol. XLII: 262–69. Copyright © 1964 by the Association for Research in Nervous and Mental Disease.

ists). In brief, for the psychiatrist, a flagrant presenting symptom is merely a license to start digging.

One effect of this enlightened approach that the sociologist might bewail has been that interest in the improprieties themselves, paradoxically, has been blunted. (After all, a symptom is only a symptom, even if it does mark the place where you start digging. If, through whatever excising, you manage to lop off one symptom, and do nothing about the dynamics, another symptom is likely to pop up; it can have a quite different face and yet wear the same leer.)

In moving so quickly from the social delict to the mental symptom, psychiatrists have tended to fail to be much better than laymen in their assessment of the impropriety of a given act—defensible in the case of extremely deviant acts but not in the case of the many milder misbehaviors. This is inescapable, since we just do not have a technical mapping of the various approved behavior patterns in our society, and what little information we have is not imparted in medical school training. Psychiatrists have failed to provide us with a systematic framework for identifying and describing the type of delict represented by psychotic behavior. At present there is a rather special and hardening language in psychiatry, involving terms such as "flattened affect," "posturing," "manneristic movement," "out of contact," and others, which solves the problem of having to write up clinical notes in a hurry but which provides the practitioner with a handful of thumbs. The moralistic language in the social sciences built around the incredible notion that persons should be in good, clear, direct or open communication with one another is, if anything, worse—as if communication were a pill one ought to swallow because it was good for the tummy.

A second effect of the enlightened psychiatric approach which the sociologist might bewail is that a very special and limited version of communication has resulted from it. Psychiatrists, because of their leaning toward an office practice and a preoccupation (at least until recently) with neurotics as opposed to psychotics, have tended to meet with their patients in two-person rooms. Even worse, they have tended to labor under the telephone-booth bias that what the patient was engaged in was somehow a type of talking, of information imparting, the problem being that the line was busy, the connection defective, the party at the other end shy, cagey, afraid to talk or insistent that a code be used. Strong patience and a good ear were apparently required in the business. Hypnosis and the "truth" drugs were also useful in clearing the lines. Lately, with the introduction of cortically embedded electrodes, we have progressed, along with Bell Telephone, to a type of direct dialing. Few professions, may I add, have so well been able to institutionalize, to sell on the social market, their own fantasies of what they were engaged in doing.

In any case, there has been a general blindness to the following fact: very often the misconduct of the patient is a public fact, in that anyone in the same room with him would feel he was behaving improperly, and, if not quite anyone, then at least anyone in the same conversation. True, the patient may misconduct himself merely because persons present are taken as substitutes for the really significant figures. But whatever the deeper target of the misconduct, and however successful the psychiatrist is in making sure that he and his patient are alone in the office, the misconduct is a public thing, potentially accessible and potentially a concern to any and all who might happen to enter the presence of the patient. And when we move from the psychiatrist's professional precincts, this fact becomes more obvious. Psychosis is something that can manifest itself to anyone in the patient's work place, in his neighborhood, in his household, and must be seen, initially at least, as an infraction of the social order that obtains in these places. The other side of the study of symptoms is the study of public order, the study of behavior in public and semipublic places. If you would learn about one side of this matter, you ought perhaps to study the other too. I am suggesting, then, that symptomatic behavior might well be seen, in the first instance, not as a tortured form of two-person communication, but as a form of social misconduct, in the sense that Emily Post and Amy Vanderbilt recognize this term.

I want for a moment to turn the psychiatric clock back and outline a slightly different approach to symptomatology and communication. Starting with the social delict of a prepatient, I propose we examine the general rule of conduct of which the offensive behavior is an infraction, then try to fill out the set of rules of which the one that gets us started is but one member and at the same time try to get a glimpse of the social circle or group that sustains the rules and is offended by the infraction of any one of them. Once that work is done, we can return to the individual offender to examine again the meaning for him of his offensive behavior. When we have made this analysis we should be in a position to understand the embarrassing fact that an individual who appears to be thoroughly crazy one day may, the next, through the magic of "spontaneous remission," come to be, in conduct, "sane" again. We should also be able to find terms that aptly and elegantly describe standard symptoms. And, as Harold Garfinkel has suggested, we should be in a position (not desirable in itself, but desirable as a test of theory) to program insanity, that is, reduce to a minimum the instructions you would have to give an experimental subject in order to enable him beautifully to act crazy, from within as it were.

Although social scientists have been classifying psychotic behavior as a type of improper conduct, a type of deviancy, for many years now, they, like their medical colleagues, have not carried the matter very far.

One issue is that although it is easy enough to call psychotic behavior social deviancy, it is even easier to see that there are many types of social deviancy that are not instances of psychotic behavior—even though brave psychiatrists and psychologists have tried to get at the sick roots of everything from crime to political disloyalty. Common criminals, we say, offend the property order; traitors the political order; incestuous couples the kinship order; homosexuals the sex-role order; drug addicts perhaps the moral order; and so forth. We must ask, then: what type of social order is specifically related to psychotic behavior?

Psychotic behavior, as suggested, runs counter to what might be thought of as public order, especially one part of public order, the order governing persons by virtue of their being in one another's immediate physical presence. Much psychotic behavior is, in the first instance, a failure to abide by rules established for the conduct of face-to-face interaction—rules established, that is, or at least enforced, by some evaluating, judging, or policing group. Psychotic behavior is, in many instances, what might be called a situational impropriety.

Given that many psychotic symptoms are instances of situational impropriety, we must ask whether all situational improprieties are instances of psychotic symptoms. If this were the case, we would have a sociologically grounded way of differentiating psychotics from other people. But, obviously, there are many situational improprieties apparently unconnected with mental disorder. There is the unmannerly conduct of the culturally alien, the arrogant, the eccentric, the insolent, the vicious, the celebrant, the intoxicated, the aged and the youthful.

Granting this, we must ask whether those situational improprieties that we call symptomatic have anything in common that is at the same time exclusive to them. In the literature there has been some effort to suggest such attributes. It is suggested that a psychotic situational impropriety is an act that one cannot easily empathize with, leading one to feel that the actor is unpredictable and untrustworthy, that he is not in the same world as one is in, that one cannot put oneself in his place.

Tempting as this approach is, I do not believe it is sound. The sharp distinction between symptomatic and non-symptomatic situational improprieties is certainly part of our folk conceptual apparatus for looking at people; the trouble is that it does not seem to have any fixed relation to the actual behavior to which it is applied. There is no consensus, except in the extreme cases, as to which of the two slots to put a behavior into. Agreement typically comes after the fact, after the label "mental illness" has been applied, or (in the other case) after its applicability has been fully discounted. Therefore, I feel that a sociological analysis of psychotic symptomatology must inevitably be a little unsatisfactory, including a range of conduct perceived to be normal as well as the range of conduct perceived to be psychotic.

Let us now begin to take a social look at symptoms. First, just what is a situational impropriety? We can twist this question around by asking: what kinds of events—proper or improper—can uniquely occur in face-to-face situations? Some possibilities are 1) physical and sexual assault, and less dramatic interferences with free body movements. Let us sidestep these possibilities for a moment, although obviously fear of the possible occurrence of these events plays an important role in our attitude to the mentally ill. 2) face-to-face communication: verbal, involving the sending and receiving of messages and non-verbal, involving the exuding and gleaning of information about the informer. Now what is it that is distinctively situational or face-to-face about verbal and non-verbal communication between persons who are present to one another: 1) reliance on the naked or unassisted sense and 2) reliance on embodied messages, ones that can be transmitted only because the body of the transmitter is present. As students of communication have suggested, these two factors, taken together, imply that: 1) there will be a simultaneous symmetry of roles (sender will be receiver, exuder will be a gleaner); 2) the communication will be very rich in qualifiers; 3) there will be considerable feed-back opportunity.

Useful as this analysis of the communication characteristics of face-to-face interaction might be, it still derives from the assumption that face-to-face interaction and communication are more or less the same thing and that an impropriety in situational conduct is somehow a pathology in communication. However, this is a very treacherous assumption, and (as already suggested) its consonance with a middle-class intellectualistic professional orientation makes it even more treacherous. I want to argue that when spoken communication occurs, the speaking occurs, or is expected to occur, only when those present to one another have come together into a special type of ritually well-marked association, a special type of huddling you can begin to think about as a conversational circle. When an impropriety such as manneristic gesturing occurs, this becomes noteworthy and hence noted not because something is being communicated, but because the rules regarding how one is to demean oneself when in the presence of others are broken. Verbal and non-verbal communication is something that is funneled through something else. This something else is the approved patterns of manner and association or co-participation in terms of which individuals are obliged to regulate their comings together. To act in a psychotic manner is, very often, to associate wrongly with others in one's immediate presence; this communicates something, but the infraction in the first instance is not that of communication but of the rules for co-mingling.

It is these rules and the resulting units of association, the resulting sanctioned modes of coming together and staying apart, which presumably provide a naturalistic framework within which so-called psychotic symptoms can be systematically located and described. What, then, are the rules of proper behavior while in the presence of others? What are the units of association, of comings together, which these rules make possible and which provide the framework in which all face-to-face events occur, including face-to-face communication?

The language of sociology traditionally deals with organizations, structures, roles and statuses, and is not well adapted to describe the behavior of persons by virtue of their presence among one another. The term "interaction," alas, has meant everything, and the units of analysis required if we are to focus on face-to-face interaction have been little considered. A translation is required, then, from structural to interactional terms, even while the key to the sociological method, the focus on rules and normative understandings, is retained. In fact, to describe the rules regulating a social interaction is to describe its structure.

As a means of beginning the analysis of face-to-face behavior, three basic interaction units may be recommended. The first is *social occasion:* an event, such as a dinner party, that is looked forward to and back upon as a unit, has a time and place of occurrence and sets the tone for what happens during and within it. Social occasions seem to merge into what the psychologist Roger Barker calls behavior settings, especially in the case of occasions that are informal and little perceived as entities in themselves.

Second, I use the term *gathering* to refer to any set of two or more individuals whose members include all and only those who are at the moment in one another's immediate presence. By the term *social situation* I shall refer to the full spatial environment anywhere within which an entering person becomes a member of the gathering that is (or does then become) present. Situations begin when mutual monitoring occurs and lapse when the next to last person has left.

When persons are in a gathering, they can come together to sustain a joint focus of visual and cognitive attention, mutually ratifying one another as persons open to each other for talk or its substitutes. Such states of talk I call *encounters* or *engagements*. These focused gatherings must be distinguished from those cases where persons are present to one another but not engaged together directly in sustaining a state of talk, constituting thereby an unfocused gathering. Focused interaction is the kind that goes on in a state of talk; unfocused interaction is the kind that goes on, say, when two persons size each other up while waiting for a bus, but have not extended to each other the status of co-participants in an open state of talk.

The rules regulating the initiation, maintenance and termination of states of talk, comprising an important part of what Bateson and Ruesch call metacommunication, have been somewhat considered in the literature, especially in connection with descriptions of so-called psychotic verbal production, and of course in small-group research and descriptions of group psychotherapy. In any case, this aspect of situational conduct fits fairly well with the occupational bias of the two-person room and the quiet talk that psychiatrists have brought to their consideration of psychotic behavior. What has been overlooked in this area, perhaps, are the rules governing encounters among the unacquainted, the rules, that is, regarding accosting and approaching strangers, and, in addition to this, rules regarding the state of being "with" someone.

Rules regarding unfocused interaction—sheer and mere copresence in the same situation—have been little considered systematically; what suggestions are available come either from descriptions of withdrawal, for example Bleuler's, or from etiquette books. Sociologists who specialize in collective behavior have focused on panics, riots and crowds, with little thought to the structure of peaceful human traffic in public places. The respect that transforms mere physical boundaries such as walls and windows into communication boundaries; the well-structured civil inattention accorded persons present, whereby one treats the other as if he has been seen but is not an object of undue curiosity; the maintenance of one's face and appearance as though one were ready at all times to receive direction and information from the setting; the expression of a proper allocation of involvement as between main involvements and side involvements (such as smoking)—these normative requirements of mere presence have not yet been systematized in any way.

Similarly, little attention has been given to the management of accessible engagements, that is, engagements that are sustained in the same social situation as are other engagements and other unengaged individuals. We have only begun to study, under the influence of ethologists, the rules about spacing, whereby the conversational circles and unengaged persons in a social situation divide up available space so as to maximize certain variables, modulating sound accordingly. We have little considered the debt that a participant in an engagement owes to the engagement relative to the situation at large, a debt which persons fail to pay when they manifest various forms of disaffection and distraction; nor, correspondingly, have we much considered the debt the engagement as a whole owes to the social situation and social occasion—obliging those in the engagement to become caught up in it but not carried too far by the progressive development of the engagement's activity.

When a patient acts in a classically psychotic way, it is relative to these various rules, and the units of association they support, that he is active. I want to argue now that there is an extremely wide range of motives and reasons for the individual indulging in such conduct. When a brain-damaged patient and a functionally ill patient manifest similar misconduct—for example, a failure to respond to the initiation of an engagement—psychiatry finds reason to confirm the belief that conduct can be a medical symptomatic thing, whether the illness is organic or functional. But surely this is an inversion of nature. It is the organic patient's behavior that mimics a socially structured delict, much as an owl's unblinking silence is read by us as a sign of wisdom, and it is the functional patient who manifests withdrawal from contact in its fuller and original form. An upper-middle-class girl who ignores the hoots, calls and invitations of slum-dwelling youths illustrates the act of being out of contact in an even more usual form. I know of no psychotic misconduct that cannot be matched precisely in everyday life by the conduct of persons who are not psychologically ill nor considered to be so; and in each case one can find a host of different motives for engaging in the misconduct, and a host of different factors that will modify our attitude toward its performance. I want merely to add that mental hospitals, perhaps through a process of natural selection, are organized in such a way as to provide exactly the kind of setting in which unwilling participants have recourse to the exhibition of situational improprieties. If you rob people of all customary means of expressing anger and alienation and put them in a place where they have never had better reason for these feelings, then the natural recourse will be to seize upon what remains—situational improprieties.

Let me try to summarize the argument. When persons come into one another's immediate physical presence, they become accessible to each other in unique ways. There arise the possibilities of physical and sexual assault, of accosting and being dragged into unwanted states of talk, of offending and importuning through the use of words, of transgressing certain territories of the self of the other, of showing disregard and disrespect for the gathering present and the social occasion under whose auspices the gathering is held. The rules of face-to-face conduct obtaining in a given community establish the form that face-to-face comingling is to take, and there results a kind of King's Peace, guaranteeing that persons will respect one another through the available idiom of respect, keep their social place and their interpersonal commitments, allow and not exploit a traffic flow of words and bodies and show regard for the social occasion. Offenses against these rulings constitute situational improprieties; many of these delicts are injurious to the rights of any and every one present and

and constitute publicly broadcast offenses, regardless of the fact that many appear to be motivated by the offender's particular relationship to particular persons present or even to absent parties. These improprieties are not in the first instance a linguistic type of interpersonal communication but examples of public misconduct—a defect not in information transmission or interpersonal relating, but in the decorum and demeanor that regulate face-to-face association. It is in this world of sanctioned forms of association that psychotic symptoms have their natural home, and it is by getting a systematic picture of the constraints of approved public conduct that we can obtain the language for neatly and effectively talking about symptomatology. Rules for behavior while in the presence of others and by virtue of the presence of others are the rules that make orderly face-to-face communication of the linguistic kind possible; but these rules, and the many infractions of them which psychotics and other cut-ups systematically exhibit, are not themselves to be considered first of all as communications; they are first of all guidelines (and their disruption) of social organization, the organized association of persons present to one another.

WHERE THE ACTION IS

"To be on the wire is life;
the rest is waiting."*

A decade ago among those urban American males who were little given to gentility the term "action" was used in a non-Parsonian sense in reference to situations of a special kind, the contrast being to situations where there was "no action." Very recently this locution has been taken up by almost everyone, and the term itself flogged without mercy in commercials and advertisements.

This paper, then, deals with a term that points to something lively but is itself now almost dead. Action will be defined analytically. An effort will be made to uncover where it is to be found and what it implies about these places.

I. Chances

Wheresoever action is found, chance-taking is sure to be. Begin then with a simple illustration of chance, and work outward from there.

Two boys together find a nickel in their path and decide that one will toss and the other call to see who keeps it. They agree, then, to engage in a *play* or, as probabilists call it, a *gamble*—in this case one go at the *game* of coin-tossing.

A coin can be used as a decision machine, much as a

* Attributed to Karl Wallenda, on going back up to the high wire after his troupe's fatal Detroit accident.

149

roulette wheel or a deck of cards can. With this particular machine it is plain that a fully known set of *possible outcomes* is faced: heads or tails, obverse or reverse. Similarly with a die: in ordinary manufacture and use,[1] it presents six different faces as possible outcomes.

Given the two outcomes possible when a coin is tossed, the probability or *chance* can be assessed for each of them. Chances vary from "sure" to "impossible" or, in the language of probability, from 1 to 0.

What a player has in hand and undergoes a chance of losing is his stake or *bet*. What the play gives him a chance of winning that he doesn't already have can be called his *prize*. The *payoff* for him is the prize that he wins or the bet that he loses. Bet and prize together may be called the *pot*.[2]

In gaming, *theoretical odds* refers to the chances of a favorable outcome compared to those of an unfavorable one, the decision machine here seen as an ideal one; *true odds* are a theoretical version of theoretical ones, involving a correction for the physical biases found in any actual machine—biases never to be fully eliminated or fully known.[3] *Given odds* or *pay*, on the other hand, refers to

[1] A die can be used like a coin if, for example, 1, 2, or 3 is called tails, and 4, 5, or 6 is called heads. Among the types of unsporting dice are misspotted ones variously called tops and bottoms, horses, tees, tats, soft rolls, California fourteens, door pops, Eastern tops, etc. These dice do not have a different number on each of the six sides, and (as with a two-headed coin) allow a player to bet on an outcome that is not among the possibilities and therefore rather unlikely to occur. Note that dice, much more frequently than coins, do land on their edges (by virtue of coming to rest against objects) and do roll out of bounds. The management of these regrettable contingencies is one of the jobs of the members of a craps crew, especially the stickman, in the sense that their very quick verbal and physical corrections are designed to make perfect a very imperfect physical model.

[2] The track has a word for it, "extension."

[3] Here and elsewhere in matters of probability I am indebted to Ira Cisin. He is responsible only for the correct statements.

the size of the prize compared to that of the bet.[4] Note that outcomes are defined wholly in terms of the game equipment, payoffs in terms of extrinsic and variable resources currently committed to particular outcomes. Thus, with theoretical odds and given odds, somewhat the same term is employed to cover two radically different ideas.

Weighting the pot by the chance on the average of winning it, gives what students of chance call the *expected value* of the play. Subtracting the expected value from the amount bet gives a measure of the price or the profit on the average for engaging in the play. Expressing this measure as a proportion of the bet gives the *advantage* or percentage of the play. When there is neither advantage nor disadvantage, the play is said to be *fair*. Then the theoretical odds are the reciprocal of the given odds, so that he who *gives* or *lays* the odds, gambling a large sum in the hope of winning a small one, is exactly compensated by the smallness of his chance of losing to the individual who *takes* the odds.

There are plays that allow a multitude of possible outcomes to choose among, each of which pays differently and may even provide the bettor differing disadvantage. Casino craps is an example. Still other plays involve a set of favorable possible outcomes that pay differently so that the expected value of the play must be calculated as a sum of several different values: slot machines and keno provide examples.

In the degree to which a play is a means of acquiring a prize, it is an *opportunity;* in the degree to which it is a threat to one's bet, it is a *risk*. The perspective here is objective. A subjective sense of opportunity or risk is quite another matter since it may, but need not, coincide with the facts.

[4] To increase the apparent attractiveness of certain bets some crap-table lay-outs state winnings not in terms of given odds but in terms of the pot; thus, a bet whose given odds are 1 *to* 4 will be described as 1 *for* 5.

Each of our coin tossers can be defined as having a life course in which the finding of a nickel has not been anticipated. Without the find, life would go forward as expected. Each boy can then conceive of his situation as affording him a gain or returning him to what is only normal. A chance-taking of this kind can be called opportunity without risk. Were a bully to approach one of the boys and toss him for a nickel taken from the boy's own pocket (and this happens in city neighborhoods), we could then speak of a risk without opportunity. In daily life, risks and opportunities usually occur together, and in all combinations.

Sometimes the individual can retract his decision to pursue a line of activity upon learning of likely failure. No chances, whether risky or opportune, are taken here. For chanciness to be present, the individual must ensure he is in a position (or be forced into one) to let go of his hold and control on the situation, to make, in Schelling's sense, a commitment.[5] No commitment, no chance-taking.

A point about determination—defining this as a process, not an accomplished event. As soon as the coin is in the air, the tosser will feel that deciding forces have begun their work, and so they have. It is true, of course, that the period of determination could be pushed back to include the decision to choose heads or tails, or still further back to include the decision to toss in the first place. However, the outcome (heads or tails) is fully determined during the time the coin is in the air; a different order of fact, such as who will select heads or how much will be chanced, is determined before the toss. In brief, an essential feature of the coin tossing situation is that an outcome undetermined up to a certain point—the point of tossing the coin in the air—is clearly and fully determined during the toss. A *problematic* situation is resolved.

The term problematic is here taken in the objective

[5] T. C. Schelling, *The Strategy of Conflict* (Cambridge, Harvard University Press, 1960), esp. p. 24.

sense to refer to something not yet determined but about to be. As already suggested, the subjective assessment of the actor himself brings further complication. He may be quite unaware that something at hand is being determined. Or he may feel that the situation is problematic when in fact the matter at hand has already been determined and what he is really facing is revealment or disclosure. Or, finally, he may be fully oriented to what is actually happening—alive to the probabilities involved and realistically concerned over the consequences. This latter possibility, where a full parallel is found between objective and subjective situation, will be our main concern.

The causal forces during the period of determination and prior to the final result are often defined as ones of "mere chance," or "pure luck." This does not presume some kind of ultimate indeterminism. When a coin is tossed its fall is fully determined by such factors as the prior state of the tosser's finger, the height of the toss, the air currents (including ones that occur after the coin has left the finger), and so forth. However, no human influence, intended and legitimate, can be exercised to manipulate the relevant part of the result.[6]

There *are* to be sure chancy situations where relevant orders of humanly directed determination are involved by virtue of skill, knowledge, daring, perseverance, and so forth. This, in fact, marks a crucial difference between games of "pure" chance and what are called contests: in the former, once the determination is in play, the participants can do nothing but passively await the outcome; in the latter, it is just this period that requires intensive and sustained exercising of relevant capacities. None the less,

[6] See the argument by D. MacKay, "The Use of Behavioral Language to Refer to Mechanical Processes," *British Journal of the Philosophy of Science*, XIII, 50 (1962), 89–103; "On the Logical Indeterminacy of a Free Choice," *Mind*, 69 (1960), 31–40.

it is still the case that during contests something of value to be staked comes up for determination; in terms of the facts and often their perception as well, the intended and effective influences are insufficiently influential to render the situation unproblematic.

A crucial feature of coin-tossing is its temporal phases. The boys must decide to settle the matter by tossing; they must align themselves physically; they must decide how much of the nickel will be gambled on the toss and who will take which outcome; through stance and gesture they must commit themselves to the gamble and thereby pass the point of no return. This is the bet-making or *squaring off phase*. Next there is the in-play or *determination phase*, during which relevant causal forces actively and determinatively produce the outcome.[7] Then comes the revelatory or *disclosive phase*, the time between determination and informing of the participants. This period is likely to be very brief, to differ among sets of participants differently placed relative to the decision machinery,[8] and to possess a special suspensefulness of its own. Finally there is the *settlement phase*, beginning when the outcome has been disclosed and lasting until losses have been paid up and gains collected.

The period required by participants in a given play to

[7] In coin-tossing this phase begins when the coin goes into the air and terminates when it lands on the hand—a second or two later. In horse racing determination begins when the barrier is opened and terminates when the finish line is crossed after the last lap, a little more than a minute in all. In seven-day bicycle races, the determination phase is a week long.

[8] Horse-racing con games have been based on the possibility of convincing the mark that the period between an outcome at the track and its announcement at distant places is long enough to exploit for post-finish sure betting, that is, "past-posting,"—a condition that can in fact occur and has been systematically exploited. It might be added that friendly 21 dealers in Nevada, after completing a deal, will sometimes look at their hole card and josh a player about a destiny which has been determined and read but teasingly delayed in disclosure.

move through the four phases of the play—squaring off, determination, disclosure, and settlement—may be called the *span* of the play. The periods between plays may be called *pauses*. The period of *a* play must be distinguished from the period of playing, namely, the *session,* which is the time between making the first bet and settling up the last one on any one occasion perceived as continuously devoted to play. The number of completed plays during any unit of time is the *rate* of play for that time.[9] Average duration of the plays of a game sets an upper limit to rate of play, as does average length of pauses; a coin can be tossed 5 times in half a minute; the same number of decisions at the track requires more than an hour.

Given these distinctions in the phases of play, it is easy to attend to a feature of simple games of chance that might otherwise be taken for granted. Once a play is undertaken, its determination, disclosure, and settlement usually follow quickly, often before another bet is made. A coin-tossing session consists, then, of a sequence of four-phase cycles with pauses between cycles. Typically the player maintains a continuous stretch of attention and experiencing over the whole four or five seconds course of each play, attention lapsing only during the pauses, that is, after the settlement of one play and before the making of another. Everyday life is usually quite different. Certainly the individual makes bets and takes chances in regard to daily living, as when, for example, he decides to take one job instead of another or to move from one state to another. Further, at certain junctures he may have to make numerous vital decisions at the same time and hence

[9] For example, assume that the nickel-finders are engaged in a sudden-death game, one toss determining who gets the nickel. If the two boys are together on this occasion for one hour, their rate of chance-taking is once per hour. Should they change the nickel into pennies and toss these one at a time, each penny only once, then the rate of chance-taking is five times greater than it was before although the resulting swing in fortune no more and probably less.

briefly maintain a very high rate of bet-making. But ordinarily the determination phase—the period during which the consequences of his bet are determined—will be long, sometimes extending over decades, followed by disclosure and settlement phases that are themselves lengthy. The distinctive property of games and contests is that once the bet has been made, *outcome is determined and payoff awarded all in the same breath of experience*. A single sharp focus of awareness is sustained at high pitch during the full span of the play.

II. Consequentiality

We can take some terms, then, from the traditional analysis of coin-tossing,[10] but this framework soon leads to difficulties.

The standard for measuring the amount of a bet or prize is set by or imputed to the community, the public at large, or the prevailing market. An embarrassment of game analysis is that different persons can have quite different feelings about the same bet or the same prize. Middle class adults may use a nickel as a decision machine, but will hardly bother tossing just to decide who keeps the machine. Small boys, however, can feel that a co-finder's claim to a nickel is a big bet indeed. When attention must be given to variations in meaning that different persons give to the same bet (or the same prize), or that the same individual gives over time or over varying conditions, one speaks of subjective value or *utility*. And just as expected value can be calculated as the average worth remaining to a nickel pot, so *expected utility* can be assessed as the utility an individual accords a nickel pot weighted by the probability of his winning it.

The expected utility of a nickel pot must be clearly distinguished from the expected utility of tossing for this pot;

[10] A sound, if popular, treatment may be found in R. Jeffrey, *The Logic of Decision* (New York, McGraw-Hill, 1965).

for individuals regularly place a subjective value—positive or negative—on the excitement and anxiety generated by tossing. Further, after the toss, the displeasure at losing and the pleasure at winning are not likely to balance each other off exactly; the difference, on whichever side, must also be reckoned on the average as part of the expected utility of the play.[11] Objective standards can be used in getting at the meaning of bets; but we must use the murky notion of utility to get at the meaning of betting.

When we move from the neat notion of the expected value of a pot to one that will be relevant for our concerns, namely, the expected utility of playing for the pot, we move into almost hopeless complexities. When an individual asserts that a given period of play involves a big gamble, or when he feels that it is chancier than another, a whole set of considerations may be involved: the scale of betting; the length of the odds (and whether he is giving them or getting them); the brevity of the span of play; the smallness of the number of plays; the rate of play; the percentage paid for playing; the variation of size regarding prizes associated with favorable outcomes. Further, the relative weight given each of these considerations will vary markedly with the absolute value of each of the others.[12]

For us this means that different individuals and groups have somewhat different personal base-lines from which to measure risk and opportunity; a way of life involving

[11] In gambling, these factors are not independent. No doubt part of the experience obtained from the toss derives from the difference between the satisfaction at contemplating winning and the displeasure at the thought of losing.

[12] Recent work, especially by experimental psychologists, has added appreciable knowledge to this area by a design which obliges individuals to show a preference among gambles involving various mixes of elements. See, for example, J. Cohen, *Behaviour in Uncertainty* (London, George Allen and Unwin, 1964), chap. 3, "Making a Choice," pp. 27–42; and W. Edwards, "Behavior Decision Theory," *Annual Review of Psychology*, 12 (1961), 473–98.

much risk may cause the individual to give little weight to a risk that someone else might find forbidding.[13] Thus, for example, attempts to account for the presence of legalized gambling in Nevada sometimes cite the mining tradition of the state, a type of venturing that can be defined as very chancy indeed. The argument is that since the economy of the state was itself founded on gambles with the ground, it is understandable that casino gambling was never viewed with much disapproval.

In simple, literal gambling, then, the basic notion of "chanciness" is shot through with a multitude of half-realized, shifting meanings. When we turn from gaming to the rest of living, matters get worse.

In coin tossing, there are *a priori* and empirical reasons for assessing the chances of either outcome in effect as fifty-fifty. The ultimate validity of this assessment need not concern those who toss coins. That's the nice thing about coins. In many ordinary situations, however, the individual may have to face an outcome matrix that cannot be fully defined. (This could arise, for example, were our two boys to pause before a deep, multi-tunneled cave, trying to decide what might befall them were they to try to explore it.) Further, even when the full set of outcome possibilities is known, the chances that must be attached to each of them may be subject to only rough assessment based on vague appeals to empirical experience.[14] Moreover, the estimator will often have little appreciation of how very rough his assessment is. In most life situations, we deal with *subjective probability* and hence at best a

[13] For this and other suggestions, I am grateful to Kathleen Archibald.

[14] Reputable firms specializing in crooked gambling devices sell variously "shaped" dice that provide the customer with a choice among five or six degrees of what is called "strength." Probably the ranking is absolutely valid. But no company has tested dice of any alleged strength over a long enough series of trials to provide confidence levels concerning the favorable percentage these unfair dice afford their users.

very loose overall measure, *subjectively expected utility*.[15]

Further, while coin tossers typically face a "fair" game, and casino gamblers a slightly disadvantageous one, wider aspects of living present the individual with much less balance in this regard; there will be situations of much opportunity with little risk and of much risk with little opportunity. Moreover, opportunity and risk may not be easily measurable on the same scale.[16]

There is an important issue in the notion of value itself —the notion that bets and prizes can be measured in amounts. A nickel has both a socially ratified value and a subjective value, in part because of what its winning allows, or losing disallows, the tosser *later on* to do. This is the gamble's *consequentiality,* namely, the *capacity of a payoff to flow beyond the bounds of the occasion in which it is delivered and to influence objectively the later life of*

[15] In the literature, following F. Knight (*Risk, Uncertainty and Profit* [Boston, Houghton Mifflin, 1921], esp. chaps. 7 and 8) the term "risk" is used for a decision whose possible outcomes and their probabilities are known, and the term "uncertainty" where the probabilities across the various outcomes are not known or even knowable. Here see R. Luce and H. Raiffa, *Games and Decisions* (New York, Wiley & Sons, 1958), p. 13ff. Following John Cohen, B. Fox (*Behavioral Approaches to Accident Research* [Association for the Aid to Crippled Children, New York, 1961], p. 50), suggests using the term hazard for objective dire chances, and risk for subjective estimates of hazard. Fox equates this with a slightly different distinction, that between risk as perceived to inhere in a situation and risk perceived as something intentionally taken on. See also Cohen, *op. cit.,* p. 63.

[16] The concept of utility, and the experimental techniques of a forced-choice between singles and pairs probabilistically linked, can attempt to reduce these variabilities to a single scheme. However these efforts can be questioned. Many actual plays are undertaken in necessary conjunction with the player remaining unappreciative of the risk (while focusing on the opportunity), or unaware of the opportunity (while attending to the risk). To place a utility on this unappreciateness in order to balance the books seems hardly an answer.

the bettor. The period during which this consequentiality is borne is a kind of post-play or *consequentiality phase* of the gamble.

A tricky matter must be considered here. "Objective value" and "utility" are both means of establishing instantaneous equivalents for consequences that are to be actually felt over time. This is achieved by allowing either the community or the individual himself to place an appraisal on this future, and to accept or to give a price for it now. I want to avoid this sophistication. When, for example, a man proposes matrimony, it is true that the payoff is determined as soon as the girl makes up her mind, reported as soon as she gives her answer, and settled up when the marriage is consummated or the rejected suitor withdraws to court elsewhere. But in another sense, the consequence of the payoff is felt throughout the life remaining to the participants. Just as a "payoff" is the value equivalent of an outcome, so "consequentiality" is the human equivalent of a payoff. We move then from pots and prizes, neatly definable, to protracted payoffs, which can be described only vaguely. This is a move from pots to consequentiality, and from circumscribed gambles to wider arenas of living.

In addition to all these limitations on the coin-tossing model, there is another and quite central one that we can only begin to consider now. The subjective experience enjoyed by small boys who toss a coin for keeps develops from the feel of light-heartedly exercising will. A decision to gamble or not gamble is made under conditions where no alien pressure forces the decision, and not gambling would be an easy, quite practical choice. Once this decision is made affirmatively, a second one is made as to possible outcome to bet on—here an illusory right, but fun none the less, and certainly not illusory in games involving skill. Once the result is in, this can be treated as a possibility that was foreseen and the gamble taken anyway. In consequence, the whole situation can easily come to be seen prospectively as a chance-taking occasion, an occasion generated and governed by the exercise of self-determination, an occasion for *taking* risk and *grasping* opportunity. In daily life, however, the individual may never become aware of the risk and opportunity that in fact existed, or may become alive to the gamble he was making only after the play is over. And when the situation *is* approached with its chanciness in mind, the individual may find that the cost of not gambling is so high that it must be excluded as a realistic possibility, or, where this decision is a practical one, that no choice is available as to which of the possible outcomes he will be betting on. Some freedom of choice, some self-determination is present here, but often not very much. The coin-tossing model can be applied to all of these situations, but only by overlooking some important differences between recreational chance-taking and real life gambles. Apart from the question of the amount at stake, our two boys who toss a coin are not engaged in quite the same type of chance-taking as is unenjoyed by two survivors who have mutually agreed that there is no other way than to toss to see who will lighten the raft; and they, in turn, are subject to chance differently than are two sick passengers who are forced by their well companions to submit to a toss decision to see which of the two will no longer share the life boat's supply of water.

III. Fatefulness

An individual ready to leave his house to keep an engagement finds he is thirty minutes early and has some "free time" to use up or put in. He could put the time to "good" use by doing now an essential task that will have to be done sometime. Instead he decides to "kill" this time. He picks up a magazine from the ones at hand, drops into a comfortable chair, and leafs through some pages until it is time to go.

What are the characteristics of this activity used to kill time with? Approach this question through another: What are the possible effects of this little piece of the individual's life on the whole of the rest of it?

Obviously, what goes on during killed time may have no bearing at all on the rest of the individual's life.[17] Many alternative lines of activity can be pursued and still his life will go on as it is going. Instead of reading one magazine, he can read another; or he can while away the time by watching TV, cat-napping, or working a puzzle. Finding he has less time to put in than he had thought, he can easily cut his dawdling short; finding he has more time, he can dawdle more. He can try to find a magazine that interests him, fail, and yet lose little by this failure, merely having to face the fact that he is temporarily at loose ends. Having nothing to kill time with, or to kill enough time with, he can "mark" it.

Killed moments, then, are inconsequential. They are bounded and insulated. They do not spill over into the rest of life and have an effect there. Differently put, the individual's life course is not subject to his killed moments; his life is organized in such a way as to be impervious to them. Activities for killing time are selected in advance as ones that cannot tie up or entangle the individual.[18]

---

[17] Although, of course, his choice of means of killing time can be expressive of him.

[18] Time off comes in all sizes, a few seconds to a few years. It comes between tasks on the job; in transit between home and work; at home after the evening meal; week-ends; annual vacations; retirement. (There is also—largely in fantasy—the time away from ordinary life that Georg Simmel calls "the Adventure.") When time off is killed, presumably this is done with freely chosen activity possessing a consummatory end-in-itself character. Whether the individual fills his time off with consequential or inconsequential activity, he usually must remain on tap at the place where serious, scheduled duties are located; or he must be within return-distance to his station. Note that time off to kill is to be distinguished from a close neighbor, the time that unemployed persons are forced to mark and cannot justify as an earned respite from past duties or imminent ones.

Killing time often involves the killer in problematic activity. The decision as to magazine or TV may be a close one whose determination is not begun until the individual is about to sit down. Here then is problematic behavior that is not consequential. (Interestingly, this is exactly the case in tossing for a nickel. Our youthful gamblers may subjectively place great value on winning the toss, yet the payoff can hardly be consequential.)

In contrast to time off we have time on and its world of collectively organized serious work, which gears the individual's efforts into the needs of other persons who count on him for supplies, equipment, or services in order to fulfill their own obligations. Records are kept of his production and deliveries, and penalties given if he fails to perform. In brief, the division of labor and the organization of work-flow connect the individual's current moments to other persons' next ones in a very consequential manner.

However, the consequentiality of properly attending to one's duties on any one occasion is very little noted. Results are, to be sure, more or less pictured in advance, but the probability of their occurrence is so high that little attention seems required in the matter. Nothing need be weighed, decided, or assessed; no alternatives have to be considered. This activity is indeed consequential, but it is well managed; it is not problematic. Incidentally, any moment, whether worked or killed, will have this element. It is a matter of total consequentiality that our coin tossers continue to inhale and exhale and do not run their heads against a concrete wall; any failure in the first and any success in the second can have very far-reaching effects on all a boy's moments to come. However, continuing to breathe and not beating one's head against the wall are objectives so continuously and unthinkingly sought and so assuredly and routinely realized, that the consequentiality of lapse need never be considered.

Time-off activities, then, can be problematic but are likely to be inconsequential, and time-on activities are likely to be consequential but not problematic. Thus both types of activity can easily be uneventful: either nothing important happens or nothing important happens that is unexpected and unprepared for.

However, an activity *can* be problematic *and* consequential. Such activity I call *fateful,* although the term eventful would do as well, and it is this kind of chanciness that will concern us here.

It must now be admitted that although free time and well-managed work time tend to be unfateful, the human condition is such that *some* degree of fatefulness will always be found. Primordial bases of fatefulness must be reckoned with.

First, there is the adventitious or literary kind of fatefulness. An event that is ordinarily well managed and unnoteworthy can sometimes cast fatefulness backwards in time, giving to certain previous moments an uncharacteristic capacity to be the first event in a fateful conjunction of two events. Should one of our youthful gamblers need a nickel to make a crucial telephone call with at the moment the nickel is found, then the chance to win the toss can become fateful. Similarly, our time-killing individual can become so caught up in a magazine story that he loses all track of time[19] and does not surface until too late —an irritation, merely, unless the appointment that is missed happens to be important. Or, leafing through the magazine, he can come upon an article on intelligence tests containing sample questions. His appointment is an examination in which one of these questions appears. A moment to fritter away is not totally cut off from the mo-

[19] In our urban society the individual is likely to check up on the time periodically and can almost always estimate the time closely. Light sleepers may even orient themselves constantly in time. Struck on some occasion how "time has flown," the individual may in fact mean only one or two hours. Finding that his watch has stopped, he may find in fact that it stopped only a few minutes ago, and that he must have been checking himself against it constantly.

ments to come; it *can* have unexpected connections with them.

Although individuals and their activities are always subject to some adventitious fatefulness, there are some enterprises whose vulnerability in this regard is marked enough to serve as a characterization of them. Where coordination and concealment are vital, a whole range of minor unanticipated hitches lose their usual quality of correctability and become fateful. Stories of near-perfect crimes and nearly exposed commando raids enshrine this source of fatefulness, as do tales of strategic goofs:

> Maidstone, England: A gang of masked men wielding blackjacks and hammers ambushed a car carrying $28,000 to a bank here yesterday but they grabbed the wrong loot—a bag of sandwiches.
>
> The cash was locked in the trunk of the car and the bag containing the bank official's lunch was on the car seat.[20]

> Three robbers who completely botched what was supposed to be a simple little bank robbery in Rodeo were sentenced in Federal Court here yesterday. . . .
>
> All three were nabbed by some 40 police officers Jan. 7 as they struggled to make off with $7710 stuffed into a laundry sack they had just taken out of the United California bank, the only bank in Rodeo . . .
>
> Pugh walked in with a sawed off shotgun and lined up the 13 employees and two customers, while Fleming, carrying a pistol, went to the vault and started filling the laundry bag with currency and, alas, coins.
>
> "The coins can't be traced," he said cleverly. He kept piling in coins until the bag weighed about 200 pounds. Then he dragged the bag across the floor to the door—and the frayed rope snapped.
>
> Both men then lugged the bag through the door,

[20] *San Francisco Chronicle*, March 10, 1966.

but it caught and ripped a hole, letting coins trail behind them as they dragged the bag to the get-away car, with Duren at the wheel.

Duren though, had parked too close to the high curb, so the three could not open the door to get the loot inside. Finally they did, by moving the car, and raced away—around the corner. There the car stopped when the three saw the clutter of sheriff, Highway Patrol and police cars.[21]

These mistakes are everyday ones and would ordinarily be easily absorbed by the reserve for correction that characterizes most undertakings. What is special about criminal enterprise (and other military-like operations) is the narrowness of this reserve and hence the high price that must be paid for thoughtlessness and bad breaks. This is the difference between holding a job down and pulling a job off; here an act becomes a deed.[22]

Second, no matter how inconsequential and insulated an individual's moment is and how safe and well managed his place of consequential duties, he must be there in the flesh if the moment is to be his at all, and this is the selfsame flesh he must leave with and take wherever he goes, along with all the damage that has ever occurred to it. No matter how careful he may be, the integrity of his body will always be in jeopardy to some degree. While reading, he may slip in his chair, fall to the floor and injure himself. This is unlikely to be sure, but should he kill time by taking a bath or earn his living by working at a lathe, in a mine, or on construction jobs, the possibility of injuring

[21] *Ibid.*, May 6, 1966.

[22] In fictional vicarious worlds, criminal jobs (as well as the structurally similar undercover operations of various government agents), are realized in the teeth of a long sequence of threatened and actual hitches, each of which has a high probability of ruining everything. The hero manages to survive from episode to episode, but only by grossly breaking the laws of chance. Among young aspirants for these roles, surely the probabilistically inclined must be subtly discouraged.

would be considerably more likely, as actuarial data show. Physical danger is a thin red thread connecting each of the individual's moments to all his others. A body is subject to falls, hits, poisons, cuts, shots, crushing, drowning, burning, disease, suffocation, and electrocution. A body is a piece of consequential equipment, and its owner is always putting it on the line. Of course, he can bring other capital goods into many of his moments too, but his body is the only one he can never leave behind.

A third pertinent aspect of the human condition concerns co-presence. A *social situation* may be defined (in the first instance), as any environment of mutual monitoring possibilities that lasts during the time two or more individuals find themselves in one another's immediate physical presence, and extends over the entire territory within which this mutual monitoring is possible.

By definition, an individual's activities must occur either in social situations or solitarily. Does which it will be, make a difference for the fatefulness of his moments?

For the special kind of consequentiality we are concerned with, the fateful kind involving the significant problematic bearing of one moment's activity upon the next, it should not matter whether the event is socially situated or not. Our concern, after all, is with the later effects of an action, not its current condition. None the less, the difference between solitary and socially situated activities has a special relevance of its own.

Just as the individual always brings his body into every occasion of his activity and also the possibility of a fortuitous linking of an already consequential event to one that would otherwise be innocuous, so he brings himself as an upholder of conduct standards like physical adeptness, honesty, alertness, piety, and neatness. The record of an individual's maintenance of these standards provides a basis others use for imputing a personal make-up to him. Later they employ this characterization in determining how to treat him—and this is consequential. Of course, most of these standards are unthinkingly and consistently maintained by adults; they are likely to become aware of these norms only when a freak accident occurs or when, in their mature and ritually delicate years, they essay for the first time to ride a horse, skate, or engage in other sports requiring special techniques for the maintenance of physical aplomb.

In some cases solitary misconduct results in a record of damage that can later be traced to the offender. In many other cases, however, no such responsibility is found; either the effects of the misconduct are ephemeral (as in gestured acts of contempt) or they cannot be traced to their author. Only the conscience of the individual can make such activity consequential for him, and this kind of conscience is not everywhere found. However, when the conduct occurs in a social situation—when, that is, witnesses are present—then these standards become immediately relevant and introduce some risk, however low.

A similar argument can be made about opportunities to display sterling personal qualities. With no witnesses present, the individual's efforts may have little identifiable lasting effect; when others are present, some kind of record is assured.

In social situations, then, ordinary risks and opportunities are confounded by expressions of make-up. Gleanings become available, often all too much so. Social situations thus become opportunities for introducing favorable information about oneself, just as they become risky occasions when unfavorable facts may be established.

Of the various types of object the individual must handle during his presence among others, one merits special attention: the other persons themselves. The impression he creates through his dealings with them and the traits they impute to him in consequence have a special bearing on his reputation, for here the witnesses have a direct personal stake in what they witness.

Specifically, whenever the individual is in the presence

of others, he is pledged to maintain a ceremonial order by means of interpersonal rituals. He is obliged to ensure that the expressive implications of all local events are compatible with the status that he and the others present possess; this involves politeness, courtesy, and retributive responses to others' slighting of self. And the maintenance of this order, whether during time off or time on is more problematic than might first appear.

A final word about social situations: The ceremonial order sustained by persons when in one another's presence does more than assure that each participant gives and gets his due. Through the exercise of proper demeanor, the individual gives credit and substance to interaction entities themselves, such as conversations, gatherings, and social occasions, and renders himself accessible and usable for communication. Certain kinds of misconduct, such as loss of self-control, gravely disrupt the actor's usability in face to face interaction and can disrupt the interaction itself. The concern the other participants have for the social occasion, and the ends they anticipate will be served through it, together ensure that some weight will be given to the propriety of the actor's behavior.

I have argued that the individual is always in jeopardy in some degree because of adventitious linkings of events, the vulnerability of his body, and the need in social situations to maintain the proprieties. It is, of course, when accidents occur—unplanned impersonal happenings with incidental dire results—that these sources of fatefulness become alive to us. But something besides accident must be considered here.

The physical capacities of any normal adult equip him, if he so wills it, to be immensely disruptive of the world immediately at hand. He can destroy objects, himself, and other people. He can profane himself, insult and contaminate others, and interfere with their free passage.

Infants are not trusted to forego these easy opportunities (which in any case they are insufficiently developed to exploit fully) and are physically constrained from committing mischief. Personal development is the process by which the individual learns to forego these opportunities voluntarily, even while his capacity to destroy the world immediately around him increases. And this foregoing is usually so well learned that students of social life fail to see the systematic desisting that routinely occurs in daily living, and the utter mayhem that would result were the individual to cease to be a gentleman. Appreciation comes only when we study in detail the remarkable disruption of social settings produced by hypomanic children, youthful vandals, suicidals, persons pathologically obsessed by a need for self-abasement, and skilled saboteurs. Although our coin-tossers can be relied upon not to hold their breath or run their heads up against a concrete wall, or spit on each other, or besmear themselves with their own fecal matter, inmates of mental hospitals have been known to engage in exactly these behaviors, nicely demonstrating the transformation of unproblematic consequential activity into what is fateful.

IV. Practical Gambles

The human condition ensures that eventfulness will always be a possibility, especially in social situations. Yet the individual ordinarily manages his time and time off so as to avoid fatefulness. Further, much of the eventfulness that does occur is handled in ways that do not concern us. There are many occasions of unavoided fatefulness that are resolved in such a way as to allow the participants to remain unaware of the chances they had in fact been taking. (The occurrence of such moments, for example while driving, is itself an interesting subject for study.) And much of the fatefulness that occurs in consequence of freakish, improbable events is handled retrospectively; only after the fact does the individual redefine his situation as having been fateful all along, and only then does he

appreciate in what connection the fatefulness was to occur. Retrospective fatefulness and unappreciated fatefulness abound, but will not be considered here.

And yet of course there are extraordinary niches in social life where activity is so markedly problematic and
consequential that the participant is likely to orient himself to fatefulness prospectively, perceiving in these terms
what it is that is taking place. It is then that fateful situations undergo a subtle transformation, cognitively reor-
ganized by the person who must suffer them. It is then
that the frame of reference employed by our two small
boys is brought into serious life by serious men. Given
the practical necessity of following a course of action
whose success is problematic and passively awaiting the
outcome thereof, one can discover an alternative, how-
soever costly, and then define oneself as having freely
chosen between this undesirable certainty and the uncertainty at hand. A Hobson's choice is made, but this is
enough to allow the situation to be read as one in which
self-determination is central. Instead of awaiting fate, you
meet it at the door. Danger is recast into taken risk; favorable possibilities, into grasped opportunity. Fateful situations become chancy undertakings, and exposure to uncertainty is construed as willfully taking a practical
gamble.[23]

[23] Decision theorists currently demonstrate that almost any
situation can be usefully formulated as a payoff matrix en-
closing all possible outcomes, each outcome designated with a
value that is in turn weighted by the probability of occurrence. The result is that conduct that might be construed as
unproblematical and automatic or as an obligatory response to
inflexible and traditional demands, can be recast as a rational
decision voluntarily taken in regard to defined alternatives.
Further, since the choice is among outcomes that have only a
probability of coming out, or, if certain, then only a probability
of being satisfactory, the decision can be seen as a calculated
risk, a practical gamble. (Characteristically, the payoff matrix
equally handles a possible outcome whose probability is a
product of nature, as when an invasion decision considers the

Consider now the occupations where problematic consequentiality is faced and where it would be easy to define one's activity as a practical gamble voluntarily taken:

1. There are roles in commerce that are financially dangerous or at least unsteady, subjecting the individual to relatively large surges of success and failure over the short run; among these are market and real estate speculators, commercial fishermen,[24] prospectors.

2. There are roles in industry that are physically dangerous: mining, high construction work,[25] test piloting, well-capping.

3. There are the "hustling" jobs in business enterprise where salesmen and promoters work on a commission or contract-to-contract basis under conditions of close competition. Here income and prestige can be quickly gained and lost due to treacherous minor contingencies: a temporary let-up in effort, the weather, the passing mood of a buyer.

---

probability of good or bad weather across the several possible landing points, or whose probabilistic features have been intentionally introduced by means of gambling equipment, as when one of the available alternatives involves dicing for a specified prize.) Resistance to this sort of formulation can be attributed to a disinclination to face up to all the choosing implied in one's act. Acceptance of this formulation involves a certain amount of consorting with the devil; chance taking is embraced but not fondled. Whatever the social and political consequence of this decision-theory perspective, a purely cultural result might be anticipated, namely, a tendency to perceive more and more of human activity as a practical gamble. One might parenthetically add that the Bomb might have a somewhat similar effect—the transformation of thoughts about future society into thoughts about the chances of there being a future society, these chances themselves varying from month to month.

[24] See F. Barth, "Models of Social Organization," *Royal Anthropological Institute Occasional Paper*, No. 23 (Glasgow, The University Press, 1966), p. 6.

[25] A recent description is G. Talese, *The Bridge* (New York, Harper & Row, 1965).

4. There are performing jobs filled by politicians, actors, and other live entertainers who, during each stage appearance, must work to win and hold an audience under conditions where many contingencies can spoil the show and endanger the showman's reputation. Here, again, any let-up in effort and any minor mishap can easily have serious consequences.

5. There is the soldier's calling[26] and the policeman's lot—stations in public life that fall outside the ordinary categories of work, and make the incumbent officially responsible for undergoing physical danger at the hands of persons who intend it. The fact that these callings stand outside civilian ranks seems to reinforce the notion of self-determination.

6. There is the criminal life, especially the lesser non-racketeering varieties, which yields considerable opportunity but continuously and freshly subjects the individual to gross contingencies—to physical danger, the risk of losing civil status, and wide fluctuations regarding each day's take.[27] "Making it" on the street requires constant orientation to unpredictable opportunities and a readiness to make quick decisions concerning the expected value of proposed schemes—all of which subject the individual to great uncertainties. As already seen, getting to and getting away from the scene of a crime subjects the participants to the fateful play of what would ordinarily be minor incidents.

[26] Which features, of course, an interesting dilemma: in battle a tradition of honor and risk-taking must be maintained, yet behind the lines the organization needs steady men in gray-flannel uniforms. See M. Janowitz, *The Professional Soldier* (New York, The Free Press, 1960), pp. 35–36.

[27] A useful autobiographical portrait of the chance-taking continuously involved in the life of a slum hustler specializing in mugging may be found in H. Williamson, *Hustler!* (New York, Doubleday, 1965). See also C. Brown, *Manchild in the Promised Land* (New York, Macmillan Co., 1965), for the Harlem version.

7. A further source of fatefulness is to be found in arenas, in professional spectator sports whose performers place money, reputation, and physical safety in jeopardy all at the same time: football, boxing, and bullfighting are examples. Sterling Moss's vocation is another:

> . . . . motor-racing on the highest level, in the fastest, most competitive company, *grand prix* driving is the most dangerous sport in the world. It is one of the riskiest of man's activities. Motor-racing kills men. In one recent year the mortality rate was twenty-five percent, or one out of four. These are odds to be compared with those cited for fighter pilots and paratroopers.[28]

8. Finally, there are the recreational non-spectator sports that are full of risk: mountain climbing, big game hunting, skin diving, parachuting, surfing, bob-sledding, spelunking.

V. ADAPTATIONS

Uneventful moments have been defined as moments that are not consequentially problematic. They tend to be dull and unexciting. (When anxiety is felt during such moments it is felt for eventful ones slated to come later.) Yet there are many good reasons to take comfort in this uneventfulness and seek it out, voluntarily foregoing practical gambles along with risk and opportunity—the opportunity if only because it is so often related to the risk. The question is one of security. In uneventful situations, courses of action can be managed reliably and goals progressively and predictably realized. By such self-management the individual allows others to build him into their own plans in an orderly and effective way. The less uncertain his life, the more society can make use of him. It is under-

[28] S. Moss (with K. Purdy), *All But My Life* (New York, Bantam Books, 1964), p. 10.

standable then that the individual may make realistic efforts to minimize the eventfulness—the fatefulness—of his moments, and that he will be encouraged to do so. He engages in *copings*.

One basic technique is physical care. The individual handles himself so as to minimize the remote danger of accidental injury to his body. He does not tip his chair too far back or daydream while crossing a busy intersection.[29] In both the matter of exercising physical care and the need for doing so, idle pursuits make the same claims as obligated, serious ones. *Some* care must always be exerted. Taking care is a constant condition of being. Thus it is one of the central concerns that parents in all societies must impress upon their young,[30] the injunction being to "take care" and not become unnecessarily involved in avoidable fatefulness.

Another means of controlling eventfulness, and one almost as much employed as physical care, is sometimes called providence: an incremental orientation to long-range goals expressed through acts that have a very small additive long-term consequence. The work of building up a savings account is an example; the acquisition of seniority at a workplace and working one's way up by the gradual acquisition of training are two others. The raising of a large family might also qualify. The important point here is that any one day's effort, involving as it does only a small increment, can be sacrificed with little threat to the whole. Here is the Calvinistic solution to life: once the individual divides his day's activities into ones that have no effect and others having a small contributive consequence, nothing can really go wrong.

Another standard means of protecting oneself against

[29] Much of this care, of course, is built into the environment by safety design. Chairs are constructed to limit the possibility of their breaking, stools of their tipping, etc. Even cars are coming to be designed to minimize possible injuries.
[30] Suggested by Edward Gross.

fatefulness is insurance in whatever form, as when house-holders invest in candles and spare fuses, motorists in spare tires, and adults in medical plans. In this way the cost of possible trouble can be easily spread over the whole course of the individual's life, a "converting of a larger contingent loss into a smaller fixed charge."[31]

Systems of courtesy and etiquette can also be viewed as forms of insurance against undesired fatefulness, this time in connection with the personal offense that one individual can inadvertently give to another. The safe management of face to face interaction is especially dependent on this means of control.

Note that the availability and approval of risk-reducing measures creates a new contingency, a new basis for anxiety. When an untoward event occurs during a moment meant to be uneventful, and the event spills over the boundary of the moment and contaminates parts of the individual's life to come, he faces a double loss: the initial loss in question plus that of appearing to himself and others as having failed to exercise the kind of intelligent control, the kind of "care," that allows reasonable persons to minimize danger and avoid remorse.

These, then, are some of the means—largely avoidant—by which the individual realistically copes with situations of fatefulness. Another issue must now be considered, which is easy to confuse with this—defensive behavior.

Anticipated fateful activity creates anxiety and excitement. This is implied in the notion that the utility of what is bet is likely to be quite different from the utility of betting it. Also, as suggested, the individual often feels remorse when something undesirable happens, the chance of which he had failed to reduce, and disappointment when something desirable does not, the occurrence of which he had failed to assure. Any practice that manages the affective response associated with fatefulness—affects

[31] Knight, *op. cit.*, p. 246.

such as anxiety, remorse and disappointment—may be called a *defense*.[32]

When we shift consideration from the management of fatefulness to the management of an affective state associated with it, we are required to review again the phases of a play. For in fact there are situations in which objectively inconsequential phases of play are responded to with a sense that they are fateful. Our individual, about to open the letter containing examination results, may feel excited and anxious to the point of engaging in little rituals of propitiation and control before casting his eyes on the awful news. Or, when the nurse approaches him with information about the condition of his wife and gender of his child, he may feel that the moment is fateful; as he may when the hospital staff returns with news gleaned from a biopsy performed on him to see whether a growth is malignant or benign. But it should be plain that these moments are not really fateful, merely revelatory. In each case the individual's fate has been determined before he entered the news-acquiring situation; he is simply apprised of what is already in force, of something that, at this late date, he can do nothing about. Opening a letter or analysing a bioptic section cannot generate or determine a condition, but only reveal what has already been generated.[33]

[32] The distinction between coping and defense is borrowed from D. Mechanic, *Students Under Stress* (New York, The Free Press, 1962), p. 51. A somewhat similar distinction is employed by B. Anderson in "Bereavement as a Subject of Cross-Cultural Inquiry: An American Sample," *Anthropology Quarterly*, XXXVIII (1965), 195:

> Stressor-directed behavior is oriented toward removing, resolving, or alleviating the impinging circumstances themselves; strain-directed behavior, toward the assuagement of the physical or psychological discomfort that is a product of these happenings.

[33] Of course, where the fate is not a matter of immediate life or death, mere apprisal of what has befallen can begin the work of adjusting to the damage, so that a *failure* to learn *now*

Just as disclosures can create the excitement and concern of fate being generated, so can settlements, that is, occasions when crucial matters known to have been determined in a particular way are finally executed. Thus, in modern Europe, a condemned man's last walk has not been fateful even though each step has brought him closer to death; his execution was merely dramatic, it was his trial that was fateful. In the eighteenth century, when many death sentences were passed and most of these commuted, the trial was not as fateful as the period following it. Very recently, of course, with the agitation against capital punishment, the post-trial period has again become appreciably fateful.

Now we can return to consider defenses, if only in a passing manner, in order to bring a much discussed topic into relationship with the subject-matter of this paper.

The most obvious type of defense, perhaps, is the kind that has no objective effect on fate at all, as in the case of ritualistic superstitions. The behavior said to be true of boxers will serve as an example:

> Since most bouts are unpredictable, boxers usually have superstitions which serve to create confidence and emotional security among them. Sometimes the manager or trainer uses these superstitions to control the fighter. One fighter believed that, if he ate certain foods, he was sure to win, because these foods gave him strength. Others insist on wearing the same robe in which they won their first fight; one wore an Indian blanket when he entered the ring. Many have charm pieces or attribute added impor-

---

about an eventual loss can itself be fateful. Here disclosure of fate cannot effect what is disclosed but can effect the timing of reconstitutive efforts. Similarly, if the quickness of the individual's response to the situation is of strategic significance in his competition with another party, then the *timing* of his learning about the outcome can be fateful, even though the disclosure of the outcome cannot influence that particular outcome itself.

tance to entering the ring after the opponent. . . .
Some insist that, if a woman watches them train, it
is bad luck. One fighter, to show he was not superstitious, would walk under a ladder before every
fight, until this became a magical rite itself. Consistent with this attitude, many intensify their religious attitudes and keep Bibles in their lockers. One
fighter kept a rosary in his glove. If he lost the rosary,
he would spend the morning before the fight in
church. Although this superstitious attitude may be
imported from local or ethnic culture, it is intensified
among the boxers themselves, whether they are white
or Negro, preliminary fighters or champions.[34]

Gamblers exhibit similar, if less religious, superstitions.[35]

Clearly, any realistic practice aimed at avoiding or reducing risk—any coping—is likely to have the side effect of
reducing anxiety and remorse, is likely, in short, to have
defensive functions. A person who coolly resorts to a game
theory matrix when faced with a vital decision is reducing a painful risk to a calculated one. His frame of mind
brings peace of mind. Like a competent surgeon, he can
feel he is doing all that anyone is capable of doing, and
hence can await the result without anguish or recrimina-
tion. Similarly, a clear appreciation of the difference between the determinative phase of a play and the disclosure
and settlement of the play can help the individual deal
with the anxiety produced during the span of the activity;
such discriminations can have defensive functions.

It is not surprising, then, that when a causal basis is

[34] K. Weinberg and H. Arond, "The Occupational Culture of
the Boxer," *American Journal of Sociology*, LXVIII (1952),
463–64.

[35] In modern society such practices tend to be employed only
with appreciable ambivalence and are no doubt much on the
decline. For the changing situation with respect to one traditionally superstitious group, commercial fishermen, see J.
Tunstall, *The Fishermen* (London, Macgibbon & Kee, 1962),
pp. 168–70.

not readily found for discounting the determinativeness of the current situation, it may be sought out; and where it can't be found, imagined. Thus, for example, we find that events determined locally may be interpreted as a consequence of prior determination. A version of this "defensive determinism" is found in the belief in fate, predestination, and kismet—the notion that the major outcomes regarding oneself are already writ down, and one is helpless to improve or worsen one's chances. The soldier's maxim is an illustration: "I won't get mine 'till my number's up so why worry."[36]

Just as causality can be sought outside the situation, so it can be sought in local forces that similarly serve to relieve one's sense of responsibility. A type of scapegoating is involved, pointing to the function of lodging causal efficacy within what is seen as the enduring and autonomous parts of the individual's personality, and thereby transforming a fateful event into something that is "only to be expected." Suffering an accident because of carelessness, the individual can say, "That's just like me; I do it all the time." About to take a crucial examination the individual can ease matters by telling himself that the exam will be fair, and so everything depends on how much work he has or has not long since done.

Further, belief in pure, blind luck can protect the individual from the remorse of knowing that something could have and should have been done to protect himself. Here is the opposite tack to defensive determinism—a kind of defensive indeterminism—but the consequences are much the same. "It's nobody's fault," the individual says. "It was just a question of bad luck."[37]

[36] See W. Miller's discussion of fate in "Lower Class Culture as a Generating Milieu of Gang Delinquency," *Journal of Social Issues*, XIV (1958), 11–12. The religious roots, of course, are to be found in John Calvin and ascetic Puritanism.

[37] An example is cited in Cohen, *op. cit.*, p. 147: "The possibility of a falling back on 'luck' may also be a great comfort

Obviously, then, a traditional statement of coping and defence can be applied in connection with fatefulness. But this neglects a wider fact about adaptation to chance-taking. When we look closely at the adaptation to life made by persons whose situation is constantly fateful, say that of professional gamblers or front-line soldiers, we find that aliveness to the consequences involved comes to be blunted in a special way. The world that is gambled is, after all, only a world, and the chance-taker can learn to let go of it. He can adjust himself to the ups and downs in his welfare by discounting his prior relation to the world and accepting a chancy relation to what others feel assured of having. Perspectives seem to be inherently normalizing: once conditions are fully faced, a life can be built out of them, and by reading from the bottom up, it will be the rises not the falls that are seen as temporary.

VI. ACTION

Although fatefulness of all kinds can be handled both by coping and by defense, it cannot be avoided completely. More important, there are, as suggested, some activities whose fatefulness is appreciable indeed if one combines the amount chanced, the rate of chance taking, and the problematicalness of the outcome. It is here, of course, that the individual is likely to perceive the situation as his taking of a practical gamble—the willful undertaking of serious chances.

Given the claims of wider obligation that commit some individuals to what they can perceive as chancy under-

---

in other circumstances. In 1962, British universities rejected some 20,000 applicants for entry. Many of them reconciled this rejection with their pride by saying that the offer of a university place depends as much on luck as on merit. The rejects are described as 'submitting applications, like a gambler putting coins into a fruit-machine, sure that the jackpot must come up at last.' "

takings, virtue will sometimes be made of necessity. This is another defensive adjustment to fatefulness. Those with fateful duties sometimes hold themselves to be self-respecting men who aren't afraid to put themselves on the line. At each encounter (they claim) they are ready to place their welfare and their reputation in jeopardy, transforming encounters into confrontations. They have a more or less secret contempt for those with safe and sure jobs who need never face real tests of themselves. They claim they are not only willing to remain in jobs full of opportunity and risk, but have deliberately sought out this environment, declining to accept safe alternatives, being able, willing, and even inclined to live in challenge.[38]

Talented burglars and pickpockets, whose skill must be exercised under pressure, look down, it is said, on the petty sneak thief, since the only art he need have for his calling is a certain low cunning.[39] Criminals may similarly disesteem fences as being "thieves without nerve."[40] So, too, Nevada casino dealers may come on shift knowing that it is they who must face the hard intent of players to win, and coolly stand in its way, consistently blocking

[38] E. Hemingway, Death in the Afternoon (New York, Scribners, 1932), p. 101, suggests that men of this stamp, being disinclined to calculate too closely, have their own disease: "Syphilis was the disease of the crusaders in the middle ages. It was supposed to be brought to Europe by them, and it is a disease of all people who lead lives in which disregard of consequences dominates. It is an industrial accident, to be expected by all those who lead irregular sexual lives and from their habits of mind would rather take chances than use prophylactics, and it is a to-be-expected end, or rather phase, of the life of all fornicators who continue their careers far enough." Penicillin has undermined this route to manliness.

[39] C. Shaw, "Juvenile Delinquency—A Group Tradition," Bulletin of the State University of Iowa, No. 23, N.S. No. 700 (1933), p. 10, cited in R. Cloward and L. Ohlin, Delinquency and Opportunity (New York, The Free Press, 1960), p. 170.

[40] S. Black, "Burglary," Part Two, The New Yorker, December 14, 1963, p. 117.

skill, luck, and cheating, or lose the precarious reputation they have with management. Having to face these contingencies every day, they feel set apart from the casino employees who are not on the firing line. (In some casinos there are special dealers who are brought into a game to help nature correct the costly runs of good luck occasionally experienced by players, or to remove the uncertainty a pit boss can feel when a big bettor begins to play seriously. These dealers practice arts requiring delicacy, speed, and concentration, and the job can easily be visibly muffed. Moreover, the player at this time is likely to be heavily committed and searching openly and even belligerently in a small field for just the evidence that is there. Skilled card and dice "mechanics" understandably develop contempt not only for *non*-dealers but also for *mere* dealers.)[41] The small-scale fishermen I knew on the Shetland Islands had something of the same feeling; during each of the five or six runs of a day's fishing they subjected themselves to a serious gamble because of the extreme variability of the catch.[42] Peering into the net as the winch brought the bag and its fish into view was a thrill, known by those who experienced it to be something their fellow islanders would not be men enough to want to stomach regularly. Interestingly, Sir Edmund Hillary, who came to practice a truly chancy calling, provides us with the following view of the work he and his father lived by, namely, beekeeping:

It was a good life—a life of open air and sun and hard physical work. And in its way it was a life of uncer-

[41] With some reverence, dealers cite as a reference model the blackjack mechanics in New York who worked next door to the hang-out of the Murder Incorporated mob, and daily "dealt down" to customers likely to be demonstrably intolerant of dealers caught cheating them. Surely those who could survive such work must have known themselves to be men of considerable poise, a match in that department for anyone they could imagine.

[42] Field Study, 1949–50.

tainty and adventure; a constant fight against the vagaries of the weather and a mad rush when all our 1,600 hives decided to swarm at once. We never knew what our crop would be until the last pound of honey had been taken off the hives. But all through the exciting months of the honey flow the dream of a bumper crop would drive us on through long hard hours of labor. I think we were incurable optimists. And during the winter I often tramped around our lovely bush-clad hills and learned a little about self-reliance and felt the first faint stirrings of interest in the unknown.[43]

When we meet these stands we can suspect that the best is being made of a bad thing—it is more a question of rationalizations than of realistic accountings. (It is as if the illusion of self-determinancy were a payment society gives to individuals in exchange for their willingness to perform jobs that expose them to risk.) After all, even with chancy occupational roles, choice occurs chiefly at the moment the role itself is first accepted and safer ones foregone; once the individual has committed himself to a particular niche, his having to face what occurs there is more likely to express steady constraints than daily re-decidings. Here the individual cannot choose to withdraw from chance-taking without serious consequence for his occupational status.[44]

However, there are fateful activities that *are* socially defined as ones an individual is under no obligation to con-

[43] E. Hillary, *High Adventure* (New York, Dutton, 1955), p. 14.

[44] Dean MacCannell has suggested that there are jobs that holders gamble with, as when a night watchman takes time off to go to a movie during time on and enjoys the gamble as much as the movie. However, these jobs are characteristically "mere" ones, taken up and left rapidly by persons not specifically qualified for them and not qualified for anything better. When these jobs are subjected to only spot supervision, gambling with the job seems to occur.

tinue to pursue once he has started to do so. No extraneous factors compel him to face fate in the first place; no extraneous ends provide expediential reasons for his continued participation. His activity is defined as an end itself, sought out, embraced, and utterly his own. His record during performance can be claimed as the reason for participation, hence an unqualified, direct expression of his true make-up and a just basis for reputation.

By the term *action* I mean activities that are consequential, problematic, and undertaken for what is felt to be their own sake. The degree of action—its seriousness or realness—depends on how fully these properties are accentuated and is subject to the same ambiguities regarding measurement as those already described in the case of chanciness. Action seems most pronounced when the four phases of the play—squaring off, determination, disclosure, and settlement—occur over a period of time brief enough to be contained within a continuous stretch of attention and experience. It is here that the individual releases himself to the passing moment, wagering his future estate on what transpires precariously in the seconds to come. At such moments a special affective state is likely to be aroused, emerging transformed into excitement.

Action's location can easily and quickly shift, as any floating crap game attests; indeed, should a knife fight develop next to a crap table, the action may shift in location even while it is shifting in kind, and yet participants will apply the same word, as if the action in a situation is by definition the most serious action in that situation at the moment, regardless of its content.[45] In asking the famous question, "Where's the action?" an individual may be more concerned with the intensity of the action he finds than its kind.

[45] Thus, Ned Polsky in "The Hustler," *Social Problems*, XII (1964), 5–6, suggests that a pool game between skilled players for a small bet will take second place to one between lesser players who are gaming for higher stakes.

Whoever participates in action does so in two quite distinct capacities: as someone who hazards or chances something valuable, and as someone who must perform whatever activities are called for. In the latter capacity the individual must ordinarily stand alone,[46] placing in hazard his reputation for competence in play.[47] But in the former he can easily share his gamble with others or even let them "take" all of it. Action, then, is usually something one can obtain "a piece" of; the performer of the action is typically a single individual, but the party he represents can contain a quickly shifting roster of jointly committed members. For analysis, however, it is convenient to focus on the case where the performer takes all his own action and none of anyone else's.

It is, of course, in the gambling world that the term action had its slang beginning, and gambling is the prototype of action. In the casinos of Nevada, the following usages can be found: "Dollar action," refers to light bettors and their effect on the day's take; and "good [or real or big] action," refers to heavier takes. Dealers who get flustered by heavy bettors are said to be unable "to deal to the action," while cool dealers are said to be "able to handle the action." Naturally, new dealers are "pulled out of the action," and when bets get heavy and multitudinous

[46] The capacity to perform tends to be imputed to the individual, but there are situations, as in gang molestations, where this capacity clearly derives from the visible backing he can readily call on. Further, there are some situations whose action arises because a set of actors have committed themselves to closely coordinated acts—as in some current robberies. The sheer working out of the interdependencies in the face of various contingencies becomes a source of action.

[47] It is quite possible for an individual to be more concerned about his reputation as a performer than for the objective value of the pot at stake. For example, casino dealers, especially in the "break-in" phase, can find it more difficult to manage dealing to a big bet during the shift than to manage the placing of the same bet as a customer after work.

at a crap table, the better of the base men may be "put on the action side." Casinos that try to avoid high limit games are said "not to want the action," while houses that can face heavy bettors without becoming nervous are said "to be able to take the action." A "high roller" known to "drop" a lot of money may find himself warmly welcomed at a casino because "we like his action." Pit bosses, ever concerned to show that they are somehow earning their keep, will, from a tactful distance, "keep their eye on the action." Someone known to cheat, or to be able to "count cards" in 21, may be asked to leave the casino permanently with the statement, "We don't want your action." Players who are indecisive "hold up the action," and one who fails to cover all of what is considered a good bet may cause another player to ask if he can "take the rest of the action." Deserving casino managers may be rewarded by being "given a piece of the action," that is, a share of ownership ("points"). In casinos with only one cluster of tables (one "pit") there is likely to be one table that because of location or special maximum is called the "action table," just as in large casinos there will be a high minimum "action pit."[48]

Although action is independent of type and concerned with amount, amount itself cannot be taken as a simple product of the size of each bet and the number of players betting. This is most evident in craps. A table whose sole player is making hundred-dollar bets can be seen as having more action than another table whose twenty players are making five- and ten-dollar bets. A table "jam up" with players, all of whom are making many different kinds of bets, can be seen as having more action than another table where ten players are betting a higher aggregate by

[48] Similarly Polsky, *op. cit.*, p. 5, reports that certain pool halls are nationally identified as "action rooms," and within one hall there will be one or two tables informally reserved for the action.

means of simple line and field bets. Correspondingly, to say that a dealer can "handle the action" may mean, either, that he can deal coolly to a very large bettor, or that he can deal accurately and rapidly when a large number of calculations and payoffs must be made quickly.

Another aspect of the gambler's use of the term action arises from the fact that action and the chance-taking it involves may constitute the source of the gambler's daily livelihood. Thus, when he asks where the action is he is not merely seeking situations of action, but also situations in which he can practice his trade. Something similar is found in the thief's and the prostitute's conception of where the action is—namely, where the risks to earn one's living by are currently and amply available.[49] Here, compressed pridefully into one word, is a claim to a very special relationship to the work world.

No doubt it was gamblers who first applied their term to non-gambling situations, thus initiating a diffusion of usage that non-gamblers have recently extended still further. Yet almost always the use seems apt. Underlying the apparent diversity in content is a single analytical property that can be sensed with sureness by persons who might be unable to define closely what it is they sense.

This diffusion of use is nowhere better seen than in the current touting of action in our mass media. In fact, contributors to the media have recently helped to clarify the inner meaning of the term and to show its applicability to new ranges of situation, giving a special accent to current popular culture. Thus a newspaper advertisement for "Teenage Day" at Whiskey à Go Go (no liquor, live music), declares:

[49] Suggested by Howard Becker. *The Dictionary of American Underworld Lingo,* ed. H. Goldin, F. O'Leary, and M. Lipsius (New York, Twayne Publishers, 1950), defines action: Criminal activity. "Shape up (be present) tonight, Joe, there's action—a Brooklyn score (robbery)."

Dance to the Big Beat music of the original Whiskey
à Go Go—WHISKEY À GO GO WHERE THE AC-
TION IS![50]

Herb Caen, reporting on East Bay doings, states that:

M. Larry Lawrence, Pres. of Hotel del Coronado, and
Stockbroker Al Schwabacher Jr. huddled at the
P'Alto Cabana the other day, which is why the ru-
mor's around that Al might buy a piece of the
Coronado's historic action.[51]

Similarly, Caen writes:

You know where the action is these nights? In Oak-
land, that's where. Or so it seemed early yesterday,
in a go-go spot at Jack London Square, where Oak-
land Mayor John Houlihan and Millionaire Bernie
Murray got into a pushing and shoving contest that
ended with Hizzoner flat on his honor in the middle
of the dance floor—as the dancers Frugged around
and over his reclining figure. . . .[52]

The *Las Vegas Sun*, underneath a picture of the contest,
reports:

BRIDGE ACTION—Women spectators closely watch
bridge experts in competition at Riviera Hotel.[53]

During another tournament, a column heading in the *Sun*
reads:

Gin Action Goes Into 2nd Round[54]

And the same paper's columnist reports:

Shirley Jones' sexy dance from the "Elmer Gantry"
movie at the Flamingo these nights is the most explosive bit of action since Juliet Prowse . . .[55]

[50] *San Francisco Chronicle*, August 7, 1965.
[51] *Ibid.*, July 22, 1965.
[52] *Ibid.*, September 24, 1965.
[53] *Las Vegas Sun*, February 10, 1965.
[54] *Ibid.*, December 4, 1965.
[55] *Ibid.*, April 20, 1965.

Newsweek titles a cover story:

SINATRA: Where the Action Is[56]

A color-page advertisement in *Look:*

> 7-UP . . . WHERE THERE'S ACTION! Seven-up is
> a real natural for the action crowd! It's got the
> sparkle that swings . . . and the quick-quenching
> action to make thirst quit. Look for it. 7-UP . . .
> where there's action![57]

And an advertisement in *California Living,* showing a girl
applying lipstick, and suggesting that "A girl's mouth is
always moving," titles the half-page:

Where the Beauty Action Is[58]

A full-page cover picture in the same magazine features
two models in a section of a department store organized
as a teen-age hang-out, above a title saying:

Check the Fashion Action.[59]

And a feature article on the San Francisco Police Department sale of unclaimed articles recovered from burglaries
reports that the auctioneer "keeps the pace lively for hun-
dreds of bidding buyers:"

> If there is no honor among thieves, neither is there a
> common denominator of thievery. Check the action at
> the police auction to see why.[60]

Financial columnists, of course, also have recourse to the
term:

[56] *Newsweek,* September 6, 1965.
[57] *Look,* August 24, 1965.
[58] *California Living,* November 7, 1965. Action figures in
other unexpected parts of the body too. My liquor merchant,
pushing a cheap Dutch imported beer, opens a trial bottle for
me, puts the bottle near my face and says: "Taste that action."
[59] *Ibid.,* February 13, 1966.
[60] *California,* April 17, 1966.

If it was panic selling that gripped the market in October, 1929, and May, 1962, then today we're surely in the throes of panic buying. Least that's how Shearson, Hammill & Co. view the current free-for-all.

"Apparently the major motivation at the moment is fear of missing or having missed a major buying opportunity," the brokerage firm observes.

"To a greater extent every day, stock buyers—we won't use the term 'investors'—are going where the action is, and it is not hard to find."

For anyone desiring a piece of the action, Shearson has this advice: . . .[61]

Heavy selling developed during the first hour and stock tickers began to lag behind the action.[62]

Those who report on government contracting can employ the term, evoking an image of occasions when decisions, allocations, and very nice opportunities are in the very process of determination:

Powerful lobbyist Tom Gray's investment firm got a $40,000 cut of the action when the Board of Supervisors approved a $2 million extension of the Fifth and Mission Garage, The Chronicle learned yesterday.[63]

These journalistic accents have significance. The cult of cars provides a case in point. One support for this world is found in professional racing and the spectator sport organized around it. Another support is found in advertising, two examples of which I cite from a recent color brochure printed by Buick:

Think of a car that's loaded with action, classic in line, agile as a cat, and luxurious beyond belief. The

[61] Lloyd Watson in *San Francisco Chronicle*, April 23, 1966.
[62] *Boston Traveler*, August 22, 1966.
[63] *San Francisco Chronicle*, August 4, 1966, front page, under the lead "A $40,000 Piece of The Action."

car you're thinking about is the Riviera by Buick. Here's a unique blend of blazing performance (325 h.p.) and solid roadability that sets the Riviera apart from all other cars. In other words, it's a car that might be equally at home on the track as on the road.

THE ACCENT'S ON ACTION! A car doesn't really come alive until you turn the key to start the engine. This is the greatest moment in owning a Buick. With any one of Buick's six engines and four transmissions you've bought yourself a piece of action that just won't quit.

These two sources of publicity contribute support for the manufacture, sale and use of sports cars and fast sedans, and this in turn provides official equipment for transforming the highways into scenes of action, places where skill, impatience, and costly equipment can be displayed under seriously chancy conditions.[64]

In this essay action will be considered chiefly in the context of American society. Although every society no doubt has scenes of action, it is our own society that has found a

[64] Driving often becomes a form of action, and the relation of everyday driving practices to the ideally dangerous world of track racing and the ideal-pushing world of car advertising is an important social topic, perhaps sufficiently appreciated only by those who have a professional interest in decreasing the accident rates. See, for example, Mervyn Jones's article, "Who Wants Safe Driving," in *The Observer,* Weekend Review, August, 16, 1964, p. 17; Cohen, *op. cit.,* chap. 5, "Gambling with Life on the Road"; and J. Roberts, W. Thompson, and B. Sutton-Smith, "Expressive Self-Testing in Driving," *Human Organization,* 25, 1 (1966), 54–63.
Driving so as to "make time" saves a remarkably small amount of time but does generate a current of underlying action; often it seems that time is being saved so that risk can be experienced. Some persons enjoy air travel for the same reason. They time their departure for the airport so as to minimize wait when they get there, and incidentally ensure some danger of missing the flight, and once on the plane they welcome for the duration of the flight a sense of slight danger to life.

word for it. Interestingly enough, we have become alive to action at a time when—compared to other societies—we have sharply curtailed in civilian life the occurrence of fatefulness of the serious, heroic, and dutiful kind.

A final word about the spread of words. In casino gambling when a player makes a large bet and loses it he sometimes speaks of what he did as "blowing it." Thus, to engage in action unsuccessfully is to "blow it." The implication is that a desirable stake (in this case monetary) that had been possessed has now been lost, and that neither possession of the stake nor its loss was particularly justified or legitimate. Blowing a big bet reflects badly on oneself, but not so badly that one can't fairly easily accuse oneself of having done so. It is this complex that has come to be generalized.

Casino personnel "breaking in" on a job feel there is much profit if they "make it" but no practical way of ensuring that they will. During this difficult phase there will be many minor infractions of rules, which can serve as sufficient grounds for being fired: coming on shift a few minutes late; declining an undignified task; mishandling chips; being irreverent concerning a house loss; expressing impatience with one's rate of progress, and so forth. Once skill and reputation have been acquired, tenure is only somewhat more secure: runs of ill luck; ill-founded suspicion of theft; change in owner-sponsorship; all can provide grounds for sudden dismissal.

Loss of a job due to what can, in fact, be seen as a meaningless lapse is also "blowing it." In contrast to the middle-class perspective that tends to define occupational position as something only deservedly acquired and deservedly lost, occupational situation for the casino worker tends to oscillate very rapidly between "having it made," and "blowing it," neither of which state is seen as particularly warranted. This perspective has extended to other areas of life, and a dealer may speak of having blown his marriage or his chance at a college education.

The logic of this racy attitude to the fundamentals of life, which implies a defense in depth to living with action, can be understood in reference to social organization in Nevada: the relative ease of divorce and marriage; the presence of a very large number of persons who have failed occupationally or maritally; a frontier tradition of asking no questions about a person's history or current livelihood; the clear possibility of getting an equivalent job across the street after being fired; the high visibility of a large number of casino employees known to have worked recently in better jobs in other casinos; the fact that sporadic bouts of big play mean sporadic realization of the ideal experience of a culture, such that however long and lean the days between bouts, this use of one's money may be the best that Nevada can offer. In any case, action is not the only term that appears to have spread outward from the gaming tables. A family of terms seems to be involved, and the entire family seems to be migrating.[65]

VII. Where the Action Is

I have argued that action is to be found wherever the individual knowingly takes consequential chances perceived as avoidable. Ordinarily, action will not be found during the week-day work routine at home or on the job.

---

[65] Along with action and blowing it, we must count the phrase "having it made," this being a source of income, whether deserved or undeserved, which allows a life of little work and considerable spending, and one sense of the phrase "to have something going for oneself," namely, an edge of some kind, as when a casino employee says that he never plays 21 unless he's got something going for him with the dealer—a condition of play, incidentally, that is very hard to stop from developing. I will not consider here a term used by casino employees in many contexts: the term, "to hustle." This is an adopted member of the casino's family of terms, having originated in an older business.

For here chance-takings tend to be organized out, and such as remain are not obviously voluntary. Where, then, is action routinely to be found? Let me summarize the suggestions already made in passing.

First, contenders find action in commercialized competitive sport. Perhaps because this activity is staged for an audience and watched for fun, it is felt that no fully serious reason could exist for engaging in the activity itself. Also, the fact that amateurs perform these spectacular activities on their own, privately and without pay, as recreation, reinforces the notion that the professionals are engaged in a self-determined free-will calling. This is the case even though it is apparent that professional and commercial interests may be staked in a business-like way on the outcome of the spectacle. Although a sports car racer may make a living at the wheel, and the decision of a company to continue or discontinue a car model may hinge on a race outcome,[66] it is still felt that drivers could take other types of jobs or at least sit out the current race, and that this sort of chance-taking is somehow voluntary.

The next place of action to consider is non-spectator[67]

[66] For example, the Corvette participation in the 1956 Sebring race, as described by the driver John Fitch (with C. Barnard) "The Day That Corvette Improved the Breed," pp. 271–86 in C. Beaumont and W. Nolan, *Omnibus of Speed* (New York, Putnam and Sons, 1958): "I knew that failure at Sebring would probably mean the end of Chevrolet's interest in racing sports cars" (p. 286).

[67] It is characteristic that risky recreational sports are "worth watching," that they will often be watched, and that the performer must accept this watching. He should be able to perform while being watched; yet he should not perform just in order to be watched and should perform in spite of having no watchers. No matter how big a crowd a sportsman gets, nor how much he is enthralled by their enthrallment, their role is unratified; they can't demand that he schedule his performance or complete it once begun. They have a right to have their watching overlooked by him, but a duty to accept his overlooking them.

risky sports. No payment is received for this effort; no publicly relevant identity is consolidated by it; and it incurs no obligations in the serious world of work. In the absence of the usual pressures to engage in an activity, it is presumably easy to assume that self-determination is involved and that the chances incurred are brought on solely because of the challenge that results. Interestingly, some of these vigorous sports are dominated by solid young-minded citizens who can afford the time, travel, and equipment. These persons seem to get the best of both worlds, enjoying the honor of chance-taking without greatly threatening their routinized week-day involvements.

Next to consider are the more commercialized places of action—places, conveniently located, where equipment and the field for its use can be rented and a slight degree of action laid on. Bowling alleys, pool halls, amusement parks, and arcade streets provide arrangements where the cost of the play and the value of the prize generate a mildly fateful context for displaying competence. Public betting at race tracks and in casinos permits the gambler to demonstrate a variety of personal attributes, although at considerable cost. The "vertigo" rides at fairs and amusement parks nakedly resolve our dilemma concerning action by providing danger that is guaranteed to be really not dangerous—what Michael Balint has nicely described as the safe excitement of thrills:

In all amusements and pleasures of this kind three characteristic attitudes are observable: (a) some amount of conscious fear, or at least an awareness of real external danger; (b) a voluntary and intentional exposing of oneself to this external danger and to the fear aroused by it; (c) while having the more or less confident hope that the fear can be tolerated and mastered, the danger will pass, and, that one will be able to return unharmed to safety. This mixture of fear, pleasure, and confident hope in face of external danger is what constitutes the fundamental element of all *thrills*.[68]

There is a final type of commercialized action involving direct participation, which I will call "fancy milling."[69] Adults in our society can obtain a taste of social mobility by consuming valued products, by enjoying costly and modish entertainment, by spending time in luxurious settings, and by mingling with prestigeful persons—all the more if these occur at the same time and in the presence of many witnesses. This is the action of consumption. Further, mere presence in a large, tightly packed gathering of reveling persons can bring not only the excitement that crowds generate, but also the uncertainty of not quite knowing what might happen next, the possibility of flirtations, which can themselves lead to relationship forma-

[68] M. Balint, *Thrills and Regressions* (London, The Hogarth Press and the Institute of Psycho-Analysis, 1959), p. 23. Balint goes on to make this interesting comment (pp. 23–24): "Let us briefly examine in what way other thrills resemble those offered in funfairs. Some are connected with *high speed*, as in all kinds of racing, horse riding and jumping, motor racing, skating, skiing, tobogganing, sailing, flying, etc. Others are connected with *exposed situations*, like various forms of jumping and diving, rock climbing, gliding, taming wild animals, travelling into unknown lands, etc. Lastly, there is a group of thrills which are connected with *unfamiliar* or even *completely new forms of satisfaction*, either in the form of a new object or of an unfamiliar method of pleasure. The obvious new object is a virgin, and it is amazing how many thrills claim this adjective. One speaks of virgin land, a virgin peak, or a virginal route to a peak, virgin realms of speed, and so on. On the whole, any new sexual partner is a thrill, especially if he or she belongs to another race, colour, or creed. The new forms of pleasure include among others: new food, new clothes, new customs, up to new forms of "perverse" sexual activities. In all these phenomena we find the same three fundamental factors described above: the objective external danger giving rise to fear, the voluntary and intentional exposure of oneself to it, and the confident hope that all will turn out well in the end."

[69] The necessity of considering this mode of action was recommended by Howard Becker.

tion, and the lively experience of being an elbow away from someone who does manage to find real action in the crowd.

When these various elements of fancy milling are combined, and the individual views the prestige and the brevity of participation against the cost of getting to the scene and the rate of expenditure necessitated during each moment of participation, a kind of diffuse action—or rather a flavor of action—results, however limited the fatefulness.[70] The individual brings into himself the role of performer and the role of spectator; he is the one who engages in the action, yet he is the one who is unlikely to be permanently affected by it.

Here hotel casinos provide an extreme example. Not only are money gambles made available, this type of action is overlaid with the consumption kind. A brief penetration into high living is laid on. Attendant-parked limousines are cluttered at the entrance. Beyond the entrance, the setting is luxurious. Liquor is served at the tables, often at no cost to the consumer. A quality buffet may be provided, allowing for discriminative gorging. A gratuity system is encouraged that elevates its users and provides scantily clad waitresses, selected for their looks, cause to be somewhat accessible. A "pit" operated signal system enables these girls to deliver drinks, cigarettes, and aspirin anywhere on the premises upon request. Keno "runners" and change girls are similarly organized to be at beck and call. Table contact is facilitated with the nationally known and with big spenders. Proximity to what some might consider the gangster element is also provided. Easy access to nationally famous entertainment is assured, and even some physical closeness to the entertainers themselves. The lounge bar is "dressed" with chorus girls clothed in their off-stage costumes. Female customers feel

[70] Services in such places *must* be priced high if this kind of action is to be facilitated. Proprietors accommodate, but for other reasons.

they can experiment with sports high-fashion, claiming an age and style they might be too modest to try out at home. In brief, the opportunity for ephemeral ennoblement abounds. However, should the consumer want to sit down during this ennoblement, he will very likely have to sit at a gaming table. There is a rich ambience, then, but each minute of it is likely to cost the risking of considerable money.

Other public service establishments, too, appear to be increasingly overlaying their services with indulgence choices heretofore considered irrelevant. Thus, our cross-country jets have added pretty girls, goodish food, movies, and free liquor.[71] Filling stations can now provide not only gas but a moment's company with a "bumper bunny." And, of course, there is the current "topless" trend, which brings, along with food, waitresses who are assuredly attractive.[72]

[71] In a feature article on "The 'Secrets' of Air Hostesses" (*San Francisco Chronicle,* April 4, 1966), under the heading "Those Cupcakes in the Sky," we read: "What we want in our hostesses is understated sexiness," says Nancy Marchand, a statuesque blonde in charge of PSA girls. "In choosing a hostess, we pay particular attention to her figure."

Passengers, said Lawrence [the President of Braniff, and a current leader in airline merchandising] are entitled to more than a safe, comfortable journey. They are entitled to a little fun.

Lawrence's definition of fun aloft included painting Braniff's fleet of jetliners a variety of Easter egg colors and wildly redecorating the aircraft interiors, ticket offices and waiting rooms. But he reserved the company's hostesses for the most fun of all. He hired famed Italian dress designer Milio Pucci, the inventor of stretch pants, to create a hostess costume with "flair, excitement and surprise."

[72] No clearer case of the indulgence overlay is to be found, I think, than The Harry's Shoeshine Palace, San Francisco (as reported in the *San Francisco Chronicle,* July 26, 1966), which provides topless shoeshines for $2.00 and an ID card. De Sade would have been impressed by this merchandising of his principles.

Certain segments of each community seem more responsive than others to the attraction of this kind of action. It is worth noting that individuals respond not as members of a local community but as like-minded, otherwise unrelated members of the great society. Strangers in town can ask the local cabby where the action is and probably gain entry when they get there. A freemasonry of individuals who would otherwise be strangers is involved, a temporary coalition against the society of the respectable in which an action seeker is likely to have friends and relations. The traditional mechanisms of acquaintanceship and personal invitation are not needed to restrict participation; the risks of participation serve instead.

Although it is possible and desirable to look for where the action is by broadly examining social organization, a much more specific effort concerns me here. I want to consider the actual social arrangements through which action is made available.

The social world is such that any individual who is strongly oriented to action, as some gamblers are, can perceive the potentialities for chance in situations others would see as devoid of eventfulness; the situation can even be structured so that these possibilities are made manifest.[73] Chance is not merely sought out but carved out. It should be added that the form of chance likely to be found here is appreciable risk to bodily welfare in exchange for the opportunity of trifling gain. Some version of "Russian roulette" is the one scene of fatefulness that

[73] Suggested by Sheldon Messinger. The garden variety, as popularized by Damon Runyon, is the small-time Broadway gambler who perceptually reconstitutes the immediate environment into a continuous series of soon-to-be-determined bettable outcomes on which propositions can be offered. The culture hero here is John W. "Bet-a-Million" Gates, the barbed-wire king, who, in 1897 on a train between Chicago and Pittsburgh, apparently won $22,000 by betting on raindrop races, a window-pane serving as a course. (See H. Asbury, Sucker's Progress [New York, Dodd Mead, 1938], p. 446.)

almost everyone is in a position to construct, and a scene that nicely illustrates chance-taking as an end in itself. Interestingly, there is currently available through L.S.D. and other drugs a means of voluntarily chancing psychic welfare in order to pass beyond ordinary consciousness. The individual here uses his own mind as the equipment necessary for action.[74] Persons who gesture with suicide use their bodies in a gamble, but here, as with drugs, chance-taking as such does not seem to be the main purpose of the undertaking.[75] The current widespread interest in the deleterious effects of smoking and of cholesterol provide a milder example of the same possibility; to various flavors can be added the extra flavor of not-giving-a-damn.[76]

In the cases so far considered, chance lies in the attitude of the individual himself—his creative capacity to redefine the world around him into its decisional potentialities. Turn now to the action possibilities that place greater demands upon the environment and are more directly facilitated by organization.

A simple beginning can be found in casino gambling, since these are places, first of all, whose physical and social organization is designed to facilitate the occurrence of action. The efficiency of these arrangements must be understood and appreciated. A player need only stride into a casino (off-street casinos are not likely to require even the opening of a door) and put money on a squaring-off or commitment area. If the dealer is not already in play, he will immediately initiate it, a momentary pause that is itself avoided in many casinos by employing shills to keep dead games going. In a matter of seconds, the

[74] Suggested by Nancy Achilles.
[75] The various kinds of gambles with life indulged by the suicidally inclined are considered in N. Farberow and E. Schneidman, *The Cry for Help* (New York, McGraw-Hill, 1961), esp. pp. 132–33.
[76] Suggested by Dean MacConnell.

player can plug himself into quite meaningful activity; sockets are available.

Further, casino plays have a remarkably short span, permitting a very high rate of play. A slots play takes only 4 or 5 seconds. A hand at 21 may take as little time as 20 seconds, by virtue of card management practices that dealers are uniformly trained to employ.[77] In all casino games it is possible, also, to engage in more than one play at a time, and, in the case of slots and craps, to phase the multiple betting so that a commitment is made and determination begun in regard to one bet while another is in the later phases of the determination process. One game, keno, available in most casinos, is specifically organized so that in almost all regions of the casino bets can be made and determination followed. Keno display boards are posted at various places and simultaneously scored electrically. Keno runners collect bets and deliver payoffs everywhere in the casino except the bathrooms. The phasing of play coincides with no other activities in the casino. Thus, whatever an individual is doing, and wherever he is doing it, he can overlay his activity with keno play and always have at least a keno number "going for him."[78]

A player can engage in all manner of calculation and divination regarding how to manage his bet, whether this involves copings, defenses, or both. But he also may, if he wants, merely push an uncounted pile of money or chips in the general direction of the commitment area and the

[77] Polsky, op. cit., p. 6, suggests that in "action rooms" billiard games are selected and even modified in order to increase the action rate, which might otherwise be too low. However, five minute plays still seem to be the shortest time except when individual shots are bet on.

[78] In American society at large, horse-racing, "the numbers," and the stock market provide means by which an individual can have one or two things "going for him" every day. Keno has a somewhat similar overlay character, but each play takes only a few minutes.

dealer will scrupulously do the rest. (I have seen a dealer assist a blind man to play, and one too arthritic to handle his own cards.) A great range of player effort is thus managed neatly by the same organization of play. This means that a player can start out very attentively watching all that happens and making elaborate calculations, find himself getting weary beyond measure after eight or nine hours of play, or drunk to the point where attendants must prop him up to prevent his falling out of his chair, and yet by merely making a few relevant gestures remain active in his gambling capacity. The organization of play in casinos is designed to service with action not only persons of widely different social status, but also those in widely differing physiological states.

Beyond these various organizational arrangements, there is the central fact that casinos, within very broad limits, routinely cover bets of any size. The player can therefore put his capital in jeopardy regardless of its size. He is assured of the opportunity of facing the excitement of a little more financial risk and opportunity than most persons of his means would be at ease with. Casinos concretely embody arrangements for allowing the individual to press himself to the margin of his own tolerance for loss or gain, thereby ensuring a real and close test, at least in his own eyes.

Some specific arrangements outside of casinos for efficiently generating opportunities for action might be mentioned. A good example can be found in the conventions associated with bullfighting. Here, the style and grace of movement and posture, the knowledge of the work, and the domination of the bull, three central qualities exhibited in bullfighting, are scored according to the danger to self that is voluntarily introduced by oneself during the movements. The extreme limits to safety must therefore be pressed:

In modern bullfighting it is not enough that the bull be simply dominated by the muleta so that he may be killed by the sword. The matador must perform a series of classic passes before he kills if the bull is still able to charge. In these passes the bull must pass the body of the matador within hooking range of the horn. The closer the bull passes the man at the man's invitation and direction the greater the thrill the spectator receives.[79]

Bullfighting is the only art in which the artist is in danger of death and in which the degree of brilliance in the performance is left to the fighter's honor. In Spain honor is a very real thing. Called pundonor, it means honor, probity, courage, self-respect and pride in one word.[80]

A somewhat similar set of arrangements can be found as the basis of action in car racing. Typically, difference in mere capacity for speed of cars similarly classed is not relevant enough to win races. A driver wins by more frequently approaching the limits where speed will take his car out of control than the other drivers are competent or daring enough to approach.[81] In fact, it is the possibility of restructuring routine activity so as to allow limits-pressing that transforms routine activity into a field of action. For example, on the highway cars often spread themselves out in a pattern whose stability is produced by each driver assessing what other drivers would not dare to do, and then, in effect, patrolling these limits; one's place in the traffic is therefore sustained. To "make time" on the road when traffic is heavy is to press beyond

[79] E. Hemingway, "The Dangerous Summer," *Life*, September 5, 1960, p. 86.

[80] Hemingway, *Death, op. cit.*, p. 91.

[81] Moss, *op. cit.*, p. 22. "The fastest driver is the one who can come closest to the point at which the car's tyres will break adhesion to the road and let the machine go into an uncontrolled slide. ('Uncontrolled' is the key word. Much of the time, the driver has deliberately broken the car loose and is allowing it to slide, but under control.)"

the point other drivers have judged as protecting their position.[82]

If margin-pressing effort is to be possible, the equipment the actor uses may have to be restricted appropriately. After all, bullfighting could hardly test a man if a Weatherby 460 were used instead of cape and sword. Similarly, if a challenge is to be made out of crossing the ocean, one must forego liners in favor of rafts. If a fish is to be constituted into a fighting opportunity, then line, hook, and rod must be selected with the nicest of self-limitation, and often are.[83] If big game hunting is to be to risky as well as costly, then telescopic sights seem hardly "fair"; in fact, the rifle itself might better be given up for bow and arrow.

Arrangements that call forth marginal effort generate the possibility of action. One further action arrangement might be considered. It is found when a series can be created by consecutive winning turns, such that each further turn adds the same additional probability of terminating the series while adding more than the previous turn's value to the series as a whole. For example, in bowling, an individual's reputation as a bowler is related to his maximum attained score. And score is dependent on number of "strikes" during any one series or string of shots, with the score mounting more than linearly with the number of strikes made in sequence. Further, a full-scoring next shot tends to be mentally assimilated to what the individual already has achieved, so failure to achieve

---

[82] Improvement in roads and in driving qualities of cars of course merely allows the driver to be "expressive" at higher speeds; whatever the conditions of road traffic, the other's territory will always be there to be pressed.

[83] B. Gilbert, "The Moment-of-Truth Menace," *Esquire*, December 1965, p. 117. Gilbert's article is a description of how far sportsmen go to find a piece of nature that can be transformed, with proper equipment limitation, into a challenge. Cave searching and rapids-running are described as examples.

it constitutes a "blowing" of a scoring sequence that the player "had going." As the gain to be made with each bowl mounts, the difficulty of maintaining skill does likewise. Something similar is to be found in casino gambling in connection with the practice of "letting it ride," namely, betting all the previous win on the next play, and continuing to do this for a sequence of plays. He who manages to "parlay" or pyramid his wins in this way is often given respect as someone who has "nerve," is "hot," and "knows when to bet." And since the bet (in an even-money game) is being doubled each time, the fifth or sixth straight win will be very much heavier than the second or third. And so the player finds that money and psychic gain increase more than arithmetically, while at the same time ever new opportunities for total loss must be faced.

A final issue must be raised concerning the organizational basis of action. Earlier I suggested that persons present in a social situation can serve not only as witnesses but also as the very objects upon which the individual acts, and that his record in this regard will be of special significance. When these other-involving acts entail fateful chances intentionally created just so they can be taken, then a special type of action results in which the persons who are present to the actor themselves provide the field for his action. Hemingway provides a wonderfully crude illustration, one that is also provided by circus performers who throw knives, and small boys who throw snow balls:

> One of the attractions Mary had set up in the park was a shooting booth she had hired from a traveling carnival. Antonio had been a little shocked in 1956 when Mario, the Italian chauffeur, had held up cigarettes in his hand in a gale of wind for me to cut off their lighted ends with a .22 rifle. At the party Antonio held cigarettes in his mouth for me to shoot the ashes off. We did this seven times with the shooting

gallery's tiny rifles and at the end he was puffing the cigarettes down to see how short he could make them.

Finally he said, "Ernesto, we've gone as far as we can go. The last one just brushed my lips."

The Maharaja of Cooch-Behar became another addict of this light-hearted amusement. He started conservatively using a cigarette holder but abandoned it immediately for the puffing school. I quit while I was still ahead and refused to shoot at George Saviers because he was the only doctor in the house and the party was just under way. It went a long way.[84]

While one person is providing a field of action for another, that other can in turn use the first individual as his field of action. When this reciprocity of use is found and the object is to exercise a skill or ability of some kind, we speak of a contest or duel. What occurs at these scenes might be called *interpersonal action*.[85]

Interpersonal action seems occasionally merely to duplicate the ordinary kind. In a pistol duel, for example, one

[84] Hemingway, "Summer," *op. cit.*, September 12, p. 76.

[85] Typically, contest arrangements require contestants to be face to face, but there are, for example, courtship contests between two suitors for the same hand wherein the opponents never meet; there are contests in the letters-to-the-editor column, and there are others (as Hemingway suggests), where the record of one party, who may be absent at the time, becomes the context of action of the other ("Summer," *op. cit.*, September 5, pp. 91–92.): "Bullfighting is worthless without rivalry. But with two great bullfighters it becomes a deadly rivalry. Because when one does something, and can do it regularly, that no one else can do and it is not a trick but a deadly dangerous performance only made possible by perfect nerves, judgment, courage and art and this one increases its deadliness steadily, then the other, if he has any temporary failure of nerves or of judgment, will be gravely wounded or killed if he tries to equal or surpass it. He will have to resort to tricks and when the public learns to tell the tricks from the true things he will be beaten in the rivalry and he will be very lucky if he is still alive or in business."

individual is the passive target field for the other, while at the same time the other is the passive target field for the first—excepting, of course, the minor stratagems of standing at an angle to present the least surface to the opponent, and using the arms as shield for the heart. In fact, a pistol duel can be analysed as an arrangement for collapsing together two separable functions: target competition and a payoff scheme for winners and losers. More often, however, reciprocality is more intimate and more interesting. The very act by which one participant exercises his capacities in the face of the other can itself provide the field for the other's competing or countering action. The figure one participant cuts will be cut out of the figure the other participant cuts. Even in Hemingway's target amusements there is a flavor of this: the coolness exhibited by Antonio in submitting to the target role requires for its field of action the marksman efforts of Hemingway.

Just as there are social arrangements for ensuring action, so there are arrangements for ensuring interpersonal action. An important example is the widespread practice of handicapping in contests.[86] This device ensures that however badly matched the contestants may be, each will have about the same chance of winning or losing and each will have to depend on pushing himself to the limit. The outcome is thus guaranteed to be not only unpredictable and therefore attention sustaining, but also a matter of *marginal effort,* the win going to the contestant who pushes himself closer to his limits than the others push themselves to theirs. The last extra bit of effort determines outcome. A handicap contest, then, is an arrangement nicely calculated to transform two individuals into fields of action for each other, with the additional bite that one person's success must be balanced by the other person's failure. It might be added that self-imposed equipment limitation in hunting and fishing can also be seen as

[86] E. Goffman, "Fun in Games," p. 67 in *Encounters* (Indianapolis, Bobbs-Merrill, 1961).

a type of handicapping; the prey is transformed into an opponent and a "fair" (or rather, almost fair) contest results. Fair games require fair game.

In various games and sports, then, individuals may use one another as fields of action, usually, in a segregated arena, physically and temporally cut off from serious life. But obviously the mutual use of one another as a field of action is more general. As a bridge from games to the world let us glance at dealings between the sexes.

All of the situations of action described so far are much more the scene of male activity than of female; indeed, action in our Western culture seems to belong to the cult of masculinity—in spite of lady bullfighters, female aerialists, and a preponderance of females in the slot machine pits of casinos.[87] There are records of a few duels fought by European women, but these encounters seem to be held up as a perversion of the fair sex, not its ornament.[88] But, of course, females are involved in one kind of action in a special way; they are the fields of play for sexual and

[87] Masculinity seems especially important as a value in Latin society, and as a value can hardly be dissociated from its basis in the biological aspects of sex. See "Honour and Social Status," by J. Pitt-Rivers, ch. 1, p. 45, in *Honour and Shame* (Chicago, University of Chicago Press, 1966, ed. J. Peristiany): "Thus restraint is the natural basis of sexual purity, just as masculinity is the natural basis of authority and the defense of family honour. The ideal of the honourable man is expressed by the word *hombría*, "manliness". . . . Masculinity means courage whether it is employed for moral or immoral ends. It is a term which is constantly heard in the *pueblo*, and the concept is expressed as the physical sexual quintessence of the male (*cojones*). The contrary notion is conveyed by the adjective *manso* which means both tame and also castrated. Lacking the physiological basis, the weaker sex cannot obviously be expected to possess it, and it is excluded from the demands of female honour." Presumably the female counterparts of the classic male virtues involve modesty, restraint and virginity, whose display would seem to comprise anything but action.

[88] R. Baldick, *The Duel* (London, Chapman and Hall, 1965), ch. 11, "Women Duellists," pp. 169–78.

courtship action. Adult males may define a female as an object to initiate a sexually potential relationship with. The risk is rebuff, misalliance, responsibility, betrayal of prior relationships, or displeasure of other males; the opportunity is for the kind of confirmation of self that success in this area alone can bring. This action is sometimes called "making out."

In our society there are special times and places set aside for making out: parties, bars,[89] dances, resorts, parks, classrooms, public events, association meetings, office coffee-breaks, church gatherings, and public streets of ill repute. Making out itself is of two kinds, according to whether the circle in which it occurs contains persons who are acquainted or unacquainted. Among the acquainted we find flirtatious exchanges and the initiation of affairs; among the unacquainted, interchanges of signs of interest and pickings-up.

Among the unacquainted, organizational facilitation of making out takes many forms: the institution of social hostess at resorts; telephone bars; bartender mediation in the buy-you-a-drink routine; etc. I cite at length the situation in Nevada casinos.

Casino tables are by definition open to any adult with money to spend. In spite of the apparent impersonality of the operation, strangers at the same table find that a slight camaraderie is generated by a joint and mutually visible exposure to fate. Big bettors, with an implied involvement because of the size of their bets, and the implied status of the visibly moneyed, render themselves somewhat accessible to fellow players and even to watchers. Imputed mutual responsibility for outcome (in the limited but constant sense in which this is imputed) adds to mutual

[89] A close statement is found in Sherri Cavan, *Liquor License* (Chicago, Aldine Press, 1966). See also J. Roebuck and S. Spray, "The Cocktail Lounge: A Study of Heterosexual Relations in a Public Organization," *American Journal of Sociology*, January 1967.

exposure and relatedness. And between the sexes additional openness prevails. Males can almost always give a little free advice to neighboring females, gradually joining with them into a coalition of hope against the dealer. Further, if a female happens to play in a way that can be interpreted as profitable to all, a bet can easily be "put up" for her and mutual involvement heightened. Similarly, when acquaintance with a female is struck up, she can be treated to play without obviously compromising her position. Her keeping all or some of her wins can then seem natural. Tables thus provide the first move in the acquaintance game and also a very graceful cover under which cash payment can be made in advance for social and sexual favors granted later in an uncommercial manner. Thus is making out organizationally facilitated.

It should be noted that there are many males who shy away from actively involving themselves in making out, even when attending places established for the purpose. There are many others who are everywhere on the lookout for these opportunities, whether in the home, at places of work, or in service contacts. And they face each day with such potentialities in mind.[90] These chronically oriented males must be classed with those who are ready to transform any event into a betting proposition, or any task into a contest of strength, skill, or knowledge.

Attempts to initiate a sex-potential relationship are, of course, only one variety of the interpersonal action that occurs in the community at large. Another important type occurs when the individual serves as a field for action by virtue of his capacity to receive and give injury of both a physical and a verbal kind. To find those who indulge

[90] Although the notion of action is certainly relevant to heterosexual contacts, it seems even more relevant to homosexual ones. Gay society apparently features the one night stand (or rather, part-of-the-night stand), much more so than straight society, with a correspondingly high rate of contingency and chance-taking regarding relationship formation.

in this sport we are likely to look to "outsiders" who, like
adolescents, have not been tightly woven into organizational structures. Presumably among them these fateful activities will be least disruptive and the most tolerable; it is
a case of having little to lose, or little to lose yet, a case of
being well organized for disorganization. The study of
corner gangs of aggressive, alienated urban youth provides
an illustration:

> The quickened tempo of the testing of relationships
> on corners, in contrast with, for example, work groups,
> arises in part because leaders do not control impor-
> tant amounts of property, because there are few
> privileges or immunities they can bestow, and be-
> cause there are no external institutional pressures that
> constrain members to accept the discipline of the
> gang.[91]

Among such youths the notion of "kicks" has its fullest
bearing. Here the culture and cultivation of recognized
sports is not present to mask the gratuitousness of the
chance-taking; the community itself is transformed into a
field for action, with special use made of peers, unpro-
tected adults, and persons perceived as symbols of police
authority. Walter Miller provides a good statement:

> Many of the most characteristic features of lower class
> life are related to the search for excitement or
> "thrill." Involved here are the highly prevalent use
> of alcohol by both sexes and the widespread use of
> gambling of all kinds—playing the numbers, betting
> on horse races, dice, cards. The quest for excitement
> finds what is perhaps its most vivid expression in the
> highly patterned practice of the recurrent "night on
> the town." This practice, designated by various terms
> in different areas ("honky-tonkin'," "goin' out on the
> town," "bar hoppin'"), involves a patterned set of
> activities in which alcohol, music, and sexual adven-

[91] J. Short and F. Strotbeck, *Group Process and Gang Delinquency* (Chicago, Chicago University Press, 1965), p. 196.

turing are major components. A group or individual sets out to "make the rounds" of various bars or night clubs. Drinking continues progressively throughout the evening. Men seek to "pick up" women, and women play the risky game of entertaining sexual advances. Fights between men involving women, gambling, and claims of physical prowess, in various combinations, are frequent consequences of a night of making the rounds. The explosive potential of this type of adventuring with sex and aggression, frequently leading to "trouble," is semi-explicitly sought by the individual. Since there is always a good likelihood that being out on the town will eventuate in fights, etc., the practice involves elements of sought risk and desired danger.[92]

A student of lower-class Boston Italians provides another statement:

For the action-seeker, life is episodic. The rhythm of life is dominated by the adventurous episode, in which heights of activity and feeling are reached through exciting and sometimes riotous behavior. The goal is action, an opportunity for thrills, and for the chance to face and overcome a challenge. It may be sought in a card game, a fight, a sexual interlude, a drinking bout, a gambling session, or in a fast and furious exchange of wisecracks and insults. Whatever the episode, the action-seeker pursues it with a vengeance, and lives the rest of his life in quiet—and

[92] Miller, *op. cit.*, p. 11. An early statement of the excitement theme in delinquency is to be found in F. Thrasher, *The Gang* (Chicago, University of Chicago Press, first published, 1927), ch. 5, "The Quest for New Experience." A more current version is to be found in H. Finestone, "Cats, Kicks, and Color," *Social Problems*, 5 (1957), esp. p. 5, who describes a group that combines disdain for the work world with a strong concern for the expression of coolness in the face of trouble. Similarly, the "focal concerns" that Miller imputes to lower class urban culture (trouble, toughness, smartness, excitement, fate, autonomy) seem very suited to support involvement in action.

often sullen—preparation for this climax, in which he is usually said to be "killing time."[93]

VIII. Character

Beginning with a boy's chance-taking, we moved on to consequentiality; from there to fatefulness of the dutiful kind (noting that this could lead to construing the situation as a practical gamble voluntarily undertaken); and from there to action—a species of activity in which self-determination is celebrated. And we saw that the fatefulness, which many persons avoid, others for some reason approve, and there are those who even construct an environment in which they can indulge it. Something meaningful and peculiar seems to be involved in action. Hemingway's description of the human situation of one of his favorite bullfighters provides a hint of what we must look for:

> We had spoken about death without being morbid about it and I had told Antonio what I thought about it, which is worthless since none of us knows anything about it, I could be sincerely disrespectful of it and sometimes impart this disrespect to others, but I was not dealing with it at this time. Antonio gave it out at least twice a day, sometimes for every day in the week, traveling long distances to do it. Each day he deliberately provoked the danger of it to himself,

[93] H. Gans, *The Urban Villagers* (New York, The Free Press, 1962), p. 29. He presents a further discussion of the appeals of action on pp. 65–69. In the literature the argument is often made that adolescent males must develop and demonstrate manliness and that the search for action serves this end. It is argued in this paper that manliness is a complex of qualities better called "character," and that it is this that must be considered in the analysis of adolescent "acting out." In any case, as Bennett Berger points out ("On the Youthfulness of Youth Culture," *Social Research*, 30 [1963], 326–27), action orientation involves a concern not only for maleness but also for youth.

and prolonged that danger past the limits it could normally be endured, by his style of fighting. He could only fight and he did by having perfect nerves and never worrying. For his way of fighting, without tricks, depended on understanding the danger and controlling it by the way he adjusted himself perfectly to the bull's speed, or lack of it, and the control of the bull by his wrist which was governed by his muscles, his nerves, his reflexes, his eyes, his knowledge, his instinct and his courage.

If there was anything wrong with his reflexes he could not fight in this way. If his courage ever failed for the smallest fraction of a second, the spell would be broken and he would be tossed or gored. In addition, he had the wind to contend with which could expose him to the bull and kill him capriciously at any time.

He knew all these things coldly and completely and our problem was to reduce the time that he had to think about them to the minimum necessary for him to prepare himself to face them before entering the ring. This was Antonio's regular appointment with death that we have to face each day. Any man could face death but to be committed to bring it as close as possible while performing certain classic movements and do this again and again and then deal it out yourself with a sword to an animal weighing half a ton, which you love, is more complicated than just facing death. It is facing your performance as a creative artist each day and your necessity to function as a skillful killer. Antonio had to kill quickly and mercifully and still give the bull one full chance at it when he crossed over the horn at least twice a day.[94]

If one examines moments when an individual undergoes these chances, whether as part of serious work or dangerous play, certain capacities, certain properties of

[94] E. Hemingway, "The Dangerous Summer," *Life*, September 12, 1960, pp. 75–76.

his make-up, appear to be of intrinsic or "primary" relevance: in high construction work, care and balance; in mountain climbing, "condition," and stamina; in bullfighting, timing and perceptual judgment; in game hunting, aim; in gambling, a knowledge of the odds; and in all cases, memory and experience. Often these primary capacities can be created by training. Significantly, the same capacities can be exercised during unconsequential circumstances, when the chancy features of actual occasions are avoided altogether or merely simulated. Thus one finds dry runs, target practice, trial efforts, war games, and stage rehearsals. Organized training uses this kind of simulation extensively. Here a good or bad showing need not be fateful in itself nor in its effect on the reputation of the actor. Similarly, primary capacities can often be exercised on occasions when effective performance is easily and unthinkingly achieved, when, in brief, the results are consequential but not problematic.

Under perceivedly fateful circumstances—consequential and problematic—and *only* in close connection with them, a second set of capacities or properties appear. An individual's sudden sense of what might shortly occur can have a marked effect on his behavior, with respect to both social ties and task performance. In the case of relations to others, the principled behavior he manages to exhibit during ordinary occasions may break down. The quick consciousness of what his principles are costing him at the moment may cause his wonted decency to falter, and in the heat and haste of the moment, naked self-interest may obtrude. Or, contrariwise, the sudden high cost of correct behavior may serve only to confirm his principledness. Similarly, in the matter of task performance, his imagining to himself the consequence of failing or succeeding can work strongly upon his capacity to exercise the primary capacities in question. The imminent possibilities may make him nervous, incapable of drawing on what he knows, and incapable of organized action;[95] on the other hand, the challenge may cause him to mobilize his energies and perform above himself. In contrast to Hemingway's friend Antonio, there is Jose Martinez who, upon his debut as a matador at Murcia, on entrance of the bull, fainted.[96]

These capacities (or lack of them) for standing correct and steady in the face of sudden pressures are crucial; they do not specify the activity of the individual, but how he will manage himself in this activity. I will refer to these maintenance properties as an aspect of the individual's *character*. Evidence of incapacity to behave effectively and correctly under the stress of fatefulness is a sign of *weak* character. He who manifests average, expected ability does not seem to be judged sharply in terms of character. Evidence of marked capacity to maintain full self control when the chips are down—whether exerted in regard to moral temptation or task performance—is a sign of *strong* character.

Primary properties and those of character both contribute to the reputation an individual acquires; both are

[95] J. L. Austin, in his "Pleas for Excuses" (*Philosophical Papers*, ed. J. Urmson and G. Warnock; Oxford, Oxford University Press, 1961), p. 141, discussing the various "departments into which the business of doing actions is organized," suggests: "There is for example the stage at which we have actually to *carry out* some action upon which we embark—perhaps we have to make certain bodily movements or to make a speech. In the course of actually *doing* these things (getting weaving) we have to pay (some) attention to what we are doing and to take (some) care to guard against (likely) dangers: we may need to use judgement or tact: we must exercise sufficient control over our bodily parts: and so on. Inattention, carelessness, errors of judgement, tactlessness, clumsiness, all these and others are ills (with attendant excuses) which affect one specific stage in the machinery of action, the *executive* stage, the stage where we *muff* it."

[96] Reported by Charles McCabe, *San Francisco Chronicle*, June 2, 1966.

therefore consequential. But there are important differences between the two. As suggested, primary qualities can be expressed in a situation that is not fateful; qualities of character—in the aspects considered here—emerge only during fateful events, or at least events subjectively considered to be fateful. One may approve of, disapprove of, or be morally neutral toward primary qualities. Properties of character, however, are always judged from a moral perspective, simply because a capacity for mobilizing oneself for the moment is always subjected to social evaluation. And, in contrast to primary properties, character traits tend to be evaluated in the extremes, referring to failures in no way expected or successes out of the ordinary; mere conformance with usual standards is not the issue. Finally, unlike primary traits, those of character tend to be "essentializing," fully coloring our picture of the person so characterized, and (as we will see later) a single expression tends to be taken as an adequate basis for judgment.

Consider some of the major forms of character that bear on the management of fateful events.

First, there are various forms of *courage*, namely, the capacity to envisage immediate danger and yet proceed with the course of action that brings the danger on. The variations are established by the nature of the risk, for example, whether physical, financial, social, or spiritual. Thus, among professional gamblers, there is respect for a quality called "gamble," namely, a willingness to submit to the rules of the game while chancing a major portion of one's current capital—presumably with the grace to carry off the win or loss circumspectly. Note that the interests served by courageous actions may be quite selfish; the issue is the actor's readiness to face great risk.

There is *gameness*, the capacity to stick to a line of activity and to continue to pour all effort into it regardless of set-backs, pain, or fatigue, and this not because of some brute insensitivity but because of inner will and determination. Boxers provide a version:

> There is also a cult of a kind of persevering courage, called a "fighting heart," which means "never admitting defeat." The fighter learns early that his exhibited courage—his ability, if necessary, to go down fighting—characterizes the respected, audience-pleasing boxer. He must cherish the lingering hope that he can win by a few more punches.[97]

It should be added that persons are not alone, and perhaps not even first, in this matter of showing heart. Bulls, properly bred, wonderfully have it; that is why they accept the matches made for them and continue to fight from an increasingly weakening position, and that is why there can be bullfights. Race horses, under a special reading of the term "class," can have it too.[98]

A fundamental trait of personal character from the point of view of social organization is *integrity*, meaning here the propensity to resist temptation in situations where there would be much profit and some impugnity in departing momentarily from moral standards. Integrity seems especially important during fateful activity that is not witnessed by others. Although societies differ widely in the kinds of character they approve, no society could long persist if its members did not approve and foster this quality. Everyone tends to claim a high standard of integrity, however rarely realized; excellence in this regard is taken for granted, and it is persons who fall short who are the ones to be designated, in this case, as having weak characters.[99] (We can find examples of integrity therefore in the littlest corners of life: when a salesperson touts an unsuitable product with less persuasion than he could have

[97] Winberg and Arond, *op. cit.*, p. 462.
[98] See M. Scott, *The Racing Game* (Chicago, Aldine Books, 1968).
[99] I am grateful to Marvin Scott for suggestions concerning the special place of integrity as a property of character.

mustered; when a girl does not break a date that sudden opportunity has made disadvantageous; when a school child admits to an offense others would have been thought guilty of; when a cab driver or barber gives back three dollars *in bills* when a two-dollar debt is paid with a five.) Somewhat similar comments can be made about "self-discipline," the capacity to refrain from excessive involvement in the easy pleasures of the table—whether in a bar, restaurant, or casino.

Earlier it was suggested that social situations carry in themselves some reputational implications, especially in connection with the standards that participants are obliged to maintain in their dealings with one another. It was said that this consequentiality was usually not problematic. However, here we must see that circumstances can sometimes render it so.

For example, the continued maintenance of the ceremonial order can occasionally become very costly, producing the questionable privilege of displaying a special version of integrity. At these times the individual will have to decide whether or not to give in under pressure, whether or not to let standards lapse. *Gallantry* refers to the capacity to maintain the forms of courtesy when the forms are full of substance. It is shown when Douglas Fairbanks, in the middle of a cinematic duel to the death, retrieves his opponent's fallen sword and hands it to him with a polite bow, the better to prevent a meaningless advantage from cutting short the opportunity for valid expression. Other competitions provide similar opportunities:

It was in 1902 that the British then-champion, Selwyn F. Edge, driving in the Paris-Vienna race, punctured an inner tube and was forced to stop for repairs. He soon discovered, however, that the tire pump which his car carried would not work. Without it, the tube could not be inflated and the car could not continue.

At this moment, the colorful Count Louis Zborowski

220

came along the road in a Mercedes, took in the situation at a glance, pulled up next to Edge's car and tossed his own tire pump to his rival. Edge went on to win the Gordon Bennett cup. Zborowski was second.[100]

It is interesting that examples of gallantry are usually of the kind I have cited, and neglect the place of this property in everyday life. In fact, a shopkeeper is gallant when he unnecessarily *and politely* refunds a large sale for a tourist who suddenly has had misgivings. Certainly a stand-by passenger is gallant when he voluntarily gives up the second last seat so that a youthful pair next in line can stay together and yet not be stranded.[101]

Gallantry, of course, is not the only quality of character that is found in connection with the costly and problematic maintenance of the ceremonial order. Just as the individual owes others courtesies, so they owe courtesies to him, and should they fail to treat him properly he may find he must risk retaliatory acts in order to show that advantage cannot be taken of him. In contemporary times the police provide excellent illustrations of this theme, since sometimes they feel they must pledge their fists, their

---

[100] S. Davis, "Chivalry on the Road," pp. 32–33, in Beaumont and Nolan, eds., *op. cit.*

[101] In casinos, gallantry is institutionalized and made the special right and obligation of the pit boss. Bets whose outcome is disputed are adjudicated by him, and the traditional, preferred style is gently to suggest to the customer how the fault could be or is his, and then when the dealer has been thusly cleared, to graciously allow the decision to go against the house. I have seen pit bosses thus conduct themselves when the bet was large enough to appreciably count in the table's take for the shift. Here of course the casino itself is concerned to acquire and sustain a reputation for what in this context is called "class," the opposite of being "cheap." (A general treatment of organizational character is provided in P. Selznick, *Leadership in Administration* [White Plains, Row, Petterson, 1957], especially pp. 38–42.)

clubs, and even their guns to ensure a nice deference from those they arrest or otherwise accost.[102]

Retaliatory acts of this sort assume, of course, that the offended person has ample authority and resources. When this is not the case then he may feel obliged to sacrifice his own substance to maintain the forms. Gallantry in reverse results: not costly courtesy but costly contempt. In the mythic extreme, dutifully employed in many action novels, the hero, stripped and bound to a chair, spits or at least sneers into the face of the villain who threatens death and torture; the hero voluntarily exacerbates a precarious situation in order to show distaste for the villain's presumption and style. More realistically, we find that servers of all kinds know that if the value of their service or of their selves is disputed, they can with majesty decline any payment or can even ask the customer to take his patronage elsewhere—a matter of cutting off one's nose in order to destroy the other's face. These pyrrhic victories are often disapproved of, along with the quality of character felt to be responsible for exacting them. And no doubt such incidents do not actually occur frequently. Yet stories of their occurrence are everywhere and seem to play a significant role in maintaining the self-respect of servers and the self-restraint of those they serve.

Of all the qualities of character associated with the management of fatefulness, the one of most interest for this essay is *composure*, that is, self-control, self-possession, or poise. This attribute is doubly consequential, for it directly effects the functioning of a primary property and is a source of reputation in its own right.

Composure has a behavioral side, a capacity to execute physical tasks (typically involving small muscle control) in a concerted, smooth, self-controlled fashion under fate-

---

[102] See W. Westley, "Violence and the Police," *American Journal of Sociology*, LIX (1953), 39–40.

ful circumstances. Money-making at pool provides an example:

> On the other hand, the hustler must have "heart" (courage). The *sine qua non* is that he is a good "money player," can play his best when heavy action is riding on the game (as many non-hustlers can't). Also, he is not supposed to let a bad break or distractions in the audience upset him. (He may pretend to get rattled on such occasions, but that's just part of his con.) Nor should the quality of his game deteriorate when, whether by miscalculation on his part or otherwise, he finds himself much further behind than he would like to be.[103]

One example of what this capacity is *not* might be cited:

> A nervous man wearing a trench coat and dark glasses stood at the check-cashing booth of the Safeway store at 4940 Mission Street last night.
>
> Reaching in his pocket, he pulled out a .32 caliber blue steel automatic. Or at least he tried. The gun caught on the pocket, firing a shot into the baseboard of the cashier's booth.
>
> Some 15 customers and ten clerks stared at the man. He licked his lips nervously.
>
> "This is a holdup," he blurted to cashier Rose Catelli, 30, of 579 Naples Street. "I want all the money in the safe."
>
> Whereupon he turned and bolted from the store, with manager Val Andreacchi and clerk Tom Holt in pursuit.
>
> Without even a glance back, the gunman wildly fired three or four more shots as he sprinted half a block up an alley to London Street, jumped into his car and sped away.[104]

Composure also has what is thought of as an affective side, the emotional self-control required in dealing with

---

[103] Polksy, *op. cit.*, p. 10.
[104] *San Francisco Chronicle*, November 17, 1963.

others. Actually what seems to be involved here is physical control of the organs employed in discourse and gesture. Sir Harold Nicolson, reviewing the qualities required of the professional diplomat provides illustrations:

> A third quality which is essential to the ideal diplomatist is the quality of calm. Not only must the negotiator avoid displaying irritation when confronted by the stupidity, dishonesty, brutality or conceit of those with whom it is his unpleasant duty to negotiate, but he must eschew all personal animosities, all personal predilections, all enthusiasms, prejudices, vanities, exaggerations, dramatizations, and moral indignations. . . .
>
> The quality of calm, as applied to the ideal diplomatist, should express itself in two major directions. In the first place he should be good-tempered, or at least he should be able to keep his ill-temper under perfect control. In the second place he should be quite exceptionally patient.
>
> The occasions on which diplomatists have lost their tempers are remembered with horror by generations of their successors. Napoleon lost his temper with Metternich in the Marcolini Palace at Dresden on June 26, 1813, and flung his hat upon the carpet with the most unfortunate results. Sir Charles Euan Smith lost his temper with the Sultan of Morocco and tore up a treaty in the imperial presence. Count Tattenbach lost his temper at the Algeciras Conference and exposed his country to a grave diplomatic humiliation. Herr Stinnes lost his temper at Spa.[105]

These men "flooded out," ceased to be their own masters, becoming, along with their principals, subject to control by others.

Along with the value of smooth movements and unruffled emotions, we can consider that of mental calmness and

[105] H. Nicolson, *Diplomacy* (New York, Oxford University Press, Galaxy Books, 1964), p. 62.

alertness, that is, *presence of mind*. This competency is important for the proper execution of many impersonal tasks, as, for example, examinations. These are meant to be a sampling device for uncovering a just and only-to-be-expected outcome. But, in fact, one's test score depends on mobilizing memory and knowledge under pressure and then fashioning an orderly comprehensive answer in less than comfortable time; the opposite of what is sometimes called "blocking."[106] Presence of mind is also important in tasks that involve other persons directly. This kind of presence of mind is what people known as wits have and the self-conscious person does not. Books of famous *mots*, brilliant statements of tact, and effective "squelches" and "put-downs" attest to the general interest in this mindedness.

Composure has still another side, the capacity to contemplate abrupt change in fate—one's own and, by extension, others'—without loss of emotional control, without becoming "shook up."[107]

Composure also has a bodily side, sometimes called *dignity*, that is, the capacity to sustain one's bodily decorum in the face of costs, difficulties, and imperative urges.[108]

[106] As part of socialization, school tests may be important not because of what pupils must learn to take them but what they may learn in the taking of them. For here, at least in our society, is perhaps the most important early training in performing difficult tasks under time-limited conditions, such that lack of mental composure is likely itself to use up limited time and to further increase its own production. Interestingly, in our society formal tests requiring *physical* composure under difficult circumstances seem to come much later in life, when at all.

[107] A consideration of this issue is given in B. Glaser and A. Strauss, *Awareness of Dying* (Chicago, Aldine, 1965, ch. 13, "Awareness and the Nurse's Composure"), pp. 226–56.

[108] Dignity can make news. Thus a *Sun-Times* release (with picture) April 17, 1953: "Viviane Romance, French screen star who refused to let actor spit in her face and curse her in movie scene, was fined $11,428 for breach of contract in Paris. Star

Here the sport of surfing (even more than skiing) is of special interest. Physical aplomb and the dignity of upright posture must be maintained on a flat narrow board against rumbling forces that press to the limit the human capacity for this kind of bodily self-control. Here the maintenance of physical poise is not merely a condition of effective performance but a central purpose of it.

A final aspect of composure might be considered: *stage confidence*—the capacity to withstand the dangers and opportunities of appearing before large audiences without becoming abashed, embarrassed, self-conscious, or panicky. Behind this is the special type of poise that pertains to dealing with the contingency of being under the observation of others while in an easily discredited role. An interesting variation is honored in the undercover world of agents, plainclothesmen, and criminals, where it may be necessary to "act natural" before a critical audience when one knows that in a few seconds the whole show may be up. It is written of one of New York's best burglars that, just after making a very big score on the tenth floor of a hotel:

> He walked back down to the ninth floor and took the elevator to the lobby. With what police call "the nerves of a burglar," he let the doorman call him a cab. "It was the first time in my life I couldn't tip the doorman," he told the police. "My pockets were so full of jewelry that I couldn't reach for any change. It was very embarrassing."[109]

Here an important set of assumptions is involved. Persons who have good reason to fear that they may be appre-

said action was 'beneath my dignity.'" A nice example of conduct some would think undignified may be found in Lillian Ross's *Picture* (New York, Dolphin Books, 1962), wherein she describes the menial tasks that Albert Band apparently performed as the assistant to John Huston and Gottfried Reinhardt. See especially pp. 32–57, 91–97.

[109] Black, *op. cit.*, p. 118.

hended shortly are inclined to bolt for it or at least look out constantly for possible danger. These quite natural tendencies can be held in check, but rarely without leaving some trace of agitation. Authorities, seeking among the apparently innocent for the actually guilty, will therefore be rightly inclined to check up on persons who appear wary, or anxious without visible cause. To look self-conscious, then, is to break the cover of "looking like anyone else." But should the individual sense that his appearance is giving him away, he will feel he has further cause to be fearful. Suppressing the urge to leave the field that this new fear creates will generate still further signs of unnaturalness, which in turn will have their circular effect.

Composure in all its different dimensions has traditionally been associated with the aristocratic ethic. In recent years, however, a version of this quality has been strongly touted by raffish urban elements under the label "coolness." Sir Harold might be disinclined to the locution but his advice to an errant diplomatist could be accurately expressed by saying, "Baby, don't blow your cool."[110] The significant point here is that we find composure a concern and a value in many different cultures and across many different strata. There seem to be two major reasons for this.

First, whenever an individual is in the immediate pres-

---

[110] Yet contemporary coolness seems to have a shading all its own. The phrasing employed assumes that although coolness is a personal trait, the possessor is in an estranged relation to it, since retaining it will always be problematic. Just as a wallet can be lost, so can one's cool. Also, the term is extended to cover not merely involvement in disruptive matters but involvement in anything at all—on the assumption apparently that for those whose social position is vulnerable, any concern for anything can be misfortunate, indifference being the only defensible tack. Finally, in the phrase "to cool it," an injunction is conveyed against behavior that might excite undesired response from others and hence, by extension, increase the threat to one's own situation and in consequence one's own cool. I might add that certain slum styles of discourse have so penetrated upwards, that language Sir Harold abjures is no doubt being employed by his hippier colleagues as evidence of their connection with the world.

ence of others, especially when he is cooperatively involved with them—as in, for example, the joint maintenance of a state of talk—his capacity as a competent interactant is important to them. The social order sustained in the gathering draws its ingredients, its substance, from disciplined small behaviors. His contribution of proper demeanor is melded in with the contribution of the others to produce socially organized co-presence. He will have to maintain command of himself if he is to make himself available to the affairs at hand and not disrupt them. Discomposure will disqualify him for these duties and threaten the jointly sustained world that the others feel they have a right to be in.

Second, whether or not the individual is in the presence of others, any task he performs involves the practiced easy use of human faculties—mind, limbs, and, especially, small muscles. Often this management must be acquired and sustained under very special circumstances: any temporary failure of control due to concern about the situation will itself provide a reason for still more self-consciousness and hence still further maladroitness and so on, until the individual is quite rattled and unable to handle the task. Sword swallowers provide a clear example. The touch and temperature of the blade make the unpracticed gag, which certainly renders the task impossible. Once this response is effectively suppressed, the learner finds that the sword causes his throat to close quite tight. Still further practice is required before these muscles become relaxed and the sword can pass without touching. The more the sword touches, the more likely an involuntary spasm, which will, of course, further increase the amount of touching.[111] (Correspondingly, of course, the more composed the swallower, the less the sword will touch and the less constrictive the passage will be, and so forth.) As has been suggested, a similar

[111] See D. Mannix, *Memoirs of a Sword Swallower* (New York, Ballantine Books, 1964), pp. 94–98.

predicament occurs under limited time conditions. Mal-adroitness can waste time, which further tightens the situation, which in turn gives still greater cause for dis-composure.

Because persons in all societies must transact much of their enterprise in social situations, we must expect that the capacity to maintain support of the social occasion under difficult circumstances will be universally approved. Similarly, since individuals in all societies and strata must perform tasks, the composure that this requires will eve-rywhere be of concern.

I have discriminated several bases of strong character: courage, gameness, integrity, composure. It should be ap-parent that these may be combined, producing decorations for the moral life of the community. A wireless operator who politely declines to leave his sinking ship and goes down while coolly improvising repairs on the transmitter, gamely driving himself even though his hands are burned, combines in his deed almost all that society can ask of anyone. He transmits an important message even though his S.O.S. may not get through.

Now I want to return to the suggestion that although properties of character are typically found during fateful moments, they are also exhibited during times of mere subjective fatefulness, when a fate that is already deter-mined is being disclosed and settled. The feelings gen-erated during these moments may require powers of self-control if they are to be managed well. And, of course, this self-possession will be of special importance when others are immediately present, since the orderly interac-tion they sustain would be jeopardized by the discom-posure of the fated one.

No better example can be found than the qualities exhibited by someone about to be hung, guillotined, shot, or gassed. Executions occur under conditions where the audience is quite labile, and where physical cooperation and psychic equanimity are required of the condemned man if things are to go smoothly. The lore of executions consequentially records persons who fought, twisted, spluttered, wailed, fainted, and were incontinent during the moments before their dispatch, proving thus to lack character:

> The people of York witnessed another unpleasant hanging when Joseph Terry fought, screamed and bit as the hangman tried to place the noose round his neck. Six men came on to the scaffold to hold him and eventually the rope was forced over his head, but in another struggle the cap fell off. At this moment the platform fell. Terry leaped and managed to get a foot on the edge of the scaffold, clinging to one of the corner-posts of the gallows with his arm. Here he managed to fight off the united efforts of the hangman and his assistants for a minute before they dislodged him. He died with his face uncovered in frightful contortions.[112]

[112] J. Atholl, *Shadow of the Gallows* (London, John Long, 1954), p. 77. The history of executions is typically written in evolutionary terms, starting with cruel deaths accorded for many crimes and moving to our time when humane death is administered for very few crimes, and there is much pressure to abolish the death penalty entirely. Actually, the history of executions could better be written in interaction terms, for the evolution of executionary techniques has largely to do with the development of devices and practices for ensuring a smooth social occasion. Given that the audience, the executioner, and the victim will all be on edge, how can the deed be managed so as to facilitate the self-containment of all three types of participants? The history of executionary practices is the story of the slowly accumulating answer. Take the art of hanging for example. Gallows came to be developed which could be erected silently overnight in the prison yard in order to minimize gruesome sights and sounds; a "table of drops" according to weight and condition of the neck so that the length of the free fall would neither leave a man to wriggle nor tear off his head but nicely break his neck—a knot and type of cord being designed to facilitate this adjustment; arm pinions to prevent the man from obstructing the fall; and trap doors sure to hold until the cord was pulled, sure to open quickly once it had, and (in one

Conversely, the lore tells of other performers who exchanged pleasantries with the audience, maintained the social niceties, assisted the hangman in adjusting the noose, and generally made matters easier for everyone present. Gallows humor literally does occur, as when an aristocrat, about to be guillotined, declines the traditional glass of rum, saying, "I lose all sense of direction when I'm drunk."[113]

The procedural difficulties unwilling execution victims can cause, and their general tendency to go to their death cooperatively, demonstrate the desire persons have to exhibit strong character. The condemned man is usually cooperative; he is a good sport; he is not a child; he accepts his losing game without getting into a huff or bursting into tears,[114] and can even show a fighter's heart, disdaining with a sneer to hedge his final bet in the traditional way, that is, with piety, prayer, and a request that those who remain forgive him and be forgiven.[115] This kind

---

of the nicest touches of all) designed not to bang back and forth in doleful reverberation of the fall.

It can be argued that the humaneness of the execution ought hardly to be significant for the victim, since the question of how one is shortly to be dispatched might well be considered of no importance compared to the fact that one *is* about to be dispatched. Only those who are left behind can take comfort that lasts in knowing that the end was practically painless and that no one enjoyed the terrible business of arranging it and witnessing it.

[113] A. Kershaw, *A History of the Guillotine* (London, John Calder, 1958), p. 71.

[114] Of course it is not only children who can be poor sports and lose their equanimity and hence their character when a game is lost. As a female chess expert tells it: "In one game, a player from the Netherlands suddenly had her queen snipped off the board by a Russian. She ran off the stage in tears." (Miss Lisa Lane quoted in "Talk of the Town," *The New Yorker*, September 19, 1964, p. 43.)

[115] Correlated with the trend toward "humane" dispatch there has been a decline in the demands for grace and character that we place upon the doomed. In the gas chamber in

of grace is the final and awful socialized act, for the condemned man smoothes out the social situation, supporting the most evanescent part of our social life—its social occasions—just at a time when he can very little longer share in what he is supporting. After all, others are present. Pass through the teeth of eternity if you must, but don't pick at them.

Understandably, during the days of public executions, the doomsday conduct of the condemned was closely watched and contributed importantly to his posthumous reputation. Heroes could thus be born, confirmed, and killed while dying. In communities where the possibility of execution is lively, this interest is still to be found, as Claude Brown suggests in his Harlem memoirs:

> It seemed like a whole lot of people in the neighborhood, cats that we'd come up with, gone to school with, were being cooked in Sing Sing. It had become a thing with people in the neighborhood to talk to these cats' mothers and relatives, cats who went to the electric chair in Sing Sing. I remember when I was younger, when I was at Warwick [prison] and right after I came out, I had heard about people I knew who had gone to the chair. We all wanted to know what they said because we wanted to find out something for ourselves. We wanted to find out if it was worth it at the last minute, if they felt it was worth it, now that they were going to die.
>
> When I was younger, a few years after Warwick, I wanted to know just whether these cats were really hard. I think most of the guys my age looked upon them as heroes when they were getting cooked at Sing Sing. We wanted to know their last words. Somebody told me that when they cooked Lollipop—

American prisons, the victim may be requested to breathe deeply soon after the cyanide drops, but no one would ask him to present a dying speech in the manner that was customary in the seventeenth and eighteenth centuries. (On dying speeches see Atholl, *op. cit.,* p. 56.)

Lollipop was a cat who was kind of crazy, and we called him Lollipop because he liked candy—just before he left, he said, "Well, looks like Lolly's had his last lick." That was it. Everybody admired him for the way he went out. He didn't scream or anything like that.[116]

In reviewing some of those personal qualities that influence the way an individual will perform on desperate occasions, I have suggested a connection between action and character. The relationship should not be pressed too far. Those who support a morality are likely to feel that it can be carried too far, even though society may benefit from the example provided by extreme devotion. It must also be admitted that there are certain positively valued qualities of character earned by sticking to an undramatic task over a long period of time, and, consequently, conduct during any moment cannot contain a rounded expression of the trait. Moreover, during dutiful fatefulness, as when men do battle, the self-distinguishing kind of intrepidity and grace exhibited by gamblers and race-track drivers will not be enough. As William James remarked in his praise of the military virtues, there is a need to surrender private interests and show obedience to command.[117] A crisis may call for not only those qualities of character that lead an individual to outdo others and set himself apart, but also for those that lead to his submerging himself into the immediate needs of the whole. Even self-interest may require the disciplined display of quite unheroic qualities. The money pool player provides an example:

> The hustler must restrain himself from making many of the extremely difficult shots. Such restraint is not easy, because the thrill of making a fancy shot that

116 Brown, *op. cit.*, p. 211.

117 W. James, "The Moral Equivalent of War," in his *Essays on Faith and Morals* (New York, Meridian Books, 1962), p. 323.

brings applause from the audience is hard to resist. But the hustler must resist, or else it would make less believable his misses on more ordinary shots.[118]

Here the deeper quality of character is to be able to appear under pressure to have less grace than one has. Finally, as already suggested, there are the qualities of character traditionally associated with womanhood. These oblige the female to withdraw from all frays in order to preserve her purity, ensuring that even her senses will be unsullied. Where action is required to ensure this virtue, presumably her male protector undertakes it.

I have been suggesting that while the individual is in a social situation he is exposed to judgment by the others present, and that this involves their assessing him in regard to primary capacities and to qualities of character. No picture of these reputational contingencies would be complete without considering the folk-beliefs prevalent in society regarding the nature of persons, for these beliefs provide the frame of reference for the trait-judgments made regarding the witnessed individual.

First, with properties of character, unlike primary properties, a single expression tends to be taken as definitive. Since properties of character are called for only on those rare occasions when eventfulness has not been avoided, additional corroborative or corrective manifestations are not immediately likely. Reliance, perforce, will have to be put on a sample of one. More important, it is part of the imagery of these traits that no exceptions are allowed. It is just when he is most tempted to deviate, that the individual has the most telling opportunity to be constant and thereby demonstrate his character; this constancy-in-spite-of-everything is, in fact, what character is all about. To say that lay imputations are impulsive and unsound, and that over time and across various situations the indi-

[118] Polsky, *op. cit.*, p. 9.

vidual might not, in fact, maintain the character he currently manifests, is quite true but quite beside the point. I am here not concerned with whether a given individual does or does not possess a specified characteristic, but with how notions about character function in daily life. In our dealings with another we assume that his currently expressed character is a full and lasting picture of him, and in his dealing with us he makes the same assumption as to how he will be viewed. Of course, excuses are offered, accountings given, and exceptions made; but this work is done in relation to the prior assumption that the current showing is crucial, and in any case is often incompletely effective.

Second, once evidence of strong character has been established, it need not be intentionally re-established, at least not right away; for the moment the actor can stand on his record. He can rely on others assuming that should the right occasion arise he would bear out the implications of his manner and act with character. But this, of course, adds its own danger to moral life, since we tend to operate in terms of optimistic views of ourselves, which would be discredited if ever put to the test.

Third, there is the belief that once an individual has failed in a particular way he becomes essentially different from that moment on and might just as well give up. A soldier indoctrinated with the idea that he has a will and that wills stand up entirely or are utterly broken, may tend, because of this, to divulge everything he knows during enemy interrogation, once he has divulged something.[119] Similarly, a bullfighter may be described as having lost all his valor after his first goring.[120] So, too, in

[119] A. Biderman, "Social-Psychological Needs and Involuntary Behavior as Illustrated by Compliance in Interrogation," *Sociometry*, 23 (1960), 138-39. A further statement is presented in E. Goffman, *Asylums* (New York, Doubleday Anchor Books, 1961), pp. 89-90.
[120] For example, Hemingway, *Death, op. cit.*, p. 89.

horse racing circles there is discussion of jockeys "losing their nerve" and either riding poorly thereafter or refusing to ride at all. Exemplary stories tell of famous jockeys who, feeling they had lost their nerve, proclaimed this fact and retired for life from racing.[121] Like tales are told of deep-sea divers. And detective fiction often describes tough cops and hoods who receive a severe beating and thereafter never quite have their old spunk. And, of course, there is the common belief that once a man's price has been discovered and paid, he no longer has any reliability left and might just as well accept bribes that are small but frequent.

Coupled with the belief in the "losability" of nerve, the destructibility of moral fiber, and "never-the-sameness," there is another: after long having no nerve or moral fiber, an individual can suddenly acquire "guts" or "heart," and from that point on continue to have it.

Cayetano Ordonez, Nino de la Palama, could manage the muleta perfectly with either hand, was a beautiful performer with a great artistic and dramatic sense of a faena, but he was never the same after he found the bulls carried terms in the hospital, inevitable, and death, perhaps, in their horns as well as five thousand peseta notes between their withers. He wanted the notes, but he was unwilling to approach the horns to get them when he found the forfeit that was collectable from their points. Courage comes such a short distance; from the heart to the head; but when it goes no one knows how far away it goes; in a hemorrhage, perhaps, or into a woman and it is a bad thing to be in bullfighting business when it is gone, no matter where it went. Sometimes you get it back from another wound, the first may bring fear of death and the second may take it away, and sometimes one woman takes it away and another gives it back. Bullfighters stay in the business relying on their

[121] J. Leach, "Unseated by Nerves," *The Observer*, March 3, 1963.

knowledge and their ability to limit the danger and hope the courage will come back and sometimes it does and most times it does not.[122]

In fiction and myth, redemption is often achieved only in the act that gives the individual strength enough to die for his principles, the decease of the redeemed one serving to maintain the contradictory assumptions that a fall from grace is permanent and that a broken person can mend himself.

Given the belief that character can be dramatically acquired and lost, the individual will plainly have reason for going through with a chancy situation no matter what the likely material or physical cost to himself, thereby manifesting what is sometimes called pride. Interestingly, our beliefs about nerve allow a little outside help in this matter: it is generally felt that a quick drink of straight liquor will allow a man to carry off a difficult action easier and better, and a surprising number of situations allow for such fortification.[123]

Given these arguments about the nature of character, it is possible to understand better why action seems to have a peculiar appeal. Plainly, it is during moments of action that the individual has the risk and opportunity of displaying to himself and sometimes to others his style of conduct when the chips are down. Character is gambled; a single good showing can be taken as representative, and a bad showing cannot be easily excused or re-attempted. To display or express character, weak or strong, is to generate character. The self, in brief, can be voluntarily subjected to re-creation. No doubt this license is practicable from society's viewpoint because, as clearly illustrated in connection with gamblers' "gamble," the price of putting on these shows is likely to provide an

---

[122] Hemingway, *Death*, p. 222.

[123] Execution practice is one illustration. See, for example, A. Keller, ed., *The Hangman's Diary* (London, Philip Allen, 1928), p. 8, under the phrase, *stärkenden Trunk*.

automatic check against those who might be overinclined to stage them. In any case, here is the chance to show grace under pressure; here is the opportunity to be measured by Hemingway's measure of men.

We can begin to see that action need not be perceived, in the first instance, as an expression of impulsiveness or irrationality, even where risk without apparent prize results. Loss, to be sure, is chanced through action; but a real gain of character can occur. It is in these terms that action can be seen as a calculated risk.[124] Statements (including mine) that action is an end in itself must be understood as locutions. The voluntary taking of serious chances is a means for the maintenance and acquisition of character; it is an end in itself only in relation to other kinds of purpose. To consider action literally as an end in itself would be to trivialize and truncate social explanation.

And now we begin to see character for what it is. On the one hand, it refers to what is essential and unchanging about the individual—what is *characteristic* of him. On the other, it refers to attributes that can be generated and destroyed during fateful moments. In this latter view the individual can act so as to determine the traits that will thereafter be his; he can act so as to create and establish what is to be imputed to him. Every time a moment occurs, its participants will therefore find themselves with another little chance to make something of themselves.

Thus a paradox. Character is both unchanging and changeable. And yet that is how we conceive of it.

It should be no less clear that our illogic in this matter has its social value. Social organization everywhere has the problem of morale and continuity. Individuals must come to all their little situations with some enthusiasm

---

[124] This argument has recently been made in connection with the risk entailed in extramarital sexual relations and in gang fights. See F. Strodtbeck and J. Short, "Aleatory Risks Versus Short-run Hedonism in Explanation of Gang Action," *Social Problems,* 12 (1964), 127–40.

and concern, for it is largely through such moments that social life occurs, and if a fresh effort were not put into each of them, society would surely suffer. The possibility of effecting reputation is the spur. And yet, if society is to persist, the same pattern must be sustained from one actual social occasion to the next. Here the need is for rules and conventionality. Individuals must define themselves in terms of properties already accepted as theirs, and act reliably in terms of them.

To satisfy the fundamental requirements of morale and continuity, we are encouraged in a fundamental illusion. It is our character. A something entirely our own that does not change, but is none the less precarious and mutable. Possibilities regarding character encourage us to renew our efforts at every moment of society's activity we approach, especially its social ones; and it is precisely through these renewals that the old routines can be sustained. We are allowed to think there is something to be won in the moments that we face so that society can face moments and defeat them.

IX. CHARACTER CONTESTS

Starting with the notion of fateful occupational duties, we can view action as a kind of self-oriented evocation in ritualized form of the moral scene arising when such duties are exercised. Action consists of chancy tasks undertaken for "their own sake." Excitement and character display, the by-products of practical gambles, of serious fateful scenes, become in the case of action the tacit purpose of the whole show. However, neither fateful duties nor action tell us very much about the mutual implications that can occur when one person's display of character directly bears upon another's, nor do we learn about the framework of understanding we possess for dealing with such occurrences. For this we must turn to interpersonal action.

During occasions of this kind of action, not only will character be at stake, mutual fatefulness will prevail in this regard. Each person will be at least incidentally concerned with establishing evidence of strong character, and conditions will be such as to allow this only at the expense of the character of the other participants. The very field that the one uses to express character may be the other's character expression. And at times the primary properties at play may themselves be openly made a convenience, pointedly serving merely as an occasion for doing battle by and for character. A *character contest* results; a special kind of moral game.

These engagements occur, of course, in games and sports where opponents are balanced and marginal effort is required to win. But character contests are also found under conditions less obviously designed for contesting, subjecting us all to a stream of little losses and gains. Every day in many ways we can try to score points, and every day in many ways we can be shot down. (Perhaps a slight residue remains from each of these trials, so that the moment one individual approaches another, his manner and face may betray the consequences that have been usual for him, and subtly set the interaction off on a course that develops and terminates as it always seems to do for him.) Bargaining, threatening, promising—whether in commerce, diplomacy, warfare, card games, or personal relations—allow a contestant to pit his capacity for dissembling intentions and resources against the other's capacity to rile or cajole the secretive into readability. Whenever individuals ask for or give excuses, proffer or receive compliments, slight another or are slighted, a contest of self-control can result. Similarly, the tacit little flirtations occurring between friends and between strangers produce a contest of unavailability—if usually nothing more than this. And when banter occurs or "remarks" are exchanged, someone will have out-poised another. The territories of the self have boundaries that cannot be literally patrolled. Instead, border disputes are sought out and indulged in (often with glee) as a means of establishing where one's boundaries are. And these disputes are character contests.

If the significance of character contests is to be appreciated, however, we must turn from games and skirmishes to constitutive features of social life. We must examine the investment an individual is obliged to make in legitimate expectations that happen to be his own, especially informal ones, and the means available in society for establishing authority, invidious position, dominance, and rank. In the interplay of righteousness and ranking, a code is to be found that cuts to the center of the self and is worth attempting to formulate ideally.

When two persons are mutually present, the conduct of each can be read for the conception it expresses concerning himself and the other. Co-present behavior thus becomes mutual treatment. But mutual treatment itself tends to become socially legitimated, so that every act, whether substantive or ceremonial, becomes the obligation of the actor and the expectation of the other. Each of the two participants is transformed into a field in which the other necessarily practices good or bad conduct. Moreover, each will not only desire to receive his due, but find that he is obliged to exact it, obliged to police the interaction to make sure that justice is done him.

When a contest occurs over whose treatment of self and other is to prevail, each individual is engaged in providing evidence to establish a definition of himself at the expense of what can remain for the other. And this dispute will embarrass not only the desire for a satisfactory place in the definitions that prevail, but also the right to be given such a place and the duty to insist thereon. A "matter of principle" is involved, that is, a rule whose sanctity derives not only from the actual conduct that is guided by it, but also from its symbolic implication as one of a whole set of rules, the system itself being in jeopardy.[125] Insisting on a desirable place is thus covered and strengthened by insisting on one's rightful place, and this is further hardened by the obligation to do so, lest the whole pattern of rules deteriorate. *Honor* can thus be engaged, namely, that aspect of personal make-up that causes the individual dutifully to enjoin a character contest when his rights have been violated—a course he must follow in the very degree that its likely costs appear to be high.[126]

The game typically starts with one player offending against a moral rule, the particular application of which the other player is pledged to maintain personally, usually because he or those he identifies with are the targets of the offense. This is the "provocation." In the case of minor infractions, the offender is likely to offer an immediate apology, which restores both the rule and the honor of the offended; the offended need only convey acceptance to abort the whole game—in fact, he may apologize himself at the same time, or accept apology before it is offered, demonstrating again the great concern of persons to stay out of this kind of action. (An important structural issue here is that it is easier to proffer an excuse and apology in one's capacity as guardian of the other's rights, when this is self-initiated, than it is to accept an affront in one's capacity as protector of one's own sanctity.) A similar termination of the game occurs when the offended conveys a

[125] See the argument by C. Fried, "Reason and Action," *Natural Law Forum*, Vol. 11 (1966), pp. 13–35.

[126] The leading case here is the sixteenth-century duel of honor. A gentleman stood by his honor, but only a small number of others were socially qualified to oblige him to satisfy his honor by means of a duel, and then, of course, the problems of arranging mutually satisfactory time, place, and equipment were so great that in countries like England few duels actually did get fought. See F. Bryson, *The Point of Honor in Sixteenth-Century Italy: An Aspect of the Life of the Gentleman* (Publications of the Institute of French Studies, Inc., Columbia University, New York, 1935); Baldick, *op. cit.*

mild challenge (enough to show he is not without honor), drawing the offender's attention to what has happened, which is followed by a sequence of apology and acceptance. "Satisfaction" is asked for and given, and little character is generated, although each party can once again affirm that he is a properly socialized person with proper piety regarding the rules of the game. Even, however, where the offense is uncommon and deep, serious consequences can be avoided. The offended person can openly express his feeling that the offender is not the sort of person whose acts need be taken seriously;[127] the offender, on being challenged, can back down with wit, so that while one part of him becomes defamed, it is another part of him that is doing the defaming—and doing it so well as to undercut the challenger's claim of having self-restorative work to do.

Since a challenge can be communicated and declined with the slightest of cues, one finds here a general mechanism of interpersonal social control. An individual who has moved slightly out of line is reminded of the direction he is taking and its consequences before any serious damage has been done. The same mechanism seems to be employed in the establishment of a pecking order regarding various kinds of rights.

If the contest is to begin in earnest, the challenge conveyed by the offended must be serious, and the other player must pointedly decline to give satisfaction. When both of these responses are present they together transform retrospectively the meaning of the initial offense, reconstituting it into the beginning of what is sometimes

[127] Tellers have foiled bank robberies by simply refusing to take seriously the threat-note to them by would-be armed robbers. Similarly policemen have countered pistol threats against themselves by simply turning their backs on the gunman, thereby removing the basis for contest. (See *San Francisco Chronicle*, July 26, 1965, p. 3, "Cop Turns His Back—And Disarms a Gunman.")

called a "run-in." This is always a two-party affair, unlike an "incident," which may centrally involve only one person. Moral combat results, with properties of character brought into play as something to be lost and gained.[128] Run-ins involve the victim himself in all the phases of the sanctioning process. In this court, the plaintiff must act as judge and executioner. As is characteristic of action in general, the unaided individual is here the efficacious unit of organization.

It should be apparent that the meaning of these various moves derives in part from the orientation the player brings to them and the readings he retrospectively makes of them.[129] Therefore there will be leeway in defining the situation, and a certain degree of mutual consent will be required before a full-fledged run-in can occur.

In today's world, when a run-in does happen, a character contest is likely to follow immediately, if indeed it is to occur. In myth and ritual, however, the parties often withdraw to meet again at a designated place, voluntarily keeping an appointment with fate, of both the corporeal and the characterological kind. In either case, bystanders are necessary and always must carefully refrain from interfering. (This ensures that the contest will be reputed as "fair," a valid scene for the play of character.)

When the run-in has occurred and the contest begun, the characterological implications of the play can unfold in different ways, and not necessarily with "zero-sum" restrictions.

---

[128] Traditional duels were more complex because of the choice-of-weapons rule. Were the offended party to challenge the offender to a duel the latter would ordinarily have the choice of weapons, an unfair advantage for someone who had already done wrong. And so the offended party would openly insult the offender, "giving him the lie," and with this provocation the original offender would then be forced to challenge the offended. Through this extensive cooperation, choice of weapon could be lodged on the right side.

[129] Suggested by P. Bourdieu, "The Sentiment of Honour in Kabyle Society," p. 200, in Peristiany, *op. cit.*

One party can suffer a clear-cut defeat on the basis of properties of character: he proves to have been bluffing all along and is not really prepared to carry out his threatened deed; or he loses his nerve, turns tail and runs, leaving his opponent in the comfortable position of not having to demonstrate how seriously he was prepared to carry through with the contest; or he collapses as an opponent, abases himself and pleads for mercy, destroying his own status as a person of character on the tacit assumption that he will then be unworthy as an opponent and no longer qualify as a target of attack.

Both parties can emerge with honor and good character affirmed—an outcome carefully achieved, apparently, in most formal duels of honor, a considerable achievement since injury was also usually avoided.

And presumably both parties can lose, just as one party may lose while the other gains little. Thus, that ideal character contest, the "chicken run," may end with both vehicles swerving, neither vehicle swerving, or one swerving so early as to bring great dishonor to its driver but no particular credit to the opponent.[130]

Obviously, the characterological outcome of the contest is quite independent of what might be seen as the "manifest" result of the fray. An overmatched player can gamely give everything he has to his hopeless situation and then go down bravely, or proudly, or insolently, or gracefully,

---

[130] A fictionalized presentation of the vehicular chicken run may be found in G. Elliott, *Parktilden Village* (New York, Signet Books, 1961), pp. 42–43. An elegant analytical treatment is provided by T. C. Schelling, *Arms and Influence* (New Haven, Yale University Press, 1966), pp. 116–25. Note that before the game can be played, persons must know how the equipment accessible to them can be used for this purpose. Some middle-class boys don't know that a lit cigarette butt held between the sides of the hands of two different boys until it burns down to the flesh provides perfect facilities for the game. (The first one to draw his hand away loses, of course, and automatically terminates the trial for both of them.) The breath-holding contest seems more widely known.

or with an ironic smile on his lips.[131] A criminal suspect can keep his cool in the face of elaborate techniques employed by teams of police interrogators, and later receive a guilty sentence from the judge without flinching. Further, a well-matched player can grimly suffer while his opponent stoops to dishonorable but decisive techniques, in which case a duel is lost but character is won. Similarly, an individual who pits himself against a weak opponent may acquire the character of a bully through the very act of winning the match. And a bully who ties is lost indeed, as this news story from Fresno, California illustrates:

> A barmaid and a bandit played a game of "chicken" with loaded pistols early yesterday and, although no shots were fired, the barmaid won.
>
> The action took place at The Bit, a proletarian beer and wine oasis on the southern fringe of town, where lovely Joan O'Higgins was on duty behind the bar.
>
> Suddenly a towering bandit walked into the establishment, ordered a beer, flashed a small pistol and commanded Miss O'Higgins to clean out the cash register.
>
> The barmaid placed $11 on the bar, an amount that failed to satisfy the bandit, whose height was estimated at six feet five.
>
> "Give me the rest," he demanded.
>
> Barmaid O'Higgins reached into a drawer for the main money bag and the .22 caliber pistol beneath it.
>
> She pointed the gun at the man and asked:
>
> "Now, what do you want to do?"
>
> The bandit, realizing that he had met his match in The Bit, blinked at the sight of the gun and left, leaving his beer and the $11 behind.[132]

[131] One of the reasons unexpected rescues are employed in action stories is that only in this way can the hero be given a chance to demonstrate that even in the face of quite hopeless odds he will not cry uncle. Second leads are allowed to prove this the hard way, being expendable in the plot.

[132] *San Francisco Chronicle*, July 14, 1966.

Just as a move is subject to interpretation, so a characterological outcome may be differently read by different participants. In negotiations between nations, for example, no unambiguous criteria may emerge for agreeing as to who won and who lost.[133] Scoring in some cases may be so flexible that each side can maintain its own view of the final outcome. Thus, some fights between rival street gangs end with both teams feeling that they won.[134] This sort of conceit is facilitated by a variable intermix of concern for the physical or manifest outcome, allowing one team to stress score in primary attributes, the other in properties of character.

The cowboy of slap-leather duel is especially instructive in pointing out the cooperativeness and regard for rules that are required on the part of all participants if the game is to be successful in generating and jeopardizing character, that is, bringing character into play. Both parties must take the game seriously; both, as suggested, must make themselves available, voluntarily giving themselves up to the game. During the combat that results, the hero, should he find himself with an easy advantage, must disdainfully give it up, restricting himself to a means of having it out that will leave the villain with no way of dodging the expressions of character that result. And the hero, upon winning a challenge or a duel, can at that very moment turn his back on his opponent, knowing that superiority once established will not be immediately rechallenged, and that in any case constant care is not dignified.[135]

[133] F. Iklé, *How Nations Negotiate* (New York, Harper & Row, 1964), p. 164 ff. See also Bourdieu, p. 207, in Peristiany, *op. cit.*

[134] J. Short and F. Strodtbeck, "Why Gangs Fight," *Transaction*, I (1964), 26.

[135] This strange fateful trust in the fair-play of the just-defeated enemy has an obvious social function. Without this trust, dominance and the pecking order would not provide a

Given these suggestions about the dynamics of the character game, let us go on to consider briefly some of the implications.

He who would avoid fateful events must avoid run-ins or wriggle safely out of ones that have not been avoided—whether he be the offender or offended. Almost everyone does such wriggling, although the Kaiser's officers are said to have barely done so. Even Casanova who, according to his own account, was a formidable swordsman and gentleman of much character, admits to such avoidance, commenting on such during an occasion when honor had just forced him into a duel with a stranger:

> We had a pleasant supper and talked cheerfully together without a word being said about the duel, with the exception that an English lady said, I forget in what connection, that a man of honour should never risk sitting down to dinner at a hotel unless he felt inclined, if necessary, to fight. The remark was very true at the time, when one had to draw a sword for an idle word and expose oneself to the consequences of a duel or else be pointed at, even by the ladies, with the finger of scorn.[136]

Another implication follows from the first. It has to do with "contest contests." The individual's tendency to avoid occasions when character is in jeopardy exposes him to being forced by someone else into a contest over whether or not there will be a contest. The aggressor, knowing that his victim is likely to seek almost any means to avoid a show-down, can force him to face up to a display of

---

practical social mechanism for establishing temporary order. Were opponents to re-contest a run-in as soon as it had been played through, no order could be established. Everyone would always be engaged either in fighting or in carefully standing guard. In any case, one finds "terminal self-exposure" on the part of the winner as a standard move in ending a wide variety of contests—wrestling matches, bullfights, cowboy duels, etc.

[136] *The Memoirs of Jacques Casanova*, tr. A. Machen (New York, Dover Publications, 1961), vol. 2, p. 958.

this weakness before witnesses, while the aggressor displays his own bravery.

The aggressor in a contest contest can begin either by committing an offense that the other can scarcely overlook, or by responding to a minor or even microscopic offense in a way that draws the near-innocent offender into a fray.[137] If the victim still declines to join battle, the aggressor may goad him with increasingly unpalatable acts, in an apparent effort either to find his ignition point or to demonstrate that he doesn't have one. We speak here of "baiting," "ranking," "sounding," or "getting a rise"; when the aggressor is a subordinate, we speak of "insolence." It should be repeated that although this sort of aggression may not be common, at least in middle-class daily life, nonetheless, all face-to-face contacts between individuals are ordered by a multitude of anticipated signs of mutual respect, which ordering can easily be transformed by an aggressor into a perilous field of fateful interpersonal action. For example, everywhere the individual goes he implants a tacit demand that the others present will respectfully keep their eyes, their voices, and their

---

[137] L. Yablonsky (*The Violent Gang* [New York, Macmillan, 1962], pp. 208–9), in describing types of gang members, describes the logical extreme: ". . . Other youths who may be included in the category of marginal gang membership are the sociopathic individuals almost *always* ready to fight with any available gang. They seek out violence or provoke it simply as they describe it: "for kicks or action." They are not necessarily members of any particular violent gang, yet are in some respects members of all. They join gangs because for them it is a convenient and easily accessible opportunity for violence. When the gang, as an instrument, is not appropriate they "roll their own" form of violence (for example, the three stomp slayers who kicked a man to death for "whistling a song we didn't like"). For example, in one typical pattern utilized by this type of gang boy, he will approach a stranger with the taunt, "What did you say about my mother?" An assault is then delivered upon the victim before he can respond to the question, which, of course, has no appropriate answer for preventing the attack."

bodies away from the circle immediately around him. Everywhere these territorial courtesies are sustained automatically and unthinkingly; yet everywhere they provide ample means at hand by which an aggressor (through the pointed, unhurried failure to accord these considerations) can test the individual's honor. Similarly, strangers in public places are bound together by certain minimal obligations of mutual aid, establishing the right, for example, to ask the time or directions, or even to request a cigarette or small coin. In granting such a plea, the individual may find that his entire package of cigarettes is calmly taken or all the change in his hand while his eye is held by the aggressor so that the affront is anchored in mutually recognized mutual awareness. Pushcart operators in slum streets may find a piece of fruit being taken in the same insolent manner.[138]

The mutual accommodation that orders human traffic can thus be seen to render vulnerable those who take it for granted. I would like to cite at length a novelistic illustration provided by William Sansom. The scene is a London drinking "club." The hero, and narrator, who plays the piano at the club, is suddenly addressed:

"As a voice above me says: 'Ain't you gonna play s'more fellah?'

It is a young man I have never seen before, a boy almost too young to be in a bar. His head sags like a pale knob of bone on a neck too thin to hold it. He wears exaggerated clothes, and a special sort of hairdress like a hedgehog's. He bunches his shoulders up to make them bigger. His eyes are dull as dead fishscales. He grits his mouth thin as if he wants to be sick.

'In a moment,' I tell him. His tone has been really insolent, but one dismisses a lot as youth.

[138] Although these various "put-on's" are directed against an individual, he will often serve in part as a symbol of a wider group—the adult world, police authority, white people, etc.

'Not too long then, fellah,' he says, still fixing me with his fishy dead eyes.

Behind him then, I started to see a kind of twin—but he was only another youth in the same cut of clothes. And then I saw that there were six or seven others standing at the bar or lounging legs stretched out from the tables. I caught Belle's [the proprietress] eye and she gave me a hopeless shrug across the room —as if this sudden phenomenon was beyond her.

'My,' I said to Marie, ignoring the young man, who still stood there, looking down at me, 'we've got company tonight.'

'You have,' said the boy sadly, 'you certainly have,' and he walked away, at a conscious stiff-legged strolling pace, to the bar. There he said something to the others, and they all looked my way and shook their heads—again, sadly, as if I were in a very bad way indeed. . . .

We watched them for a moment. Every glance and gesture was carefully aggressive. They stuck out their legs so that Andrew carrying a tray of drinks had to circle round to save tripping—and watched him silently as he did so. One leaned over and took a tray of chips off someone else's table—unsmiling, pointedly unapologetic. Another at the bar began flipping olive stones at the bottles. Belle told him to stop. He apologized with an exaggerated bow and flipped another stone straight away.

'For God's sake *play* something,' said Belle.

I got up. It had been a mistake to talk about them so openly. They knew they were being discussed, and now, as I went to the piano, saw that their orders had been obeyed. You could almost feel them spreading themselves. So I began to play the dimity notes of *Humoresque* to put them back a little.

Of course, it did not work. The common quality of all these young men is their watchfulness. They sit and watch everything with dull dislike. This gives them that famous 'pinched' look. As my tinkling established itself, one of them sauntered across, hands in pockets, chin down, and stood above me. He simply stated, as an order, the name of a disc-hit. Apart from this plain rudeness, a pianist's biggest bugbear is to be asked for another tune when he is already playing —so I gritted my teeth and tried to close my ears. He nudged my right arm off the notes with his elbow and said simply; 'mush.' And repeated, louder, his request."[139]

I am suggesting that minor behaviors can be employed as a serious invitation to a run-in or show-down. One type of truncated act should be mentioned specifically. It is the use of the style of standing or walking as an open invitation to action to all others present. Thus there is a "delinquency strut" which in effect communicates an authority challenge to adults present, simultaneously conveying not only that the first move has been made but also that it has not been faced up to by those at whom it was and is directed.[140] The special swagger of the bullfighter in the ring, Sandunga, is the stylization of the same expression.

Since communications or expressions, not substantive matters, are involved in these games, there is little to keep the symbol from becoming increasingly attenuated in duration and visibility until it has practically disappeared. In consequence, a sequence of moves can be exchanged between two players and a winner established with hardly any visible activity at all, as implied, of course, in G. H. Mead's analysis of communication.

Earlier it was suggested that an individual can become reputed among his peers as an action seeker—always on the make for any desirable girl he happens upon, or ready

[139] W. Sansom, The Cautious Heart (New York, Reynal and Company, 1958), pp. 100–2.
[140] Sometimes called "walking pimp." On this and other collapsed moves employed by delinquents, see the useful study by C. Werthman, Delinquency and Authority, M.A. Thesis, Dept. of Sociology, University of California, Berkeley, 1964, p. 115, and throughout chapter LV, "Gang Members and the Police."

to "make something" of the slightest affront, or to see everywhere something that can be bet on. Similarly, an individual may acquire the reputation for always being available *to others* for a particular type of interpersonal action, ready at all times to provide a definitive test of anyone seeking definition. The Western "gunfighter" is often portrayed as the archetypical example. Well-known pool players find themselves cast in this role. Bet-a-Million Gates apparently attracted bettors in the same way.[141] Today the police, being committed (as already suggested) to obtaining immediate deference from all civilians they contact, and to enforce this demand with an immediate willingness to invoke physical sanctions, sometimes find themselves forced into the tester's role. Male movie stars who are type-cast into tough hero roles may be utilized as testers by those who chance to meet them in public places. Highly regarded jazz musicians who allow the practice of "cutting," provide another example, at least for those who write about them.

Whether an individual constantly seeks out character contests or is constantly sought out for them, we can anticipate that he won't last long; anyone so inclined will eventually be removed from competition by the workings of probability. So long as each play involves an appreciable gamble, the persistent chance-taker ought not to plan on a long future. The action role is itself long-lived, but its performers can last only briefly, except on television.

Just as there is specialization of persons, so there is specialization of signs. Particular affronts can be defined as those an honorable individual ought not to tolerate. There are critical points understood by all those involved as the ones past which things will have gone too far; once they are reached, the offended person must disallow excuses, feel things seriously, and take steps to re-establish

---

[141] See Lucius Beebe, *The Big Spenders* (New York, Doubleday, 1966), p. 85.

the normative order if he is to preserve his honor. Among the many words an honorable cowboy can hear, he must, however peaceful his intent, recognize the few that everyone knows are "fighting" ones. Once such specialized function is given to acts, they can be employed by aggressors as an unavoidable call to action. Performed in a measured and pointed way, these acts test the recipient's honor, that is, his readiness regardless of price to uphold the codes by which he lives. The actual offense is understood by all parties to be incidental, a mere convenience; the chief significance of the act is to serve as a frontal test of the individual's tacit claim to honor.[142] Thus a conventionalized statement, "You lie in your throat," was the traditional *mentita*—the act by which an offended party forced the offender to challenge the speaker to a duel.[143] Spitting in the other's face is a less gentlemanly and more common example. In current American race relations, the white person's use of the word "nigger" is equally provocative. Other acts serve as tests in more circumscribed groups. A teacher in an urban slum school who affirms the school rule against lateness exposes himself to a pupil's strolling in late and coolly looking him in the eye to underline the challenge.[144] These testing acts are favorite moves in contest contests.

Just as a test can be fashioned out of an offensive act performed by one individual against another, so it can be generated by demanding under threat that an individual

[142] These acts of insolence and pointed insubordination are to be contrasted to bodily acts of deference, acts which are specialized too, but which serve to attest to the actor's current willingness to accept the status quo.

[143] Bryson, *op. cit.*, ch. IV. As suggested, the offended party could not challenge the offender because this would give the offender the choice of weapons. Offenders were thus tacitly assumed to be honorable enough to allow themselves to be maneuvered into the challenger role.

[144] An incident of this kind is described in Werthman, *op. cit.*, pp. 68–69.

act in a way he thinks improper. To establish an individual in a subordinate status, an aggressor may coerce him into openly performing an undignified obeisance or service on the assumption that once he allows himself to give-in he can (and he knows he can) be relied upon henceforth to accede to any demand made of him.[145] As with the jockey, "nerve" is then thought to be lost, but this time in regard to interpersonal activity and its ceremonial order. And, of course, as long as both parties share these beliefs, the social game will be played accordingly.

In considering action I said that, although there is a relation between action and character, some forms of character arise in opposition to the spirit of action. The same qualification must be made in regard to interpersonal action and character contests. There are situations in which approval is given to an individual's refusal to be drawn into a fray of honor, and "immaturity" is imputed to challengers. It is always possible for the individual to decline to accept the whole ritual frame of reference and, moreover, put a bold face on it, especially when his peers support this style of response:

> But it must be emphasized that, despite prevalent stereotypes, juvenile gangs are not all conflict oriented, and value systems may vary among them as among other human groupings. A "retreatest" gang, which built its value system around the effect of dope, provides a dramatic contrast.
>
> Although criticized and ridiculed repeatedly by other gangs for their cowardice and lack of manhood, the retreatests seldom responded to taunts, and always retreated from combat. They did not worry about their reputations as fighters—they had none—and did not think them important—in fact, they thought the conflict oriented gangs to be "square." Directly chal-

[145] See the treatment of "obedience tests" in Goffman, *Asylums, op. cit.,* pp. 17–18.

lenged to join other white gangs in repelling Negro "wade-in" demonstrators on a beach in Chicago, they got "high" on pills and unconcernedly played cards during the entire incident.[146]

[146] Short and Strodtbeck, "Why Gangs Fight," *op. cit.*, pp. 27–28. See also their, "The Response of Gang Leaders to Status Threats," *American Journal of Sociology*, LXVIII (1963), 576–77. A literary example is provided in Louis Auchincloss's novel, *Sybil* (New York, Signet Books, 1953), pp. 122–23. A man (Philip) at his club with his mistress draws an acquaintance (Nicholas Cummings) aside and asks if he would like to meet her. Nicholas declines, and the following dialogue occurs:

"You'd better watch your step, Cummings," he said ominously. "You're talking about the young lady whom I intend to marry."

But Nicholas simply continued to fix him with his chilly stare.

"It's hard for people to know that, isn't it," he inquired, "when you're still married to my cousin?"

There was a weighty pause.

"Well, anyway," Philip said heavily, not knowing what honor might require in so awkward a situation, "you'd better cut those cracks about Julia. Unless you want your block knocked off."

Nicholas, however, was remorseless.

"Do you regard the term 'mistress' as a 'crack'?" he demanded. "I'm sorry. I had thought it accurate. You're not going to deny that she *is* your mistress, are you? Because I should tell you that as your wife's lawyer, although in no way at her instigation, I have made it my business to find out exactly what your relationship with Miss Anderson is. The word 'mistress' appears to cover it exactly. Can you suggest a better? At any rate I must insist on my right so to describe her whenever I have occasion to discuss your affairs with those who may be concerned. If you object, you are at liberty to seek redress, either legally in a slander suit or illegally, as you threaten, in an assault upon my person."

Philip's breath was now coming in pants. There was no rule for handling a person who so boldly defied the most elementary precepts of good fellowship.

"Would you like to step outside," he demanded, "and settle this thing like a gentleman?"

"I most certainly would not," Nicholas replied. "I have not come to my club to give you an opportunity to start a brawl in the street."

Something similar occurs in middle-class bars, where an offended person may feel it beneath him to "seek satisfaction," at least with the particular opponent of the moment—thus democratizing the chivalric notion that only one's social equals are worth challenging. The victim will be content to lecture his adversary briefly on how "sick" he must be. In social worlds where honor *is* highly valued, and men must be prepared to put up their lives to save their faces, fashions of morality may quickly change, and the act of proving such attributes as one's "masculinity" may decline in significance.[147] There has even developed

Philip stood there for a moment more, looking at him uncertainly.

"Oh, go to hell," he retorted. "God damn lawyers," he answered as he moved away. "Shysters. All of them."

[147] Brown, *op. cit.*, pp. 211, 253–56, 261, provides a nice description of ways in which Harlem youth in the 1930s and '40s were taught the necessity to defend their money and their women with lethal fighting, and how, in the '50s in conjunction with the rising significance of drugs, the coercive power of the code declined markedly. This is but a small version of larger histories. The duel of honor, for example, while very popular in France, very rarely occurred in the Northern States, being muchly disapproved by the citizenry. In England, in 1844, the article of the Mutiny Act which obliged officers to uphold their honor by dueling was repealed and replaced by ones that forbade it. The third of the new articles nicely outlines the modern anti-umbrage perspective:

"Approbation is expressed of the conduct of those who, having had the misfortune to give offense to, or injure or insult others, shall frankly explain, apologize, or offer redress for the same, or who, having received offense, shall cordially accept frank explanations or apologies for the same; or, if such apologies are refused to be made or accepted, shall submit the matter to the commanding officer; and, lastly, all officers and soldiers are acquitted of disgrace or disadvantage who, being willing to make or accept such redress, refuse to accept challenges, as they will only have acted as is suitable to the character of honourable men, and have done their duty as good soldiers who subject themselves to discipline" (Cited in Baldick, *op. cit.*, p. 114). Baldick comments thusly:

"With surprising suddenness, these articles, which were rec-

the literary ideal of the "anti-hero" who confidently de-clines all opportunity to display costly virtues, shows sub-terranean pride in fleeing from his moral obligations, and takes no chances. Of course, when an individual declines a challenge with coolness or fails to become incensed at an offense he is demonstrating self-command under diffi-cult circumstances, and therefore establishes character of a kind, although not the heroic kind.

In sum, although character contests that can be fought without relevance to physical force are not uncommon, the classic punch-out and slap-leather varieties belong mainly to cinematic places. None the less, the logic of fights and duels is an important feature of our daily so-cial life. The possibility, however slight, that matters might degenerate in that direction provides mutually present persons with a background reason to hedge expressions of hostility; they have here a constant guide to what is not going to be allowed to happen. (In fact, joking ref-erence to "stepping outside" can be used as a strategic move to cut back into unseriousness a threatening de-velopment in social discourse.) Through a multitude of joint accommodations, the voice of our reason prevails at the cost of hardly any dishonor.

X. Conclusions

The traditional sociological view of man is optimistic. Once you get the beast to desire socially delineated goals under the auspices of "self-interest," you need only con-vince him to regulate his pursuits in accordance with an

---

ognized as constituting a British 'Code of Honour,' combined with the obvious determination of judges and juries to convict duellists of murder, the sarcasm of the Press, and the sheer pressure of public opinion, succeeded in suppressing duelling in Britain . . . the duel as a thriving, honoured and respected institution to all intents and purposes ceased to exist in Britain in the middle of the nineteenth century" (*ibid*).

elaborate array of ground rules. (Important among these rules, I want to add, are "situational proprieties," that is, standards of conduct through whose maintenance he exhibits regard for the current situation.) Accordingly, the main trouble the individual can cause is to fail to acquire appropriate wants, or wilfully to fail to abide by the rules in going about satisfying such wants as he has acquired. But obviously other difficulties must be considered. This essay has dealt with one of them.

Whether an individual is concerned with achieving a personal goal or sustaining a regulative norm, he must be in physical command of himself to do so. And there are times when his aliveness to the contingencies in the situation disrupt his dealings with the matters at hand: his capacity to perform ordinary mental and physical tasks is unsettled, and his customary adherence to standard moral principles undermined. The very intelligence that allows him to exert foresight and calculation in the pursuit of his ends, the very qualities that make him something more complex than a simple machine, assure that at times what he intelligently brings to mind will disrupt his capacity to perform and disarray his usual morality.

The ability to maintain self-command under trying circumstances is important, as is therefore the coolness and moral resoluteness needed if this is to be done. If society is to make use of the individual, he must be intelligent enough to appreciate the serious chances he is taking and yet not become disorganized or demoralized by this appreciation. Only then will he bring to moments of society's activity the stability and continuity they require if social organization is to be maintained. Society supports this capacity by moral payments, imputing strong character to those who show self-command and weak character to those who are easily diverted or overwhelmed. Hence we can understand the paradox that when an immoral deed is accomplished by a well-executed plan that excludes impulsive temptation, the culprit may be half-admired; he can be thought a very *bad* character even while it is appreciated that he is not a *weak* one.[148]

A central opportunity to show strong character is found in fateful situations, and such situations necessarily jeopardize the risk-taker and his resources. (An already-decided fate that is now being settled is useful too, but still more costly.) The actor is therefore likely to avoid this chance-taking and squirm out of occasions he has not avoided. In our society, after all, moments are to be lived through, not lived. Further, fateful activity is often itself disruptive of social routines and cannot be tolerated by organizations in large amounts. (Thus, in Europe, duelling throve under monarchies, but monarchs and their leading generals led in trying to curb the institution, partly because of the duelling toll on key personnel.) In domestic and occupational life, most of these hazards seem to have been safely eliminated.

However, there is some ambivalence about safe and momentless living. Some aspects of character can be easily affirmed, but other aspects can be neither expressed nor earned safely. Careful, prudent persons must therefore forego the opportunity to demonstrate certain prized attributes; after all, devices that render the individual's moments free from fatefulness also render them free from new information concerning him—free, in short, from significant expression. As a result, the prudent lose connection with some of the values of society, some of the very values that portray the person as he should be.

So some practical gambles may be sought out, or, if not sought out, at least made into something when they occur in the ordinary course of affairs. And enterprises are undertaken that are perceived to be outside the normal round, avoidable if one chose, and full of dramatic risk and

---

[148] A good recent example is provided by the heroes of timing who brought off the Great Train Robbery in England. On the regard held for them, see J. Gosling and D. Craig, *The Great Train Robbery* (Indianapolis, Bobbs-Merrill, 1965), pp. 173–75.

opportunity. This is action. The greater the fatefulness, the more serious the action.

Fatefulness brings the individual into a very special relationship to time, and serious action brings him there voluntarily. He must arrange to be in a position to let go, and then do so. The circumstances into which he thus thrusts himself must involve matters that are problematic and consequential. And—in the purest case—his dealings with these circumstances must be resolved or paid off during the current span of what is for him a subjectively continuous experience.[149] He must expose himself to time, to seconds and minutes ticking off outside his control; he must give himself up to the certain rapid resolution of an uncertain outcome. And he must give himself up to fate in this way when he could avoid it at reasonable cost. He must have "gamble."

Serious action is a serious ride, and rides of this kind are all but arranged out of everyday life. As suggested, every individual engages in consequential acts, but most of these are not problematic, and when they are (as when career decisions are made that affect one's life) the determination and settlement of these bets will often come after decades, and by then will be obscured by payoffs from many of his other gambles. Action, on the other hand, brings chance-taking and resolution into the same heated moment of experience; the events of action inun-

---

[149] Persons differ according to how long they hold their breath for a continuous experience. Zealots and true believers seem to be inclined to stretch things out a bit, sustaining a span of experience and enthusiasm where others would exhale and mark life off into different plays. Of course poets and the religious are wont to argue that if the individual compares the very considerable time he is slated to spend dead with the relatively brief time allowed him to strut and fret in this world, he might well find reason for viewing all of his life as a very fateful play of very short span, every second of which should fill him with anxiety about what is being used up. And in truth, our rather brief time *is* ticking away, but we seem only to hold our breath for seconds and minutes of it.

date the momentary now with their implications for the life that follows.

Serious action is a means of obtaining some of the moral benefits of heroic conduct without taking quite all of the chance of loss that opportunity for heroism would ordinarily involve. But serious action itself involves an appreciable price. This the individual can minimize by engaging in commercialized action, wherein the appearance of fatefulness is generated in a controlled fashion in an area of life calculated to insulate its consequences from the rest of living. The cost of this action may be only a small fee and the necessity of leaving one's chair, or one's room, or one's house.

It is here that society provides still another solution for those who would keep their character up but their costs down: the manufacture and distribution of vicarious experience through the mass media.

When we examine the content of commercialized *vicarious* experience we find a startling uniformity. Practical gambles, character contests and serious action are depicted. These may entail make-belief, biography, or a view of someone else's currently ongoing fateful activity. But always the same dead catalogue of lively displays seems to be presented.[150] Everywhere opportunity is provided us to identify with real or fictive persons engaging in fatefulness of various kinds, and to participate vicariously in these situations.

Why is fatefulness in all its varieties so popular as an

[150] James Bond is given a fateful undertaking. He checks with his seniors at an exclusive club whose services he handles very firmly. James Bond takes a room at a plush hotel at a plush resort in a plush part of the world. James Bond makes the acquaintance of an unattainable girl and then rapidly makes the girl, after which he shows how coolly he can rise above her bedside murder. James Bond contests an opponent with cars, cards, 'copters, pistols, swards, spear guns, ingenuity, discrimination of wines, judo, and verbal wit. James Bond snubs the man about to apply a hot iron. Etc.

ingredient of living once-removed? As suggested, it provides excitement without cost, if the consumer can identify with the protagonist.[151] This process of identification seems facilitated by two factors. First, fateful acts, by definition, involve the actor in use of facilities whose full and effective agent is the actor himself. The single individual is decision maker and executor, the relevant unit of organization. Presumably an individual, real or fictional, is easier to identify with, at least in bourgeois culture, than is a group, a city, a social movement, or a tractor factory. Second, fatefulness involves a play of events that can be initiated and realized in a space and time small enough to be fully witnessed. Unlike such phenomena as the rise of capitalism or World War II, fatefulness is something that can be watched and portrayed in toto, from beginning to end at one sitting; unlike these other events, it is inherently suited to watching and to portraiture.

Consider the following story told by a Negro journalist, driving across the country in order to write a story about what such a trip would be like for a person like him:

> I didn't linger long in Indianapolis, nor in Chicago, which was now held fast in the grip of a bitter lake-

[151] There are of course great differences through time and across cultures regarding what persons will allow themselves to enjoy vicariously. I don't think execution watching is now considered much of a privilege, but there is no doubt that it was once a neater example of thrills through vicarious participation. Thus in eighteenth-century England:

"The curiosity of men about death led intellectuals and people of fashion to be fascinated by the scaffold. Pepys was a frequent spectator and Boswell, Johnson's biographer, is said to have used his great gift for making friends with the famous to the Keeper of Newgate for no other purpose than to get good seats at hangings. On one occasion when he was able to ride to Tyburn with the condemned man he considered himself as fortunate as a modern sports fan with a couple of tickets for a world heavyweight fight. His pleasure was shared by Sir Joshua Reynolds riding in the coach beside him" (Atholl, *op. cit.*, p. 53).

side winter. Then I was cutting across Ohio, driving dully, the seat belt tight against my waist. In mid-afternoon I saw a patrol car coming up behind me. I checked my speedometer and it read seventy, the limit. I held steady at this speed, expecting the trooper to pass me, but when I glanced around I found him keeping pace with me. Then he signaled me to pull over.

After Kentucky, I had been followed by police or troopers in Georgia, Tennessee, Mississippi; I had been pulled over in Illinois and California. Followed, pulled over and made to know that I was a lone black man in a big car, and vulnerable as hell. I had had enough. I snatched off the seat belt and rolled down the window. It didn't give me room enough, so I practically kicked the door open.

"What's the matter?" I shouted at the trooper. He didn't answer as he walked to the car. And then I decided to commit it all—my body, too, if he wanted it—for I would not take any more harassment.

"Let's see your license."

"I asked you what the trouble was." That was not what he wanted. The ritual said that I should hand my license over to him without a word.

"I want to see your license."

I gave it to him, smelling the odor of a man about to exercise the insolence of office. It was the old game: "You black, me white, and I'm cop besides."

He fingered the license and then, leaning casually in the window, said, "John, what's your occupation?"

I laughed. What does occupation have to do with an alleged traffic violation? Was the nature of my work supposed to tell him that I had money enough to pay him off? Was it to let him know that I was the "right kind" of Negro, one with political connections that could make it hot for him? Was I supposed to be job-less and transporting drugs, a corpse, or young girls across the state line? Police and troopers of America, comes a slow day, you can always find a Negro or two wandering through your state. Brighten up that day by making like exactly what you are.

"My name," I shouted, "is Mr. Williams." I'm sure that cops and troopers use the familiar address with many people who are white, but this one I smelled out. "John" was synonymous with "boy." He snatched his arm from the window. I flung my authorization for the trip at him. I watched him as he read it, and thought, not only am I not the "right kind" of Negro, not only will I not pay you off, but I am about five seconds away from total commitment—which means five seconds from beating your head.

He glanced over the top of the sheet. "Mr. Williams, you were doing eighty coming down the road. When I caught up with you, you were doing eighty-two."

"You're a liar. I was doing seventy. Eighty? Take me in and prove it."

"Mr. Williams—"

"Tired of taking all this crap from you guys."

"Mr. Williams—"

"You're going to run this nonsense and yourselves right into the ground."

Cars were slowing as they passed us. The trooper's face took on an anxious look. Yes, I was rambling in my anger, but I was ready to go. What is more, for the insults I delivered, he would have taken me in *had he been right*. Instead, he returned to his car and I drove on—at seventy miles an hour.[152]

Mr. Williams really has this experience and then makes himself and it available in a popular magazine. A dramatic reporting nicely covers the relevant events, as would a cinematic or stage version. We readers become vicariously involved, safely removed from what we live by. What is for him a character contest, a moment of truth, is for us a means to massage our morality.

[152] J. Williams, "This Is My Country Too," Part II, *Holiday*, September 1964, p. 80.

Whatever the reasons why we consume vicarious fatefulness, the social function of doing so is clear. Honorable men in their scenes of fatefulness are made safely available to all of us to identify with whenever we turn from our real worlds. Through this identification the code of conduct affirmed in fateful activities—a code too costly or too difficult to maintain in full in daily life—can be clarified and reasserted. A frame of reference is secured for judging daily acts, without having to pay its penalties.

The same figure-for-identification very often engages in all three kinds of fateful activity: dangerous tasks, character contests, and serious action. Therefore we can easily come to believe in an intrinsic connection among them, such that he whom character leads to one type of fateful activity will be the sort of person in the sort of life who finds it necessary and desirable to engage in the other two as well. It is easy to fail to see that the natural affinity of the hero for all types of fatefulness probably does not belong to him but to those of us who vicariously participate in his destiny. We shape and stuff these romantic figures to satisfy our need, and our need is for economy—a need to come into vicarious contact with as many bases of character as possible for the same admission price. A living individual misguided enough to seek out all types of fatefulness is merely adding flesh and blood to what originated as consumer packaging.

This suggests that rules of social organization can be given support by and give support to our vicarious world of exemplary fatefulness. The hero of character is not likely therefore to be the man on the street:

> Consider the strain on our moral vocabulary if it were asked to produce heroic myths of accountants, computer programmers, and personnel executives. We prefer cowboys, detectives, bull fighters, and sports-car racers, because these types embody the virtues

which our moral vocabulary is equipped to celebrate: individual achievement, exploits, and prowess.[153]

Because the portrait is needed, a place must be found for the portrayer. And so, on the edges of society, are puddles of people who apparently find it reasonable to engage directly in the chancy deeds of an honorable life. In removing themselves further and further from the substance of our society, they seem to grasp more and more of certain aspects of its spirit. Their alienation from our reality frees them to be subtly induced into realizing our moral fantasies. As suggested of delinquents, they somehow co-operate by staging a scene in which we project our dynamics of character:

> The delinquent is the rogue male. His conduct may be viewed not only negatively, as a device for attacking and derogating the respectable culture; positively it may be viewed as the exploitation of modes of behavior which are traditionally symbolic of untrammeled masculinity, which are renounced by middle-class culture because incompatible with its ends, but which are not without a certain aura of glamour and romance. For that matter, they find their way into the respectable culture as well but only in disciplined and attenuated forms as in organized sports, in fantasy and in make-believe games, or vicariously as in movies, television, and comic books. They are not allowed to interfere with the serious business of life. The delinquent, on the other hand, having renounced his serious business, as defined by the middle class, is freer to divert these subterranean currents of our cultural tradition to his own use. The important point for our purpose is that the delinquent

[153] B. Berger, "The Sociology of Leisure: Some Suggestions," *Industrial Relations*, 1, 2 (1962), p. 41. Yablonsky, *op. cit.*, pp. 226–27, makes a similar point in a discussion of what he calls the "sociopathic hero."

response, "wrong" though it may be and "disreputable," is well within the range of responses that do not threaten his identification of himself as a male.[154]

Although fateful enterprises are often respectable, there are many character contests and scenes of serious action that are not. Yet these are the occasions and places that show respect for moral character. Not only in mountain ranges that invite the climber, but also in casinos, pool halls, and racetracks do we find places of worship; it may be in churches, where the guarantee is high that nothing fateful will occur, that moral sensibility is weak.

Looking for where the action is, one arrives at a romantic division of the world. On one side are the safe and silent places, the home, the well-regulated role in business, industry, and the professions; on the other are all those activities that generate expression, requiring the individual to lay himself on the line and place himself in jeopardy during a passing moment. It is from this contrast that we fashion nearly all our commercial fantasies. It is from this contrast that delinquents, criminals, hustlers, and sportsmen draw their self-respect. Perhaps this is payment in exchange for the use we make of the ritual of their performance.

A final point: Vicarious experience re-establishes our connection to values concerning character. So does action. Action and vicarious experience, then, so different on the

---

[154] A. Cohen, *Delinquent Boys* (Glencoe, The Free Press, 1955), p. 140. Here it would hardly be possible to find a better example than the writer, Norman Mailer. His novels present scenes of fateful duties, character contests, and serious action; his essays expound and extol chance-taking, and apparently in his personal life he has exhibited a certain tendency to define everything from his marriages to his social encounters in terms of the language and structure of the fight game. Whatever the rewards and costs of life-orientation to gambles, he appears to have reaped them. In this fantasization of one's own life, Hemingway of course was the previous champ.

surface, seem to be closely allied. Evidence might be cited.

Take clothing. Female dress is designed to be "attractive," which must mean in some sense or other that the interest of unspecified males is to be aroused. And with this arousal the basis is laid for one type of action. But the actual probability of this action occurring is very often very low. Fantasies are thus invigorated, but reality is not. A clearer version of the same vicarious tease is the wide current sale to horseless cowboys of Stetson hats, high-heeled boots, Levi's, and tattoos.[155] Delinquents who carry knives and own "a piece" similarly exhibit a heightened orientation to action, but here perhaps appearances have a better chance of intruding on reality.

Lotteries, the "numbers," and casino keno are commercialized expressions of long-shot gambles offered at a very small price. The expected value of the play is, of course, much smaller even than the price, but an opportunity is provided for lively fantasies of big winnings. Here action is at once vicarious and real.

When persons go to where the action is, they often go to a place where there is an increase, not in the chances taken, but in the chances that they will be obliged to take chances. Should action actually occur it is likely to involve someone *like* themselves but someone *else*. Where they have got to, then, is a place where another's involvement can be closely watched and vicariously enjoyed.

Commercialization, of course, brings the final mingling of fantasy and action. And it has an ecology. On the arcade strips of urban settlements and summer resorts, scenes are available for hire where the customer can be the star performer in gambles enlivened by being very slightly consequential. Here a person currently without social connections can insert coins in skill machines to

---

[155] See, for example, J. Popplestone, "The Horseless Cowboys," *Trans-Actions*, May–June 1966.

demonstrate to the other machines that he has socially approved qualities of character. These naked little spasms of the self occur at the end of the world, but there at the end is action and character.